THE OLD CITY

BAR ANGEL

Address: Carrer Ocata 2bis,
Ribera - El Born
(near França statio
Telephone: +34 93 269 049
Hours: Mon. 8pm-midnight;
Tues.-Sat. 9am-4pm
& 8pm-midnight;
closed Sunday

Free Range Pork (and Peas)

Santi Hoyos, owner of this modest, brightly lit eatery, is an expert in the ingredients and products he uses. He knows the provenance and defining qualities of every loaf of bread, egg, fish or handful of peas that passes through the doors and has chosen each of these for those very reasons. When he was a partner at the bar Mudanzas, he would spend six months a year traveling around Spain with a notebook under his arm, researching and tasting products in all the different regions. At Bar Angel, the food he serves is exactingly prepared – mostly grilled, never fried – so that the ingredients can speak for themselves, without distractions or obfuscations.

This care is perhaps most evident in the seafood and meat dishes. All the pork on the menu – cuts such as pancetta, *papada*, or jowl, and *presa*, shoulder blade – is pure Iberian pork from the renowned small producer Maldonado, which raises the animals in the Sierra de San Pedro mountains in Albuquerque, Extremadura. The tuna – Hoyos offers the *galta*, cheek, and *morrillo*, neck – is sustainably fished and comes from the Catalan company Balfegó. Also on offer: expressive wines from small Catalan makers, wonderful Italian cheeses, such as the Tomino that came with a subtle zucchini carpaccio anointed with an especially aromatic truffle oil, Galician potatoes and preserved sardines and fresh, local mackerel marinated Barceloneta-style with peppers and paprika.

To maximize everyone's enjoyment of this magnificent produce, Bar Angel offers a cozy, laid-back atmosphere. Hoyos told us that he started this place for the locals, for those in the neighborhood who loved eating the traditional food of the region but were sick of badly cooked, cheap tapas made from poor-quality ingredients. Bar Angel is the kind of place he wanted to hang out in. And now, we do too.

Introduction

This book got its start, naturally, over lunch, when we asked ourselves a simple question: Why are small, traditional eateries – where some of the best meals in any city await – so often overlooked? Why, in a city like Barcelona, with such rich culinary districts, are some of these areas and their bounty of good food rarely explored and celebrated?

In response, we launched Culinary Backstreets, devoted to collecting the best undiscovered local eateries you might not always find on your own. We're talking serious food for serious eaters, hold the frills.

Beyond tapas – and what you will find listed in most guidebooks – lies a wide range of unique Spanish regional cuisines and restaurants and, more importantly, spots that reflect Barcelona's role as the heart of Catalan identity. With this booklet as your trusty introduction to the culinary backstreets of Barcelona, you will know what to eat and where to eat it.

Because prices tend to change, we have decided to generally not include them in our reviews. Most of the spots covered vary from very inexpensive to modest. More importantly, we consider all of our selections high in value. Alcohol is generally among the offerings, unless otherwise indicated in the review. In general, we recommend making reservations for dinner.

Welcome to Barcelona's Culinary Backstreets.

Bon Profit!!

Ansel Mullins & Yigal Schleifer
Founders, Culinary Backstreets

CONTENTS

Beyond the Center (South)

Beyond the Center (North)

Specials

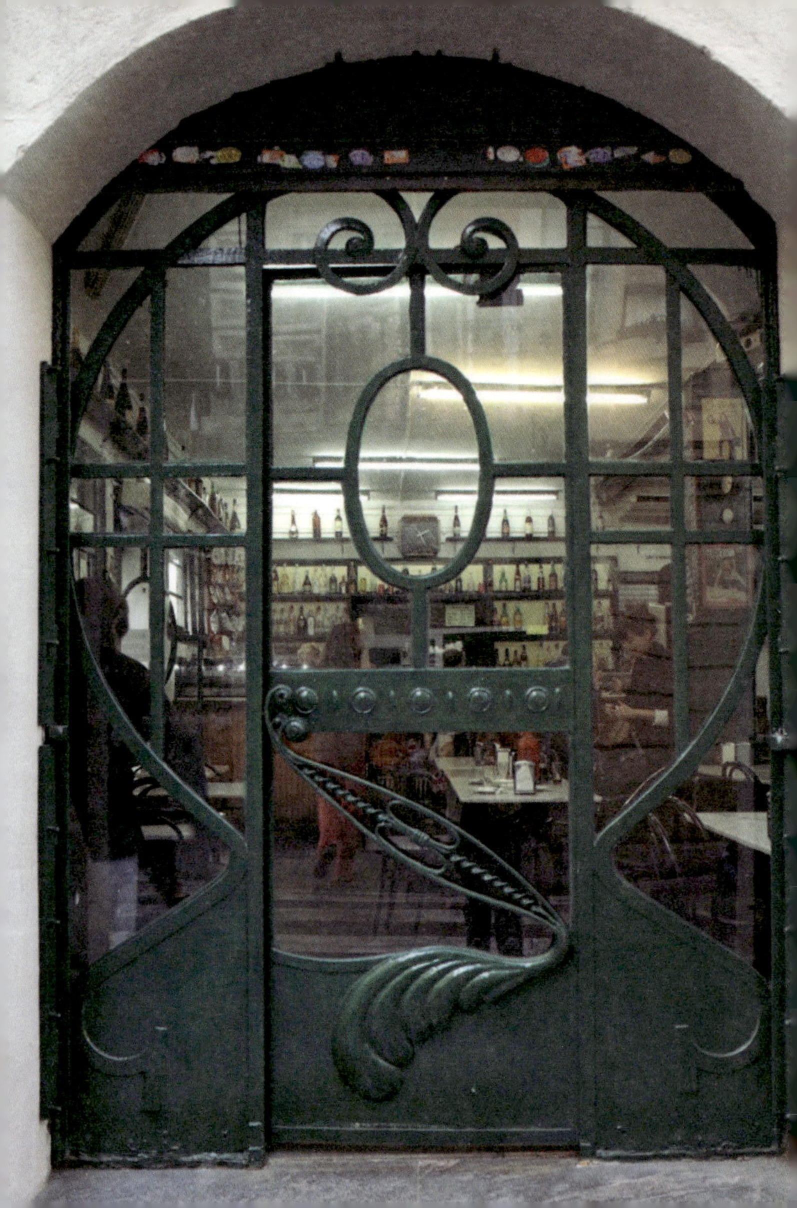

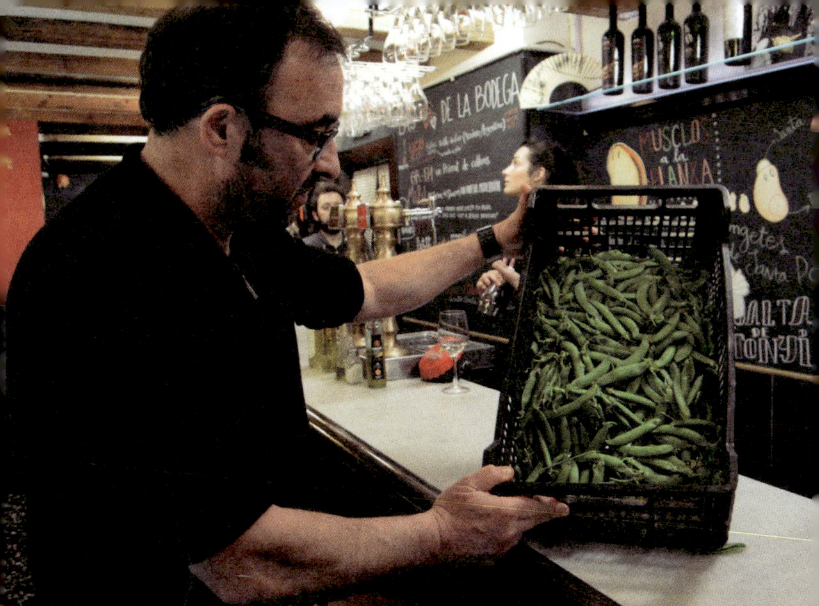
DE LA BODEGA

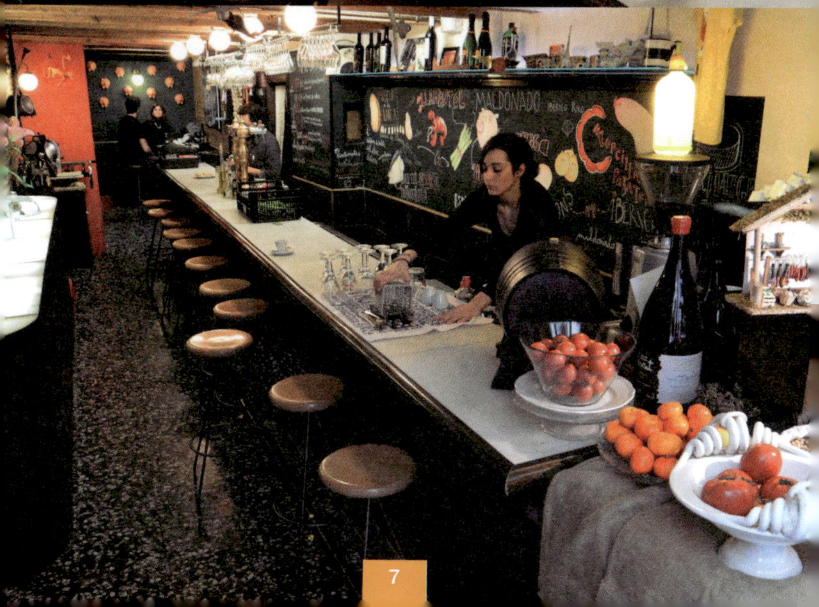
MALDONADO

BAR MUNDIAL

Address: Plaça Sant Agustí Vell 1, Sant Pere-El Born
Telephone: +34 93 319 9056
Hours: 1-4pm & 8:30pm-midnight

Heavyweight Champ

The perpetually packed Bar Mundial is one of Barcelona's elder statesmen, opening for business in 1914 and now run by third-generation owner Paco Tort. His grandfather managed the young boxers whose old black-and-white photos line the walls.

Ten years ago, Tort brought in the chef Andreu Rosillo, whose CV was full of experience at high-end restaurants, to lend a more refined touch to the kitchen. Today, Rosillo's disciple, Joana Salinas, brings the menu up to date with the Asian flavors he loves, as in the grilled langoustines with ginger. Salinas also adds a bit of sophistication to more traditional Mediterranean flavors, such as with the grilled cuttlefish flambé with rum, truffles and foie gras. The famous tapa of eggplant chips with goat cheese and honey has been drawing customers in since its introduction to the menu four years ago.

Rosillo also makes calamari *a la romana*, a typical dish throughout Spain, whose name refers to its origins with the Portuguese Roman Jesuits, who in the 16th century were battering and frying fish and vegetables for Lent, as they had taught the Japanese during their missions in Asia ("tempura" comes from the Latin tempora ad quadragesimae, or "in Lent time" in English). The squid is sliced into rings, dipped in a mixture of flour and egg and fried in sunflower oil, whose neutral flavor allows that of the seafood to shine. Rosillo also cooks *chipirones*, or baby squid, the same way, giving them a light, satisfying crunch.

Perhaps the best-loved items at Bar Mundial are the tellerinas and escupiñas, two types of shellfish that come from the coasts of Maresme and Menorca, respectively. They're grilled just until tender and tasty, with an added one-two punch of garlic and parsley. We love to eat them accompanied by a zippy white – something refreshing, like Albariño or Verdejo.

Rosillo's cooking is the kind we call *para chuparse los dedos* – finger-licking good. Or, as Tort's grandfather might call it, a total knockout.

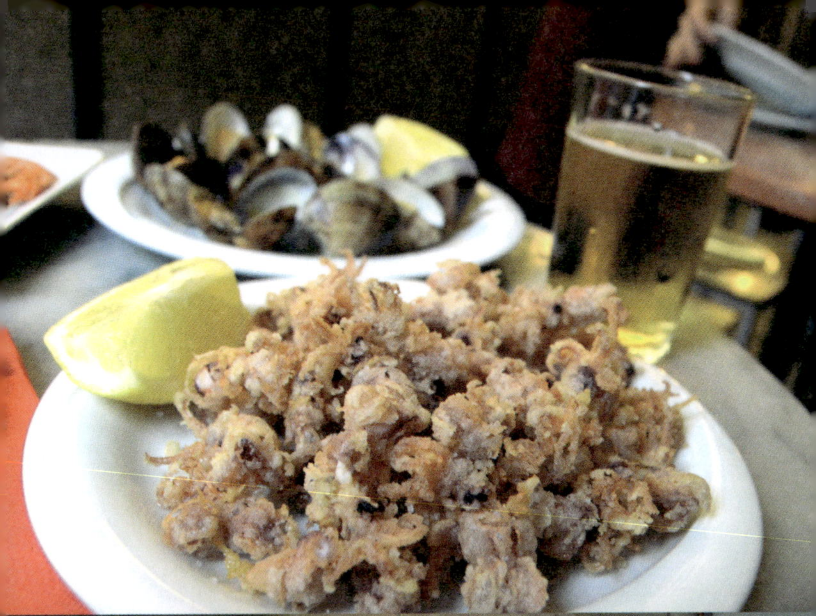

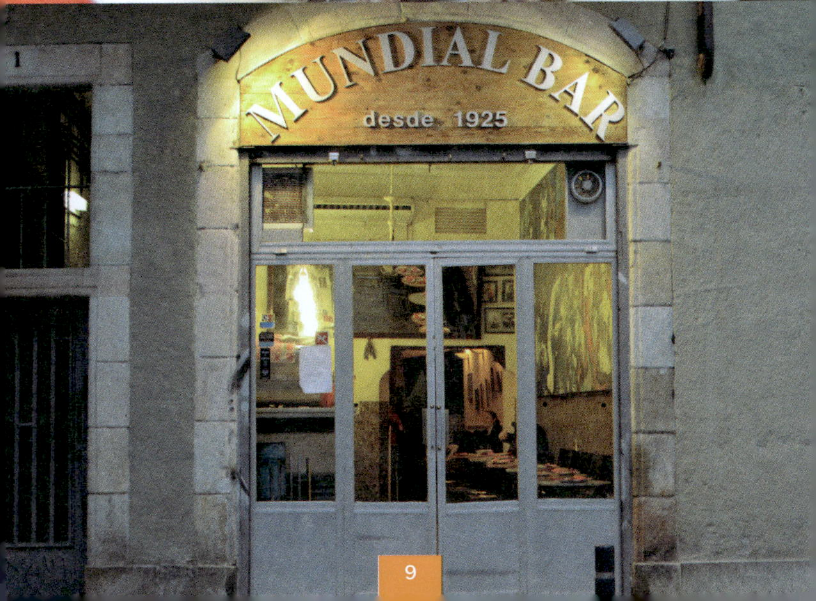
MUNDIAL BAR
desde 1925

CAN SOLÉ

From Fishermen to Famosos

Address: Carrer Sant Carles 4, Barceloneta
Telephone: +34 93 221 5012
Hours: Tues.-Thurs. 1-4pm & 8-11pm; Fri.-Sat. 1-4pm & 8:30-11pm; Sun. 1-4pm; closed Monday

Since the late 18th century, this quiet street corner in the salty seaside neighborhood of La Barceloneta has borne the name Can Solé. Its conversion from a shop to a restaurant in 1903 set in motion a century-old trajectory – from fisherman's tavern of humble stature to famous culinary institution, offering some of the best classic Catalan cooking, rice dishes and seafood in Barcelona. Throughout the elegant downstairs dining room, framed photos of celebrities (*famosos*) who have visited Can Solé give guests a glimpse back at more than a century of Barcelona's most celebrated citizens.

Chef Mari Carmen Durán follows the seasons, so when the artichokes of Catalonia flood into Barcelona in late winter/early spring, she serves a heaping plate of golden, paper-thin slices of crispy-fried artichoke hearts, blanketed in shaved foie gras *mi cuit*. This was soon followed on our visit by a platter of the famous *trompetes de la mort amb xipirons* (black trumpet mushrooms with baby squid), along with a plate of ultra-fresh *navalles a la planxa*, razor clams grilled and served plain to allow the flavor of the sea to be the star.

Can Solé has a multitude of rice dishes from which to choose – from the *arròs negre* (black rice, creamy and jet black due to the addition of squid ink) to the restaurant's signature dish, the *arròs caldós Can Solé*, which is more brothy than paella and cooked in a wide iron *cassola* (casserole). When ordering the arròs caldós, you choose your protein from an extensive list, be it sea cucumber, sea urchin, prawns, scallops, crab or clams. We ordered the luxurious lobster paella, with perfectly tender rice and delicious bits of *socarrat* (crispy rice grains) that become crusted around the edges and the bottom of the pan. Paella is all about the rice and the broth, with the seafood or meat playing a supporting role, and the version here pays the utmost respect to tradition.

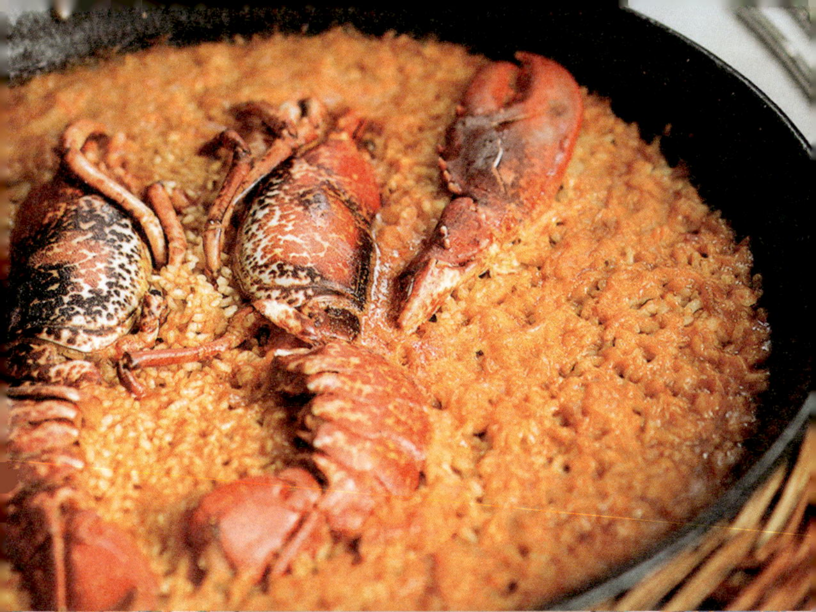

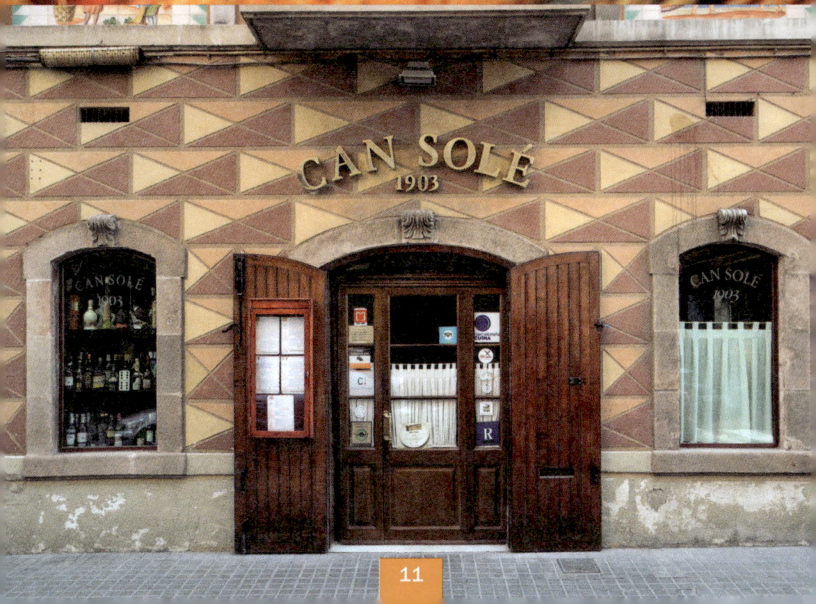
CAN SOLÉ
1903

EL PASSADÍS DEL PEP

Address: Pla de Palau 2,
La Ribera-El Born
Telephone: +34 93 310 1021
(reservations recommended)
Hours: 1-4pm & 9pm-midnight;
closed Sunday

Simple Pleasures

El Passadís del Pep may be located in one of the most visited quarters of Barcelona, but it's out of sight down a long corridor for anyone who isn't looking for it. From the moment you sit down, the "house" offers you your first bottle of cava, and the celebration of food and life begins. There is no menu and there are no "daily specials," just whatever they decide to cook that day.

The restaurant, whose name means "Pep's Corridor," was opened in 1979 by the late Joan Manubens, an iconic local restaurateur, and is still run by his family. The restaurant specializes in *cocina de mercado*, or market cuisine, prepared in a simple, traditional Mediterranean style. As if in a ballet, the show begins when the waiters start to dance around you and the food arrives at the table in a continuous flow of abundance: Iberian cured ham, anchovies, typical Catalan bread rubbed with tomato; sautéed baby squid with rice and garlic; choice shellfish such as *cañaíllas* (a kind of sea snail), velvet crabs or spider crabs prepared in such a delicate way that all the natural flavor is retained.

The long first act ends and the second act begins. Stewed chickpeas with ham, artichokes and Basque peppers in olive oil might appear on your table, or perhaps a delicious stew of wild rabbit with mushrooms. Or how about *caldereta de bogavante*, a traditional dish with squid and clams in olive oil, a tiny touch of garlic, parsley and a little bit of lard to add intensity and richness to the flavors, all of which complement the star of the dish: a fresh lobster from the Bay of Biscay, cooked in salted water or even seawater.

The choice of wine from the excellent cellar is the only aspect of the meal that is left up to you. The "house" will also make recommendations of wine pairings but you are given the "freedom to combine them as you like." The important thing here is to enjoy the meal, which the warm, comfortable atmosphere encourages.

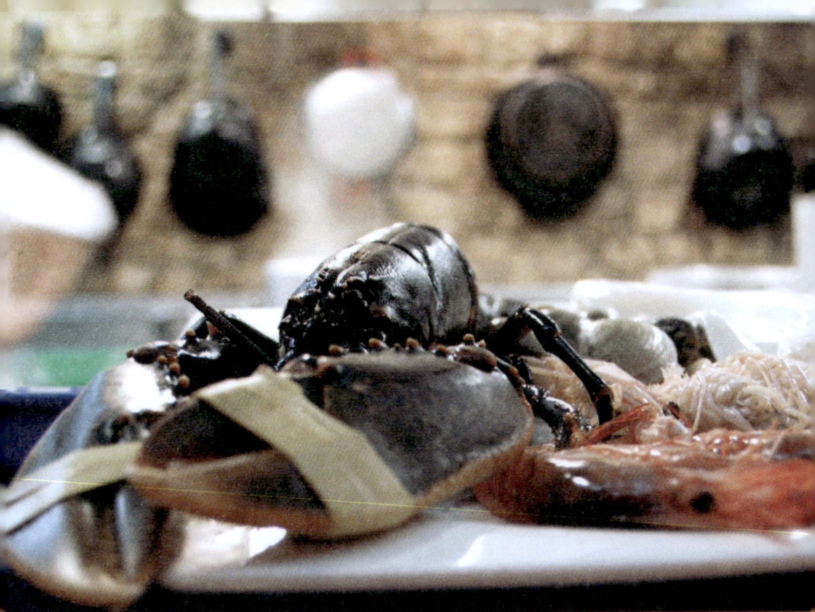

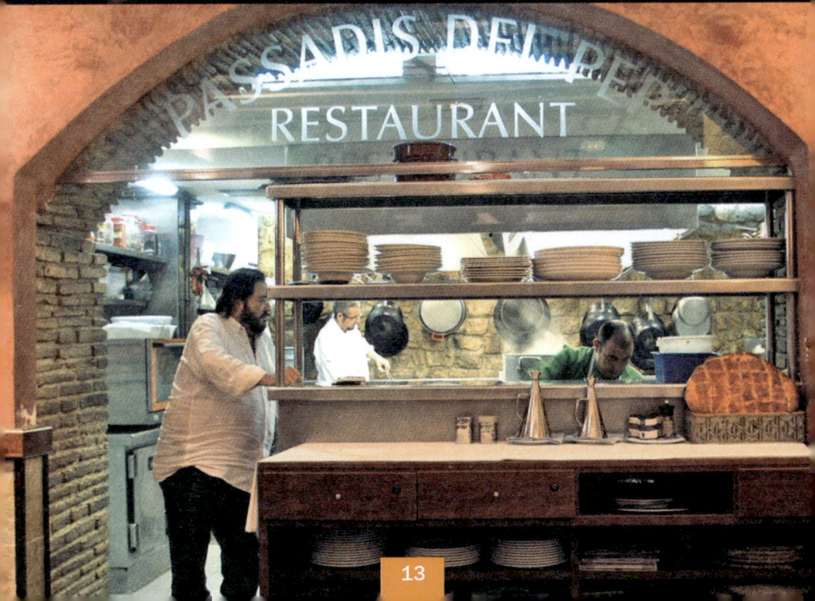
PASSADIS DEL
RESTAURANT

LA COVA FUMADA

The Bomb Squad

Address: Carrer del Baluard 56, Barceloneta
Telephone: +34 93 221 4061
Hours: Mon.-Wed. 9am-3:20pm; Thurs.-Fri. 9am-3:20pm & 6pm-8:20pm; Sat. 9am-1:20pm; closed Sunday & holidays; closed in August

One of the most beloved gastronomic icons in Barcelona's port area, La Cova Fumada is a place to take off your tie, eat with your hands and relinquish your smartphone, lest the screen get covered with grease from your fingers.

The atmosphere has remained almost unchanged since the 1940s. In those difficult years just after the Spanish Civil War, the customers were people from the neighborhood and workers at shipyards and the nearby factories who came to have a glass of wine and to heat up their own food in the open "cheap kitchen." The same spirit still pervades the tiny venue today, from the seven old, marble-topped tables and the cramped open kitchen to the almost prehistoric blackboard.

La Cova Fumada is legendary for its food. Maria Pla, grandmother of the current owners, brothers Josep Maria and Magí Solé, is said to have invented the famous and now ubiquitous potato bomb, a breaded and deep-fried ball of mashed potato with pork served with aioli or a spicy cayenne sauce. It's just one of many classics on the menu, which includes tender and tasty fried artichokes, cooked chickpeas, stewed beans from Cartagena, *butifarra negra* (black sausage) and salt cod. Sardines, mackerel, prawns, squid and octopus are all served with a touch of olive oil and are best eaten with some *pa amb tomàquet* (bread rubbed with oil and tomato). The only change in the menu in the last 70 years is the introduction of seasonal seafood, such as fresh clams or crayfish.

La Cova Fumada is a place with what Spaniards call *solera*, a sort of vintage character and maturity. And nobody in the Solé Pla family would ever think of changing this.

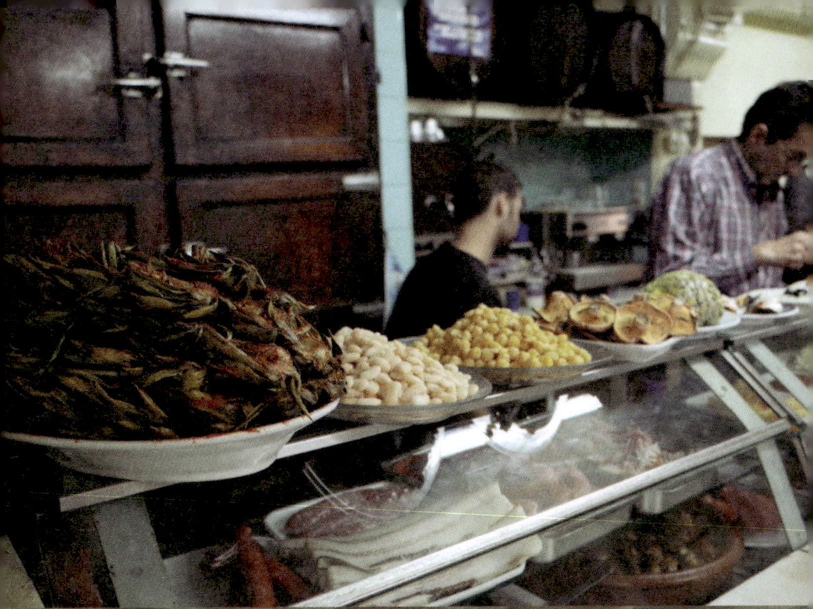

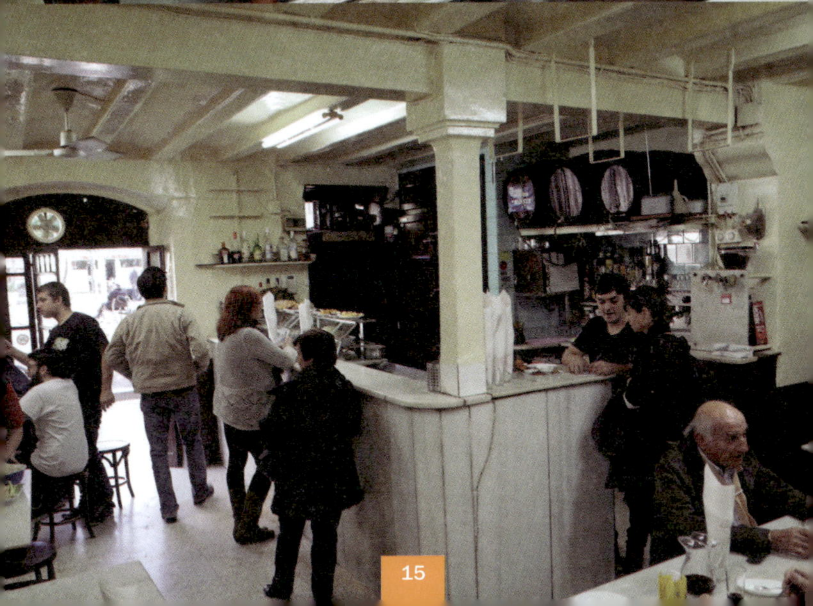

LA ESTRELLA

Grand Dame

Address: Carrer Ocata 6,
La Ribera - El Born
Telephone: +34 93 310 2768
Hours: Tues.-Sat. 1:30-4pm
& 8:30-11pm;
closed Sunday & Monday

Josefa Chiquillo opened La Estrella in 1920 as a kind of travelers' inn and began cooking for guests in 1924. Her great-grandson, Jordi Baidal, and his wife, Josefa Villada, run the restaurant today, serving simple but refined Catalan cooking, with a little French and Italian influence, thoughtfully prepared from quality local products. The atmosphere is formal but relaxed, quiet and friendly. Eating here feels like eating in someone's home.

One of La Estrella's most beloved specialties is the starter of chickpeas with prawns, served in a clay casserole. The chickpeas have been divested of their papery skins and are tender and delicate, the grilled prawns offer their sweet, marine flavors, and everything is bound by a rich, earthy garlic confit mousseline. The last time we visited La Estrella, Baidal surprised us with some *canyuts*, small razor clams from the Ebro Delta, which he grilled and served with a traditional *picada* of toasted almonds and hazelnuts crushed in a mortar with olive oil. This technique has been used since medieval times to thicken sauces and intensify flavors.

Cod, a cornerstone ingredient of Spanish and Catalan cooking, is another standout at La Estrella. Baidal cooks the *morro*, considered the best part and found along the back, close to the head, of specimens that are more than 10 years old. (The very best morro usually comes from cod that's between 20 and 30 years old.) Many of his cod preparations are based on old Catalan recipes, such as those served with that garlic mousseline or *romesco* sauce (made from red pepper, almonds and bread) or with spinach and pine nuts. The wonderful Lenten cod, stewed with artichokes, chickpeas, hard-boiled eggs, olive oil, onion, garlic, tomato and paprika, is a masterpiece.

Like an aged cheese or cellared wine, La Estrella has only gotten better with time.

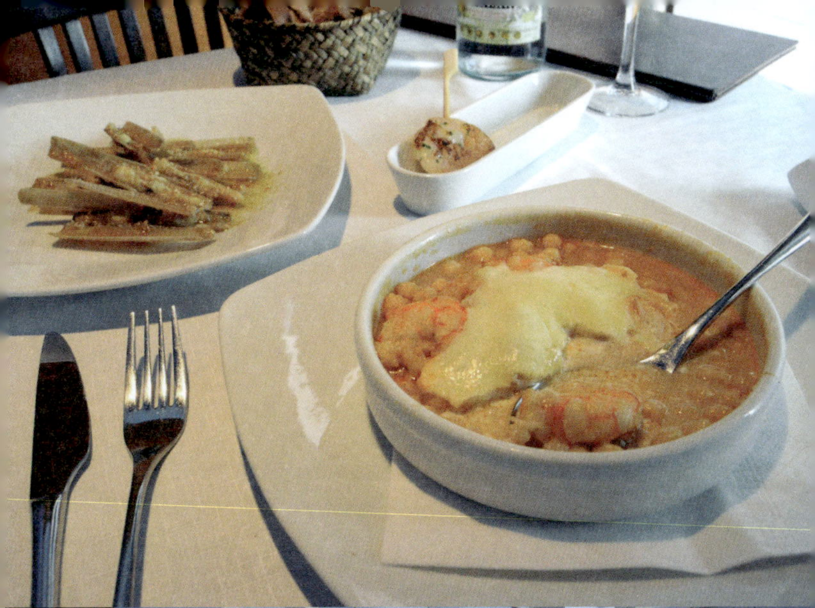

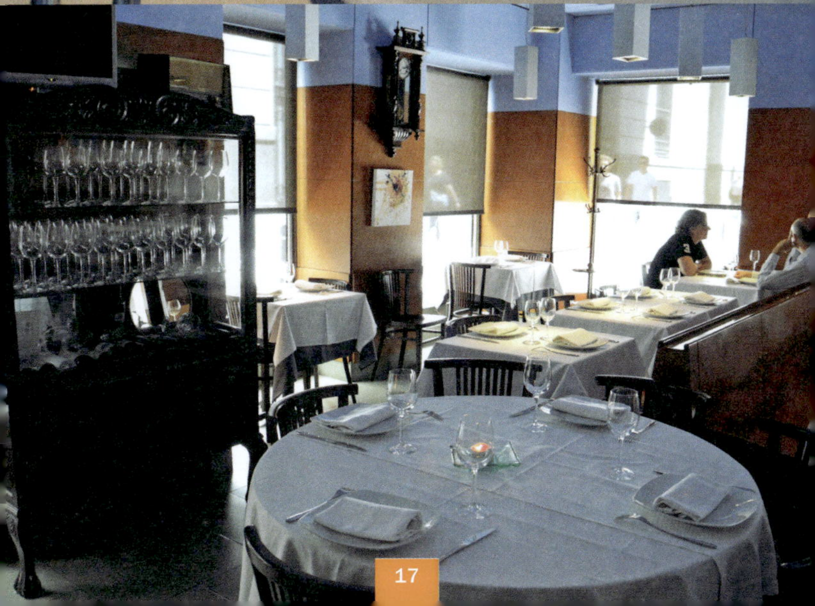

LA PINEDA

The Sausage Club

Address: Carrer del Pi 16,
Barri Gòtic
Telephone: +34 93 302 4393
Hours: Mon.-Sat. 9am-3pm
& 6-9:30pm;
Sun. 11am-3pm

The sign over the entrance says La Pineda was established in 1930, but it has actually been around much longer. In the 19th century it served as a place to slaughter pigs and prepare meat. Around the turn of the century, it became a *colmado*, a small store selling dry goods and *conservas* (tinned or jarred foods). As the years passed, La Pineda began to focus more on selling *embutidos* (sausages) and cheeses along with the conservas. The proprietors also installed a marble-topped bar in the back and started serving snacks and drinks.

In 1976, Antonio Segovia, then 14, arrived in Barcelona and began working at La Pineda. After a few years, he was joined by his younger brother José, and now, nearly 40 years later, they run the place. The brothers have put together a top-notch list of suppliers, and their meats, cheeses and tinned seafood are all of excellent quality. There is *morcón*, a cured, paprika-flavored sausage from Jabugo, white and red *longaniza* from Murcia and *chistorras*, fast-cured, fat-laced sausages from Pamplona.

But what we really can't resist are the *butifarras*, traditional Catalan sausages made with pork, salt, pepper and other spices. A seemingly infinite number of other ingredients can be added, including honey, pine nuts and *calçots* (spring onions). On any given day at La Pineda there are at least four different varieties of butifarra on offer. Our favorite, the butifarra with *ceps* (porcini mushrooms), is succulent and rich, accented by a spicy, mushroomy depth that makes us close our eyes and sigh with contentment. It's even better washed down with a glass of the house-made *vermut*.

We're not the only butifarra fanatics at La Pineda. In 2010, a group of younger customers went so far as to form the Buticlub, a "butifarra appreciation society," with La Pineda serving as club headquarters.

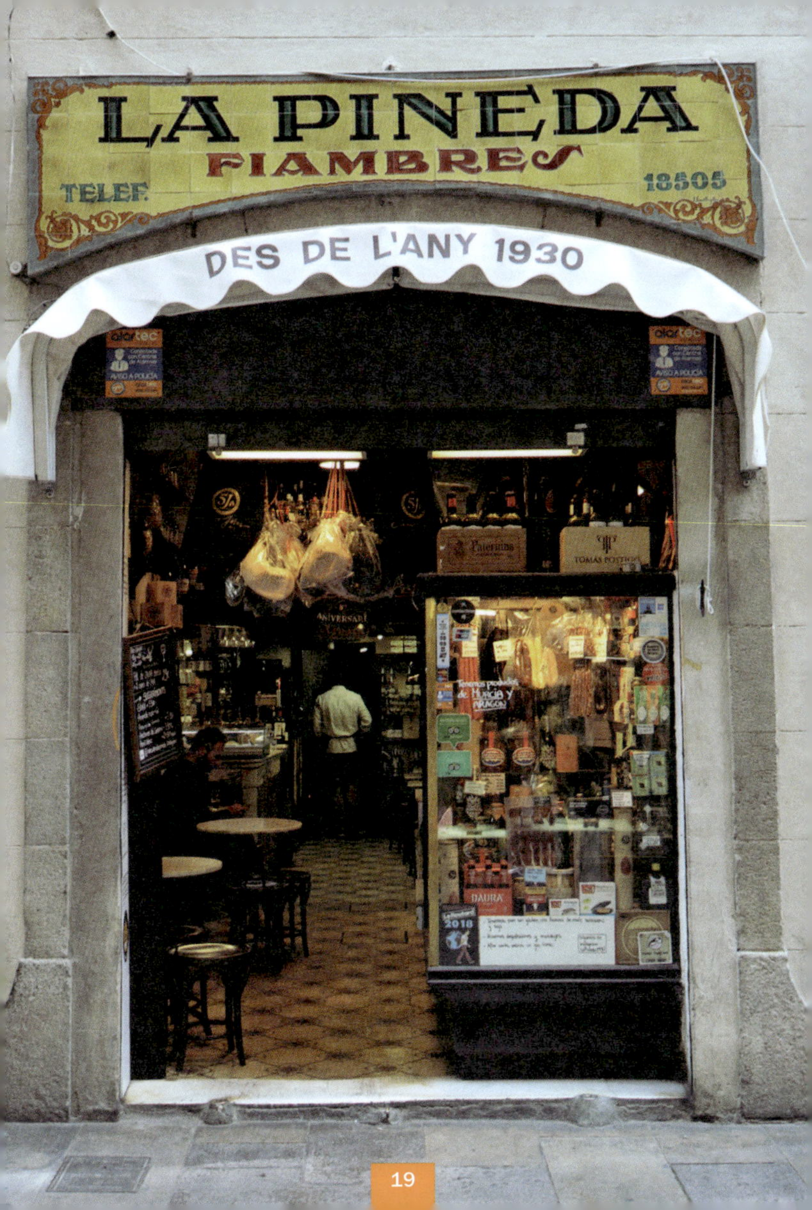
LA PINEDA
FIAMBRES
TELEF.
18505
DES DE L'ANY 1930
DAURA
2018

SAGÀS

Hands-on Cuisine

Address: Pla de Palau 13, El Born
Telephone: +34 93 310 2434
Hours: Sun.-Thurs. 12:30pm-00:30am; Fri. & Sat. noon-1am

Specializing in high-end sandwiches, acclaimed Catalan chef Oriol Rovira's restaurant Sagàs Pagesos i Cuiners ("Farmers and Cooks") embraces the farm-to-table philosophy, with a menu that is both distinctively Catalan and international in scope. According to Irene Baños, the second maitre d' at Sagàs, Rovira feels that in recent years much of the cuisine coming out of Catalonia has been too "*elaborado,*" and he wanted to provide something more simple but just as tasty. The sandwich was thus the perfect solution. In addition, because sandwiches must be eaten with the hands, Rovira believes diners are able to get more in touch with what they are consuming.

The menu at Sagàs is divided into two sections: "Origens" and "Mundo." The first offers a selection of sandwiches based on traditional Catalan cuisine, while the latter features concoctions inspired by cuisines from around the world, such as Sicilian smoked sardines, Mexican *chicharrón* and even a Texas Chili Cheese Burger. There is also a selection of desserts and a mid-sized drinks menu that includes a variety of "Gin Tonics," wines, beer and cava (Spanish sparkling wine).

The most popular sandwich on the "Origens" menu is the "Porchetta" – roasted pork served on *pa de coca*, a traditional Catalan flatbread – and we could certainly see why. The crunch of the *coca* and the tender juiciness of the flavorsome pork was a killer combination. We were similarly impressed by the "Botifarra de Perol," Catalan sausage stuffed with locally gathered mushrooms and served on a toasted baguette. From the "Mundo" menu, we tried the Vietnamese "Báhn Mì," a baguette filled with porchetta, spicy red Sriracha sauce, carrots, ginger and cilantro. By this time, with sauce dripping off our chins and covering our fingers, we had more than achieved Rovira's goal of "getting in touch" with our food. For dessert, we finished up with a wicked Catalan combination of chocolate, olive oil and salt served on warm toasted *pa de coca.*

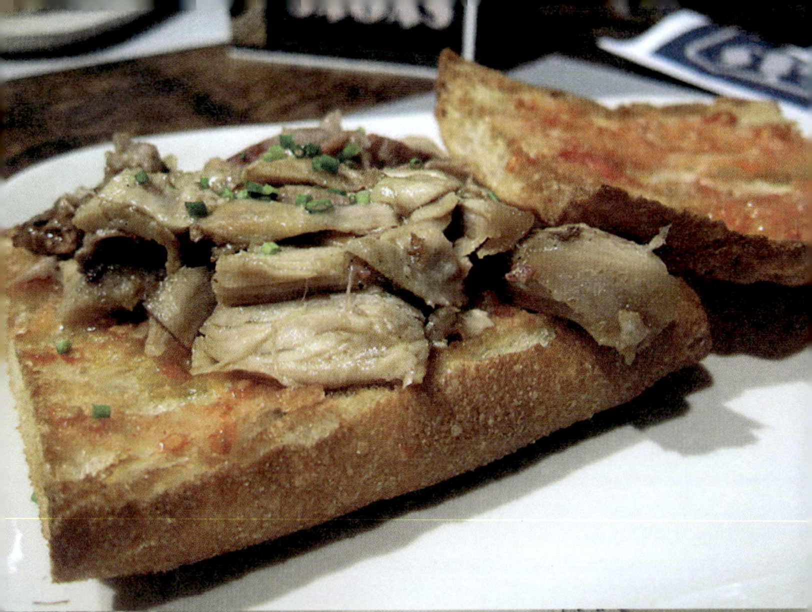

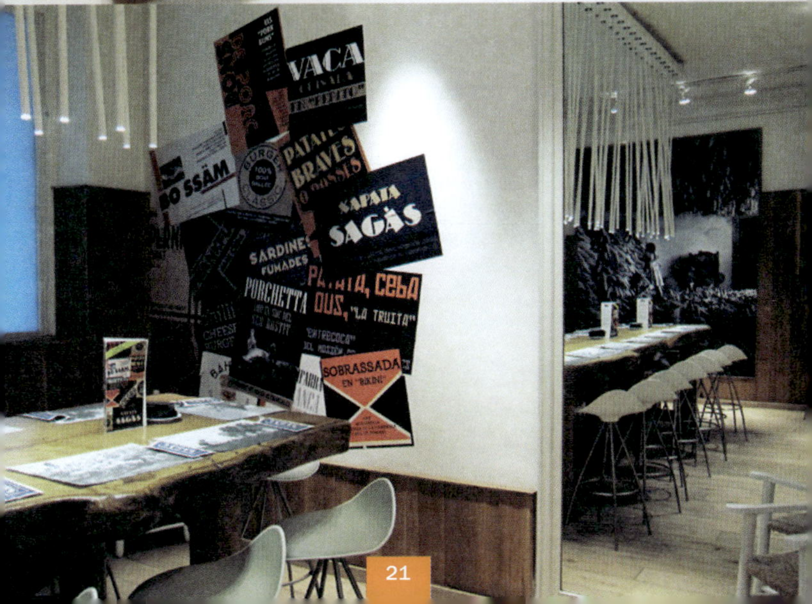
VACA
BO SSÄM
PATATES BRAVES
XAPATA SAGÀS
SARDINES FUMADES
PORCHETTA
PATATA, CEBA OUS, "LA TRUITA"
SOBRASSADA EN "BIKINI"

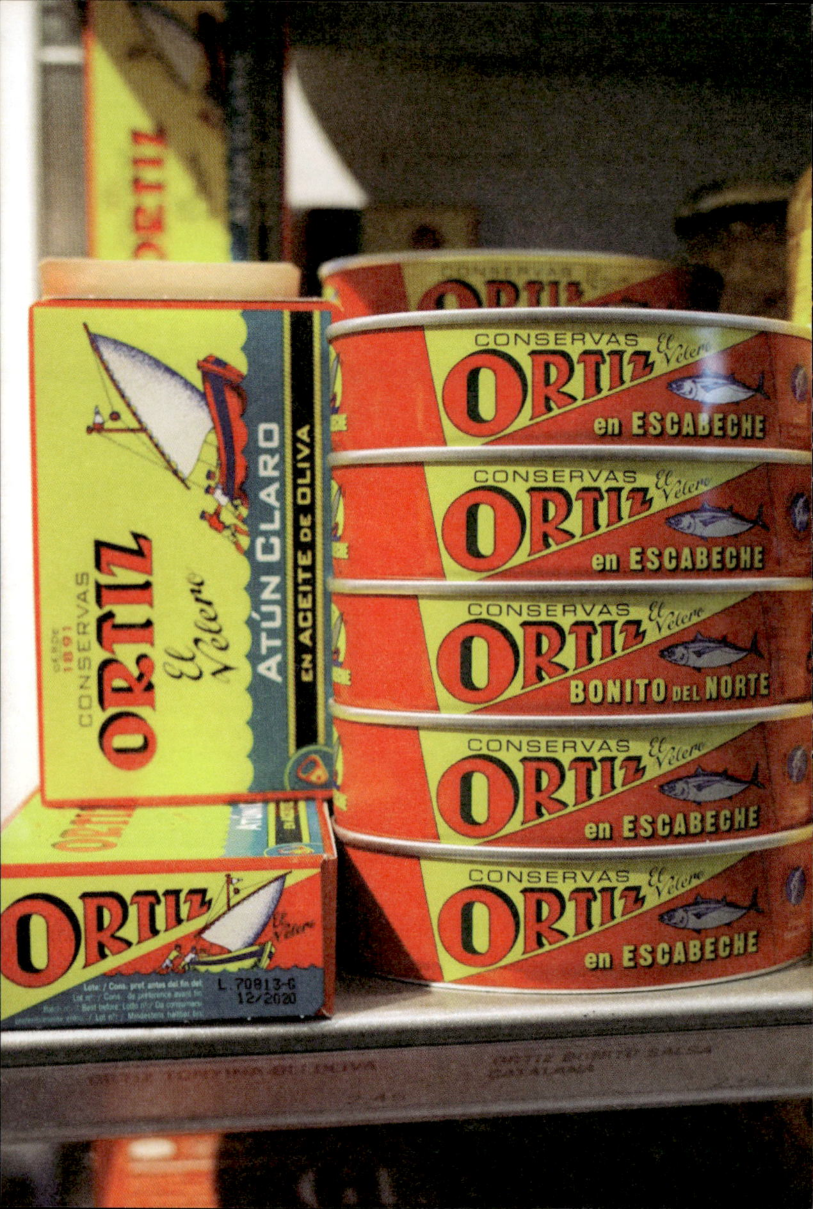

DESDE 1891
CONSERVAS
ORTIZ
El Velero
ATÚN CLARO
EN ACEITE DE OLIVA
CONSERVAS
ORTIZ
El Velero
en ESCABECHE
CONSERVAS
ORTIZ
El Velero
en ESCABECHE
CONSERVAS
ORTIZ
El Velero
BONITO DEL NORTE
CONSERVAS
ORTIZ
El Velero
en ESCABECHE
CONSERVAS
ORTIZ
El Velero
en ESCABECHE
ORTIZ
El Velero
L.70813-G
12/2020

THE EIXAMPLE DISTRICT

BAR BODEGA GELIDA

Address: Carrer Diputació 133, Eixample (corner Comte d'Urgell)
Telephone: +34 93 453 1061
Hours: Mon.-Fri. 7am-10pm; Sat. 7am-4pm; closed Sunday, holidays and August

Old Faithful

At the beginning, Gelida was just a bodega where Joan Llopart Pujó, who came from the village of Gelida in Penedés, offered Catalan wine, cold cuts and a few traditional Catalan dishes cooked by his grandmother, like *butifarra amb mongetes* (boiled sausage with beans).

These days, Gelida, now run by Llopart Pujó's son Alberto, is a modest yet charming old-school "all in one," where you can buy bulk wine, have a drink with tapas or sit and enjoy a complete meal with dessert. The atmosphere is homey and pleasing, relaxed between meal times but hectic at lunch and dinner. The day begins early with *esmorzars de forquilla,* traditional hearty "fork breakfasts," and the same dishes are offered all day. Customers can come in for a *callos* (tripe stew) fix whenever they need it. Gelida's specialty is traditional Catalan cooking, particularly stews, but there are also a few salads, soups, grilled fish and salt cod dishes, plus tapas, omelets and sandwiches.

Paella is served on Tuesday and here, it's a surf-and-turf version with ribs, squid, mussels, prawns and peas. On Friday and Saturday, Gelida serves *cargols* (snails) stewed in a spicy sauce made with chorizo, ham and herbs. On Wednesday, there's pig feet. The restaurant's most iconic Catalan dish might very well be *cap i pota*, the famous cartilaginous stew made with beef head and leg, plus some chorizo and a powerful *sofrito* to make a dense and soft spicy sauce, perfect for dipping bread in.

Another great classic is fricandó, a dish with medieval origins – a very different version of which turns up in French cooking – made with thin beef chops that are fried, coated in flour and then stewed with a sofrito of garlic, onion and tomato (the original went without), ranci wine (a fortified sweet wine) and moixernons (St. George's mushrooms), the delicate fungi that give this recipe its distinctive flavor.

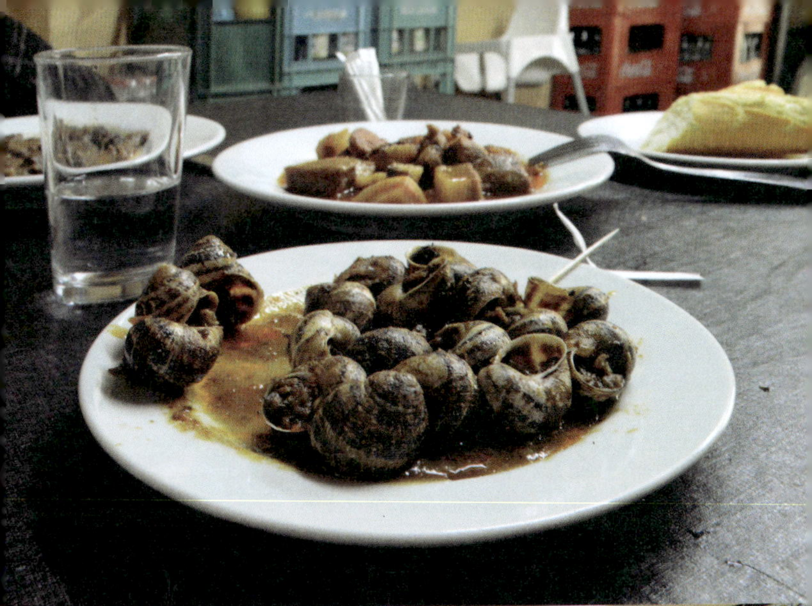

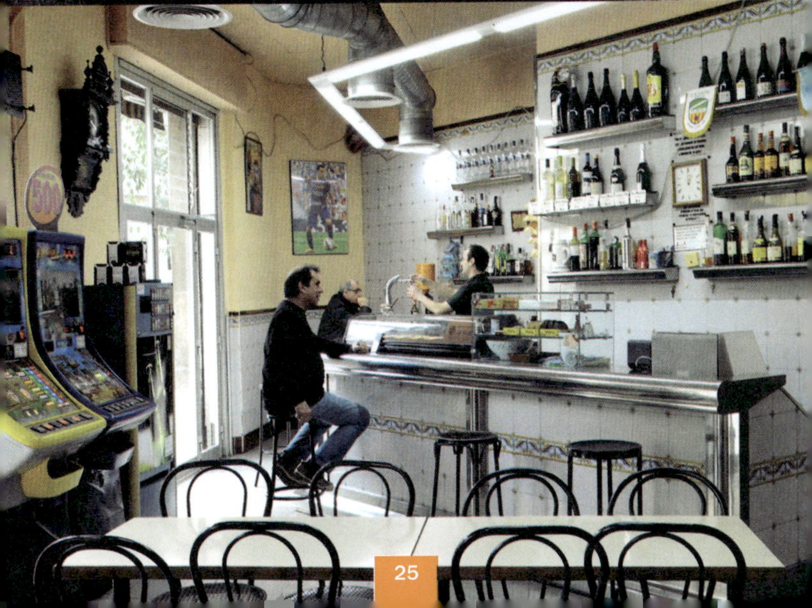

CAN VILARÓ

Address: Carrer Comte Borrell 61, Sant Antoni-Eixample
Telephone: +34 93 325 0578
Hours: Mon.-Sat. 8am–4pm; closed Sunday

No Guts, No Glory

Can Vilaró, a third-generation traditional eatery located in front of Sant Antoni market, pays tribute to offal, cuts of pork, lamb and beef that most Catalan people seem to have turned their backs on these days. The interior is bare-bones, but owner Dolors, her über-friendly husband Sisco and their hardworking daughters, Aida, Alba and Anna, make regulars and newcomers feel like they are eating at Grandma's house.

The faces of Dolors's legion of fans certainly glow with happiness when they have her superb *cap i pota*, a traditional Catalan stew made with calf's head and leg and chickpeas, as well as *lletons amb mongetes* (sweetbreads with baked beans), *fetge amb salsa* (liver with sauce), *tripa amb cigrons* (tripe with chickpeas), *peus de porc amb bolets* (pig's trotters with wild mushrooms), *cervells a la romana* (battered lamb brains), *callos* (beef tripe and pork feet stew) or *conill amb herbes* (rabbit with herbs) for breakfast or lunch.

For not-so-adventurous eaters, this popular restaurant offers more everyday dishes, such as breaded chicken, pork rib stew, sardines, cod salad, baked cod and squid in sauce. There isn't a set lunch menu but there are daily specials: *escudella* (a traditional Catalan soup) and *carn d'olla* (a stew of seasonal vegetables, beef bones and pork sausages) on Mondays; *fideus a la cassola* (casserole noodles) on Tuesdays; *llenties amb xoriç* (lentils with chorizo) on Wednesdays; *arròs a la cubana* (rice with fried egg and tomato sauce) on Thursdays and Fridays; and *fricandó* (beef fillets with wild mushrooms cooked in a beef broth sauce) on Saturdays.

When asked about Can Vilaró's future, Dolors says, "If this market becomes a tourist trap like La Boquería, I don't think Can Vilaró will last another 100 years, to be honest. Tourists want to eat paella, not offal." We hope she's wrong, but in the meantime, we plan to eat as many bowls of *cap i pota* as we possibly can.

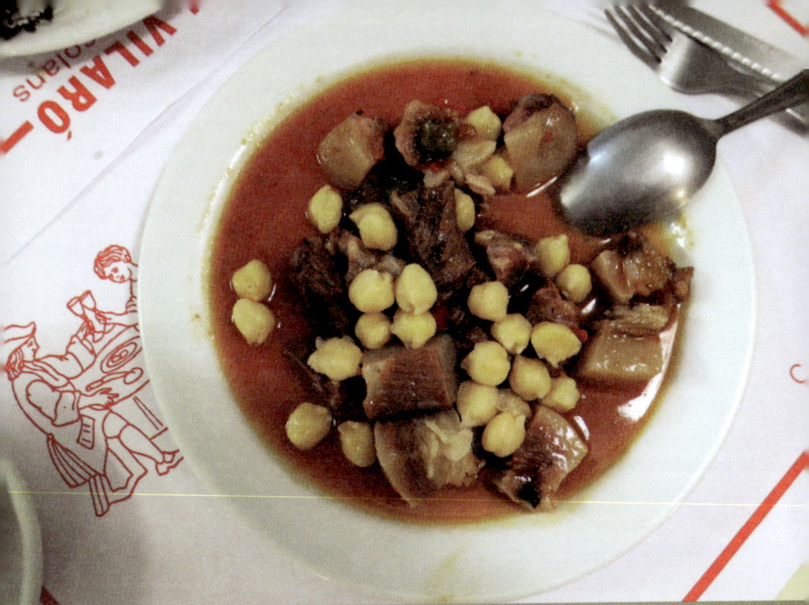
VILARÓ

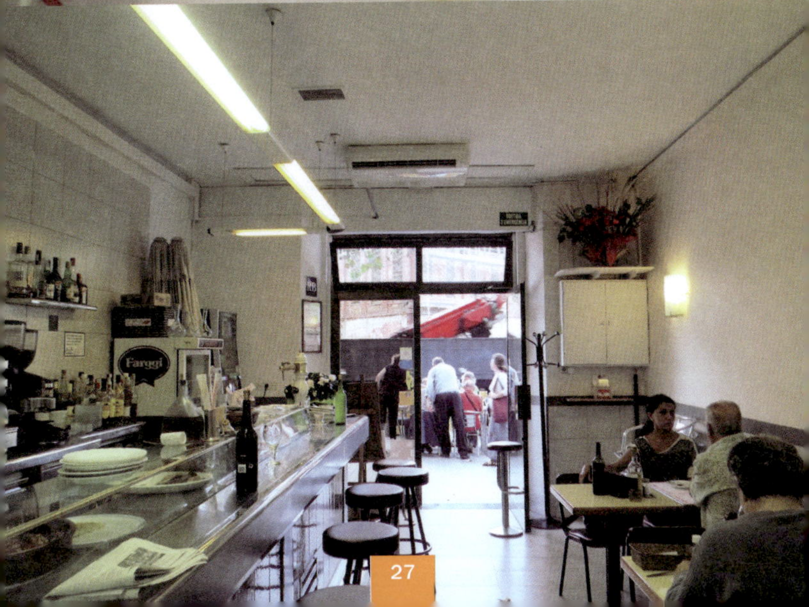
Farggi

ELS ENCANTS

Flea Market Finds

Address: Avinguda Meridiana 69, Eixample
Telephone: +34 93 246 3030
Hours: Mon., Wed., Fri. & Sat. 9am-8pm; some food stalls closed July 22 to August 3

One of the oldest still-functioning flea markets of its kind, Els Encants offers all kinds of fascinating objects for perusal, and the best way to fuel up for looking through it all is to head up to the top floor. There, long communal tables and benches sit in front of a wide variety of restaurant stalls offering takeaway made from excellent ingredients.

One of our favorite vendors, located in a corner of the top floor, is **Stop&Mos**, which specializes in *pintxos*, such as egg and chorizo, *escalivada* (eggplant with onions) and anchovies, as well as hot and cold sandwiches made with the wonderful bread of Forn Baluard. Slices of black beer bread or the traditional Catalan *coca del Mossén* might form the foundation for roast beef, a burger, Catalan cold cuts (chorizo, *fuet, sobrassada de Mallorca, butifarras,* etc.), Iberian ham, cheeses, omelets and vegetables.

Just next door is **Gall Encantat**, a stall specializing in poultry dishes – besides chicken, there's magret duck and foie gras, croquettes, sandwiches, salads and much more, including homey pies for sale.

On the other side of the top-floor space is **Peixet als Encants**, where the seafood and fish on offer include fried anchovies and squid, a delectable seafood *fideuà* with especially well-cooked pasta, grilled sardines, mussels *a la marinera*, fish soups and other freshly prepared specialties.

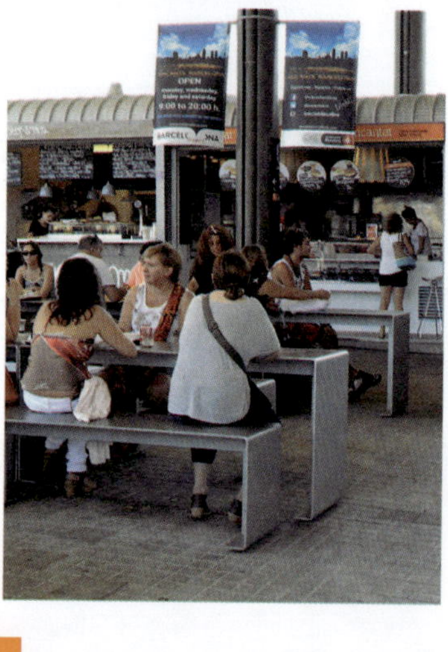

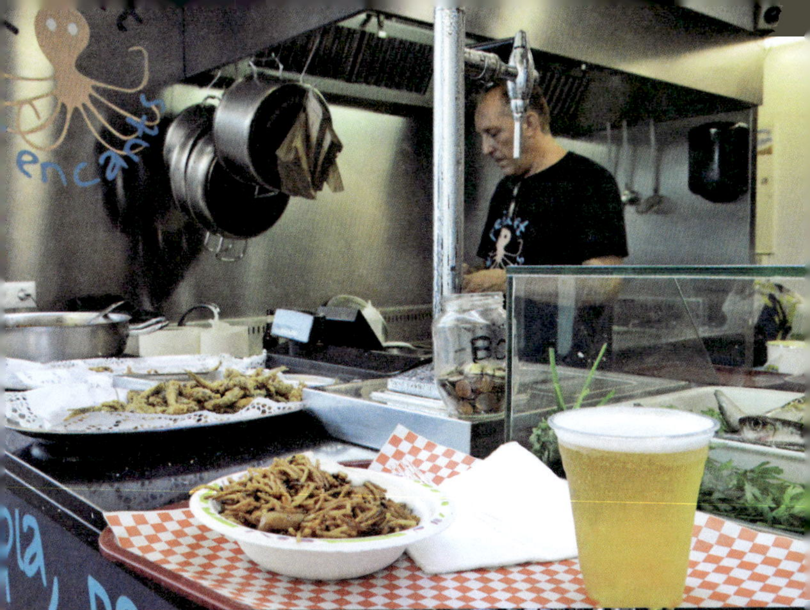
encants

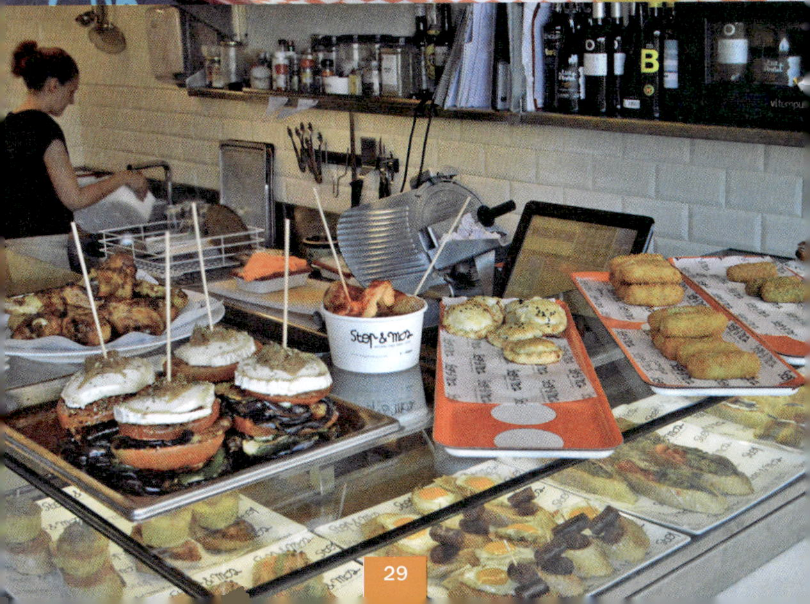
Stop & Mos

ENTREPANES DÍAZ

Address: Carrer Pau Claris 189, Eixample
Telephone: +34 93 415 7582
Hours: Tues.-Sun. 1pm-midnight, closed Monday

Sandwich Central

Kim Díaz, a well-known local restaurateur and owner of Bar Mut tapas bar and El Mutis cocktail bar, wanted to pay tribute to one of the most humble and sadly underrated Spanish snacks, the sandwich, by giving it the respect it deserves.

It took months for Díaz to find the right bread rolls, at Forn de Sant Josep, an old bakery a few blocks away. Then came the right chef, Víctor Lema, able to turn classic plated dishes into nearly 20 absolutely mouthwatering gourmet sandwiches. Customers' top five favorite sandwiches are *calamares* (calamari with squid ink mayonnaise), *rabo de buey* (oxtail), *cochinillo* (roast suckling pork), *kokotxas al pil-pil* (lower part of the cod chin cooked in parsley and garlic) and Antxón (red pork sausage and poached egg).

Despite the sandwich being the main theme of this bar, Díaz hasn't neglected to include a wide range of equally delicious offerings on the menu. Among the tapas are classics such as *croquetas, callos* (pork tripe cooked with chorizo and paprika) and *patatas bravas,* as well as more Andalusian ones: *ortiguillas* (deep-fried anemones), *cazón en adobo* (marinated school shark) and *tortitas de camarón* (deep-fried shrimp pancakes). Brunch at Entrepanes Díaz means eggs: eggs Benedict, scrambled eggs and omelets. Among the daily specials there are always meat, fish and pasta options. Desserts are as delicious as the rest of the menu: Amaretto ice cream, *crema catalana* and chocolate marquise are the highlights. Drinks include *caña* (a small glass of draft beer), Spanish red and white wine, French rosé and champagne, Catalan cava and homemade vermouth.

Black-and-white photos, a marble bar and tables, red stools, mirrors and blackboards fill up this little corner joint while the chatty and cheerful veteran waiters offer impeccable service and lively conversation to regulars and newcomers. Businesspeople and the thirty-something hipster crowd congregate here throughout the day, giving it a classy and yet informal vibe.

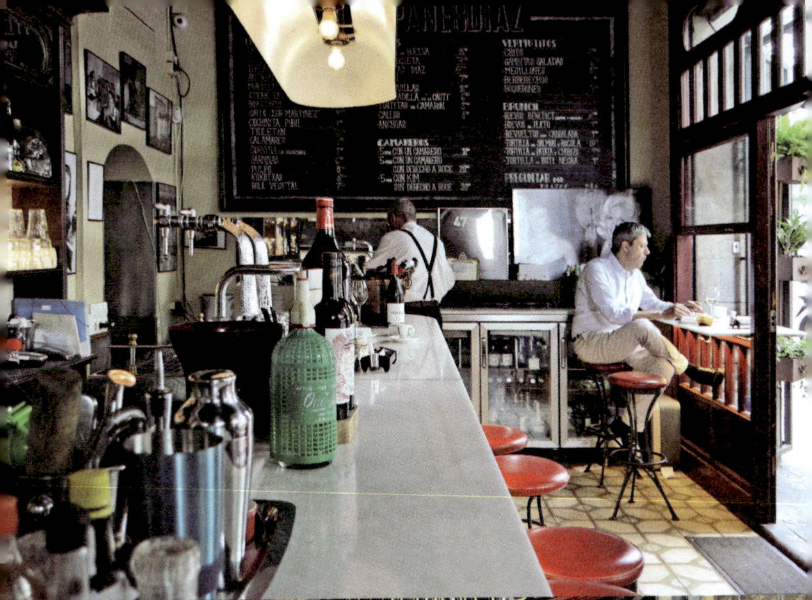
CAMARONES
BRUNCH

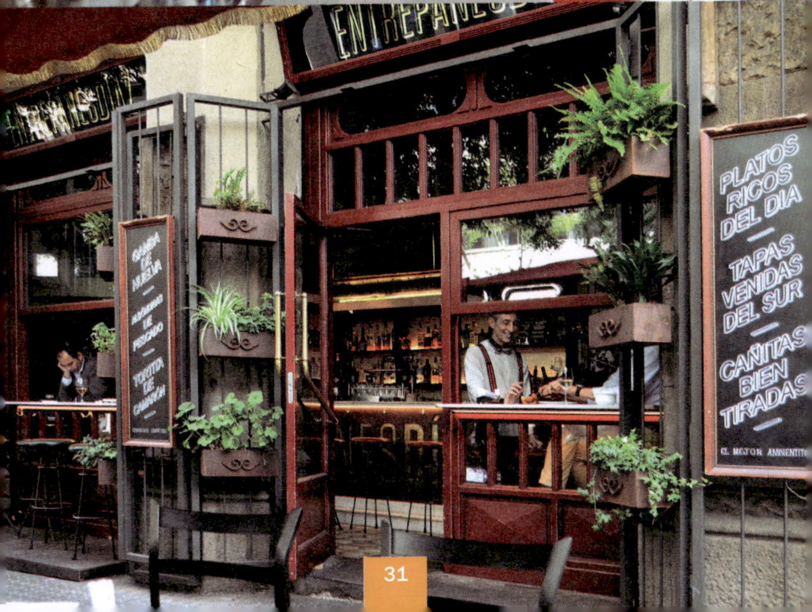
GAMBA DE HUELVA
ALBÓNDIGAS DE PESCADO
TORTITA DE CAMARÓN
PLATOS RICOS DEL DIA
TAPAS VENIDAS DEL SUR
CAÑITAS BIEN TIRADAS
EL MEJOR AMBIENTITO

HORCHATERÍA SIRVENT

Original location:
Address: Carrer del Parlament de Catalunya 56, Eixample
Telephone: +34 93 441 2720

Branch:
Address: Carrer de Balmes 130, Eixample
Telephone: +34 93 215 1913
Hours: 9am-10:30pm

Nectar of the Gods

Be it kvass in Russia or boza in Turkey, every nation seems to have one of their own, a locally loved drink that to most outsiders comes off as a particularly strange brew. In Spain, that drink is called *horchata* in Spanish and *orxata* in Catalan, a unique and deliciously refreshing concoction made from *chuflas* (tigernuts), water and sugar, and served chilled.

In Barcelona, there's really only one place to try the stuff: Horchatería Sirvent. In fact, no visit to the city is complete without stopping by this Barcelona institution, founded in 1920 by Tomás Sirvent and now managed by members of the third generation of the Sirvent family. The faithful line up here in droves during the summer months, waiting with ticket in hand to sip the best *orxata de xufla* in town. Sirvent's horchata is made the traditional way, that is, as it's made in Valencia, which boasts ideal conditions for growing chufas. Just as "little green peppers" are associated with Padrón in Galicia, the Valencian town of Alboraya is renowned for the sweet, intense flavor of its tigernuts, which are actually small tubers.

To many an acquired taste, *orxata* goes down sweet with a slightly bitter aftertaste. Catalans routinely triple-park their cars to run in for a Venti-size cup to go or for larger, family-size containers. Horchata will keep in the refrigerator for two to three days.

In addition to horchata, Sirvent also offers *torró* (a kind of nougat), ice cream and *granizados*, which are semi-frozen drinks similar to a Slurpee. While the *granizado de café* we tried was uninspired and too sweet, the *granizado de limón* was like chunky lemonade, a perfect remedy for the hot sun.

Sirvent is closed for three months during winter and reopens in April following *Semana Santa* (Easter). The original location at Carrer del Parlament 56 feels more authentic, often like a block party. But for a quick fix, especially for those averse to lines, the Balmes location serves the same artisanal *orxata*.

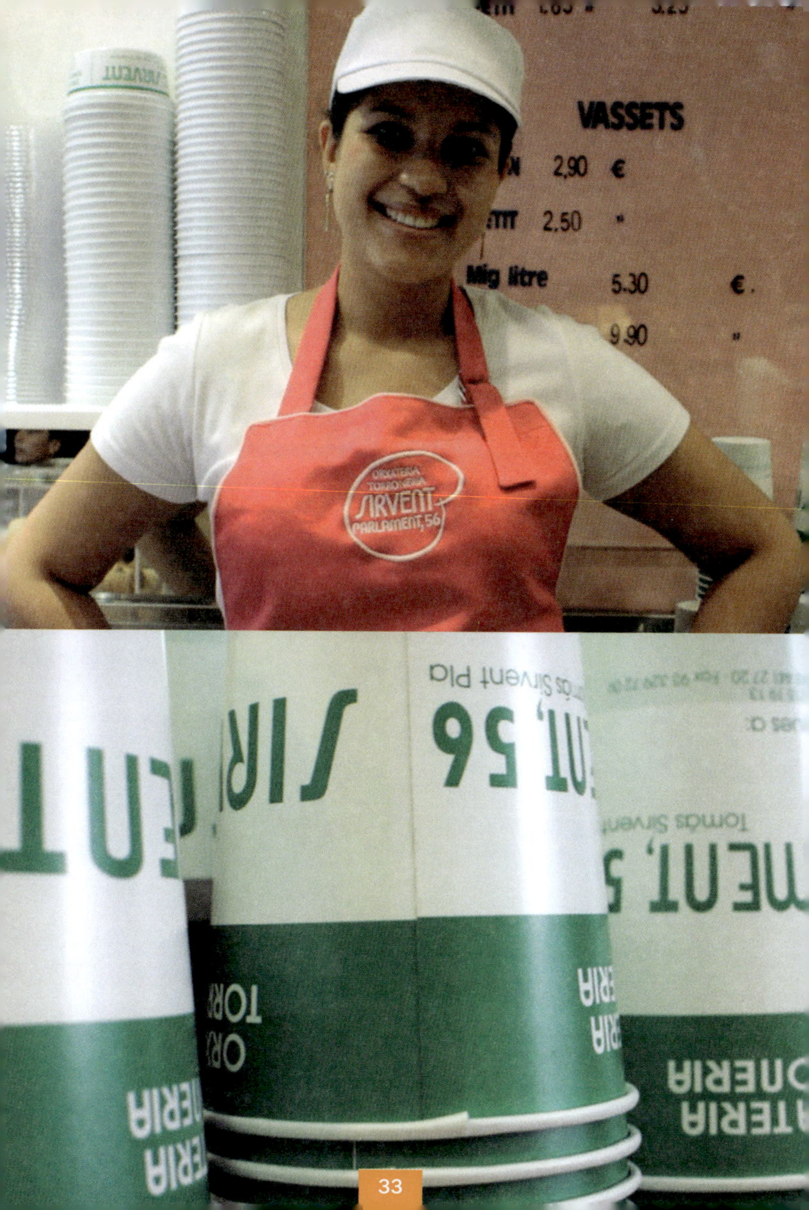
VASSETS
2,90 €
2,50
Mig litre 5.30 €.
9.90
SIRVENT
PARLAMENT, 56

EL JABALÍ

Address: Ronda de Sant Pau 15, Sant Antoni
Telephone: +34 93 441 1082
Hours: Tues.-Sun. 9am-1am; closed Monday

Hams and Roses

Ever since this combination delicatessen, butcher shop and tapas bar first opened in 1958, the main star of the show here has been the Iberian acorn-fed ham, *jamón ibérico de bellota*. Emilio García and his son Jordi make regular trips to two ham hot spots, Salamanca, in the Castile and León region, and Huelva, in Andalusia, to select their favorite cuts. Then, depending on demand, they bring back the hams they need and leave the rest in *secaderos*, naturally ventilated warehouses, in the villages where the ham is sourced to keep them curing in optimum conditions. The resulting ham has a deep red color, a sweet, intense flavor and a rich layer of fat with a characteristic astringent finish.

In addition to ham, El Jabalí ("The Wild Boar of Ronda") offers a delightful menu of tapas made from the delicatessen products it carries – aged Castilian and creamy Catalan cheeses, Iberian *chorizo*, Catalan *botifarra* sausages.

We are particularly fond of the ham "bomb": a ball of Iberian ham, minced onion and potato that is breaded, deep-fried and served with a spicy, vinegary tomato, garlic and cayenne-spiked sauce. There's a superb Russian salad made with excellent canned Spanish tuna, ham and freshly cooked carrots, potatoes, beans and peas, all bound together with a delicate mayonnaise. It demonstrates just how transcendent this maligned dish can be.

Traditional preparations include Catalan beans with botifarra and cod and *callos* (spicy pork tripe), as well as salads like the classic *esqueixada*, made with tomatoes, onions, peppers and olives mixed with cod (in this case fresh, as opposed to the more usual *bacalao*).

Open from morning to late at night, El Jabalí remains a good place to stop and eat something before or after going to a show at one of Avinguda del Paral·lel's theaters.

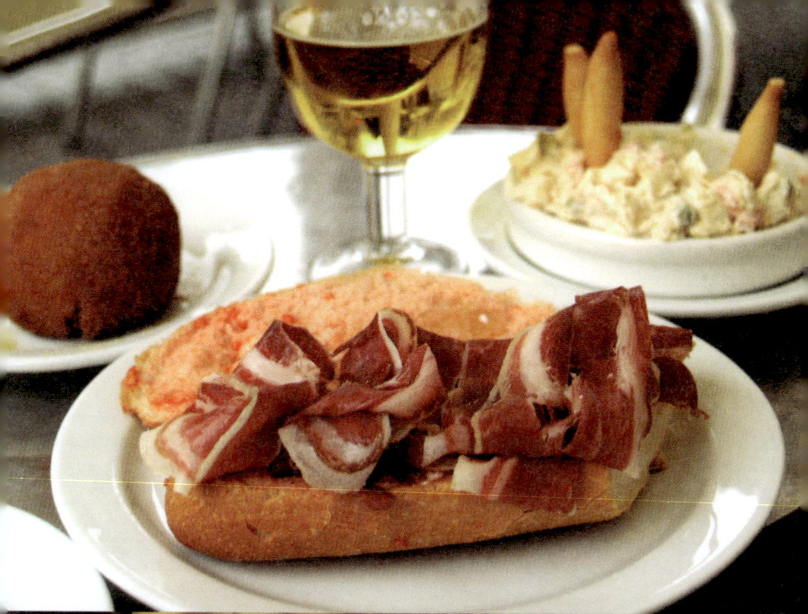

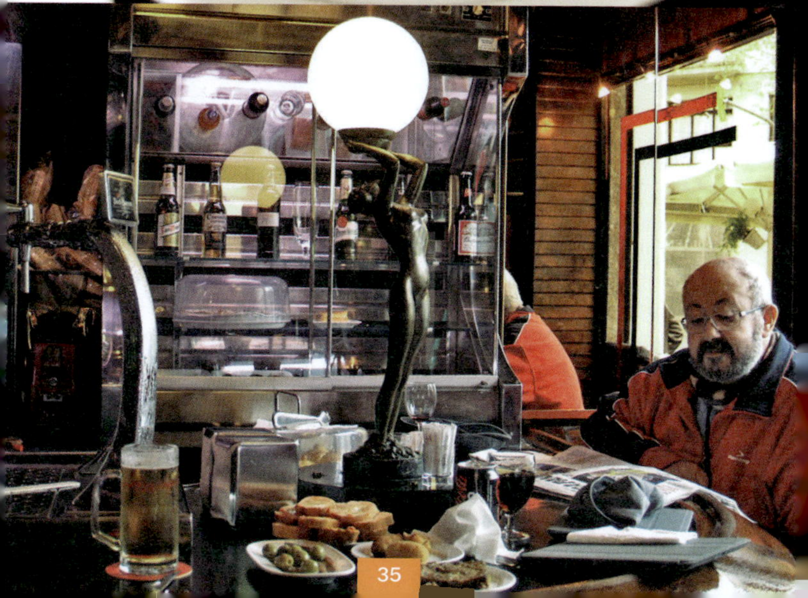

SENSE PRESSA

Stress-Free Dining

Address: Carrer Enric Granados 96, Eixample
Telephone: +34 93 218 1544 (reservations required)
Hours: Mon.-Sat. 1:30-3:30pm & 9-11:30pm

In 2005, José Luís Díaz was thinking about retiring after working for many years in great local restaurants. He wanted to leave behind the stress of big kitchens, but still to cook the recipes that he loved with a different rhythm and with more time and care. And so he opened Sense Pressa (literally "Unhurried"), a cozy, modest eatery.

Each night, Díaz and his team cook around 25 covers (by reservation only) in a single, leisurely seating for customers who come from all over the city to eat in Sense Pressa's comfortable, welcoming atmosphere, where the solicitous attention and the unhurried tempo are both important parts of the meal.

The cuisine here is based in Spanish multiregional traditions, with that magic combination of simplicity and remarkable ingredients. Lamb, pork, Atlantic and Mediterranean fish and seafood from the best sources are given classic treatments that have been thoughtfully reconsidered to improve the dish and the experience. Díaz offers a fixed menu and also a roster of dishes that change daily with the season.

The star here is the absolutely wonderful dish of chickpeas with a "broken" fried egg and *espardenyes,* a kind of sea cucumber. Díaz invented the dish, taking as inspiration another seafood-legume combination, the classic clams with beans. The chickpeas are profoundly luscious and creamy. The egg unifies all the ingredients but also allows their individual identities to shine. The sea cucumber has a much more intense flavor than that of clams, and so calls for a counterpart that can stand up to it – hence the chickpeas.

Among other great dishes we've enjoyed recently at Sense Pressa were a refreshing and tasty cold tomato soup with lobster and delightful squash blossoms, stuffed with cod *brandada,* battered and fried and served with a light romesco sauce.

We can't leave Díaz's restaurant without having the chocolate soufflé, a flourless marvel of a generous size. It's yet another reason to linger at the table.

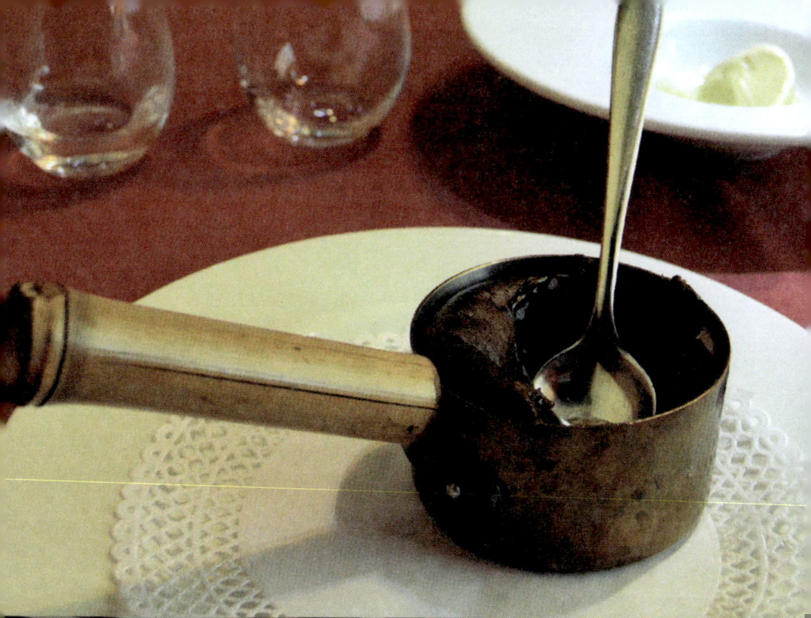

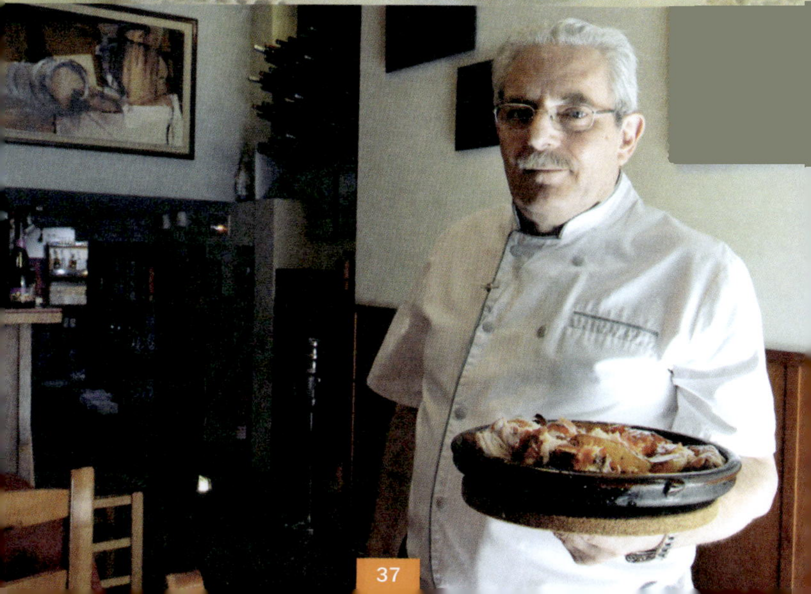

SERGI DE MEIÀ

Back to the Land

Address: Carrer de Aribau 106, Eixample
Telephone: +34 93 125 5710
Hours: Tues.-Sat. 8:30-11:30am, 1:30-3:30pm & 8:30-10:30pm
closed Sunday and Monday

Sergi de Meià, in his own words, "started in cuisine the day he was born," growing up as he did in his mother's restaurant. His mother, Adelaida Castells, is still a fundamental part of the team at de Meiá's restaurant and is in charge of the most traditional recipes they make. Those dishes are part of a concept dedicated to Catalan cuisine that is a tribute to local products, mixing tradition and modernity in the same pot.

De Meià works directly with 87 Catalan farmers to get the best authentic ingredients for his kitchen, which offers both the menu of the day and a surprise tasting menu – as well as a vegan version – that takes diners through the four Catalan provinces.

We started with a spoon of squash cream with a nutty Catalan *picada,* made of minced almonds and hazelnuts, and crowned with a flower, followed by a wonderful 19th-century dish: a salad composed of a soft, juicy onion cooked for eight hours at a low temperature, some herbs and a great bittersweet sauce of muscat vinegar and raisins. Next came a *ceviche* made of cute organic mini vegetables and chickpeas, all dressed with lemon. We loved de Meiá's version of *all i pebre,* "garlic and paprika," a traditional fish casserole from the Delta de l'Ebre in northern Valencia and southern Catalan with smoked eel chops in a delicious cream with caramelized pine nuts. Staying gastronomically close to the sea, we then had a wonderfully intense clam rice from the same region, with caramelized cuttlefish. The final dish was a nod to the mountains: very traditional meatballs from Pobla del Segur with another picada of minced almonds and hazelnuts, saint George mushrooms from the Pyrenees and aromatic herbs, including rosemary.

The two desserts complement the experience with a selection of Catalan artisan cheeses and a couple of lovely soft chickpeas flour fritters with Catalan cream. The perfect finish for a *tour de force.*

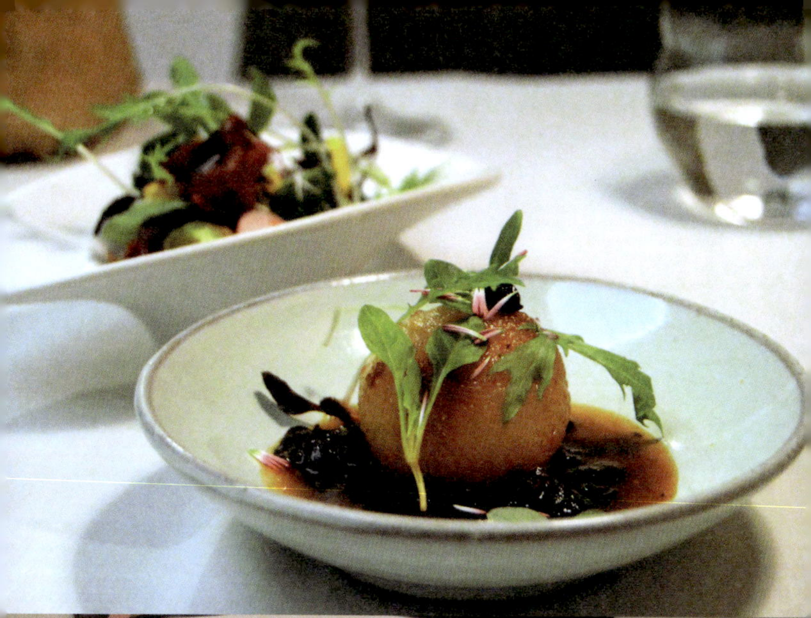

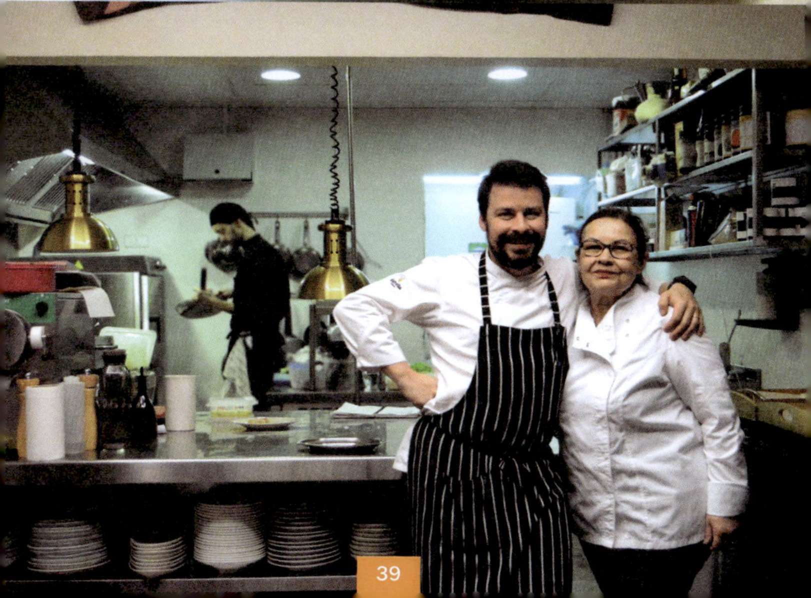

TAKTIKA BERRI

Address: Carrer de València 169, Eixample
Telephone: +34 93 453 4759
Hours: 1-4pm & 8:30-11pm; closed Sat. night & Sunday

Always a Party

Taktika Berri, a family-run Basque restaurant, specializes in *pintxos*, tapas affixed to a piece of bread with a toothpick and traditionally presented open-air, on plates spanning the length of the bar. Patrons are handed an empty plate and are free to help themselves. Once you have finished, simply mosey up to the register and the *camarero* will count the number of toothpicks, or pintxos consumed.

A pintxo crawl is a fine start to an evening, so order a Txakoli – a cloudy white Basque wine that pairs well with anything from the ocean and also olives – and dive in.

With tumbler in hand, sidle up to the bar and try *la gilda*, the quintessential pintxo: anchovy, olive and *guindilla* pepper. Next, look for its cousin, featuring *boquerones*, roasted green pepper and egg, plus a dollop of mayonnaise, vinegar and herbs. The foie gras we tried was rich, buttery and smooth – in a word, excellent. *Tortilla de bacalao* was oily but tasted light; it was so popular, it flew off the plates. *Morcilla* (blood sausage), a thick, black sausage made of pig's blood, rice, onions and spices, sounds gross, but it's not. It was served with a smoky salsa with a note of chipotle, a perfect complement. Though not our favorite, *xistorra*, a spicy Catalan sausage made with paprika, is a safe option for carnivores.

The bar is as important if not more so than the *comedor* in the back, which serves more filling dishes. Some of the *platos estrellas* from the restaurant include *tortilla de patatas/bacalao* (Spanish potato/cod omelet), *pochas* (white beans), *tronco/cogote de merluza* (hake) and *chuletón* (chops). Reservations are required, so call in advance. Eating at the bar is permitted during the day, but at night, service is restricted to pintxos. Get here early because, from the second the door opens at 8:30 each evening, the bar teems with locals anxious to bite into the best Basque tapas in town.

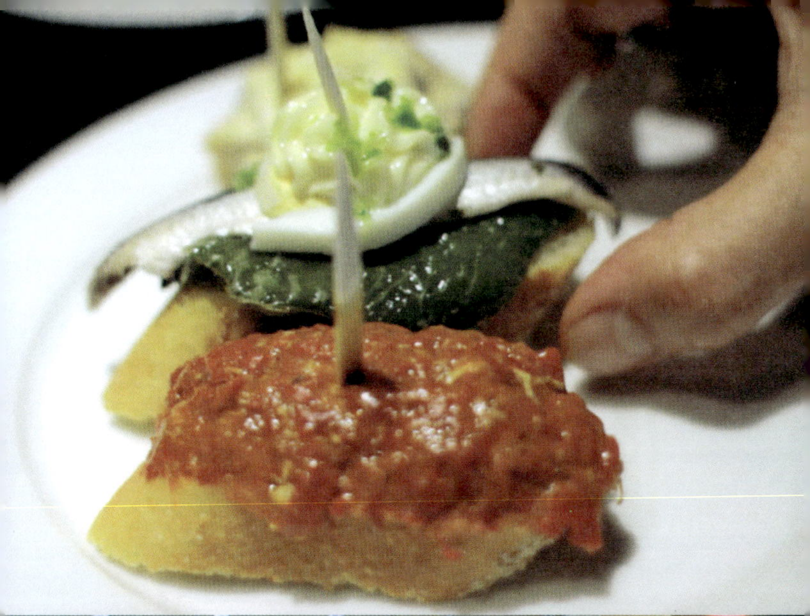

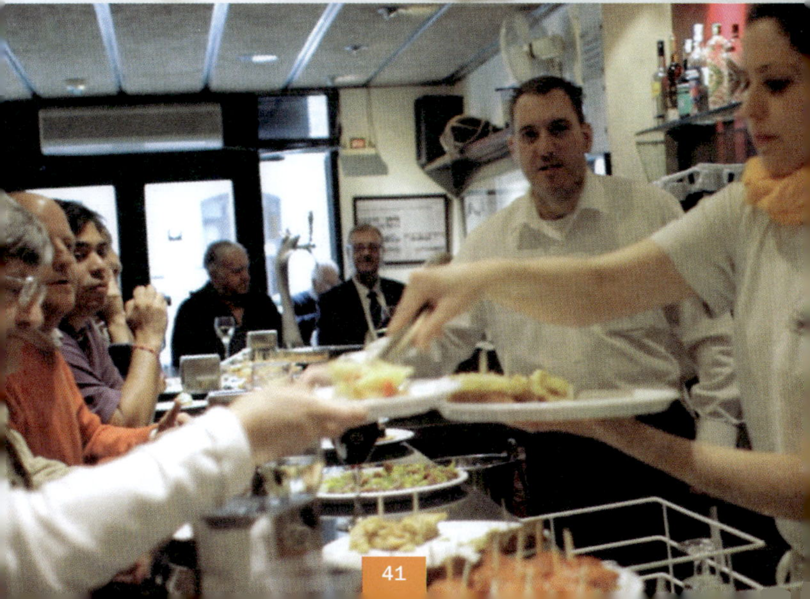

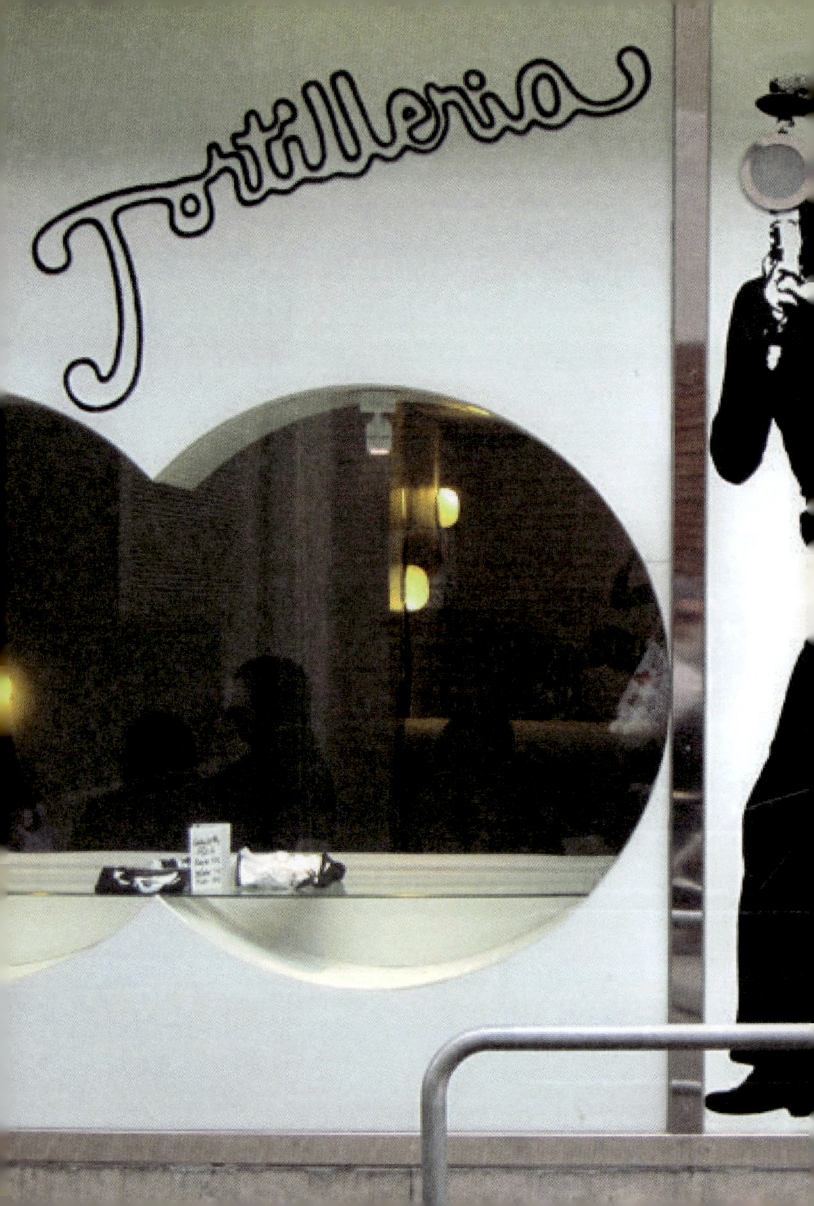
Tortilleria

UPPER BARCELONA

CASA JORDI

Friendly Takeover

Address: Passatge de Marimon 18, Sant Gervasi
Telephone: +34 93 200 1118
Hours: Mon.-Sat. 1-4pm & 8:30-11:30pm; Sun. 1-4pm

A fine example of a classic 20th-century Barcelona restaurant, Casa Jordi is decorated in the old *masía* (traditional Catalan farmhouse) style over two floors but adapted to urban dimensions. The food, market-to-table cuisine with a seasonal menu and daily specials, is rooted in traditional Catalan cooking, Barcelona's classic dishes, blending the popular and rustic, simple and refined. One can see and taste as well the French influences that have been present in the city over the last couple of centuries and have become integral to local traditions, as well as fundamentally Spanish preparations and ingredients, such as exquisite Basque *kokotxas* (cheeks) of hake or Iberian ham from Extremadura or Huelva.

The formula here remains the same as when the restaurant first opened in 1968: no pretensions, just highly enjoyable, straightforward and excellent cooking in an old-school place with white tablecloths and warm, professional service. The recipes and presentation, likewise, are virtually the same as they were when Casa Jordi opened, with a few minor differences (a teriyaki sauce, a basket to serve croquettes, a Kobe beef hamburger). Among the essential dishes on the menu are *esqueixada* (shredded salt cod with tomatoes, onions, olive oil and vinegar), the roasted vegetable dish known as *escalivada*, rustic *cargols a la llauna* (snails grilled in a tin casserole), sole and prawns *al cava*, duck *magret à l'orange* with honey and rosemary and *tournedó* with Café de París sauce.

The kitchen delivers on all these and more with a refined hand. The classic *fricandó* sauce was robust and tasty, amply flavored with Saint George mushrooms, and came with very tender, pleasingly thin veal filets. The ham croquette combines a wonderfully crunchy exterior with a creamy interior, while the local artichokes were meaty within their light, crisp tempura coat. We loved the grilled squid, which were perfectly tender and flavorful with just a touch of garlic and parsley – a prime example of how lovely simplicity can be.

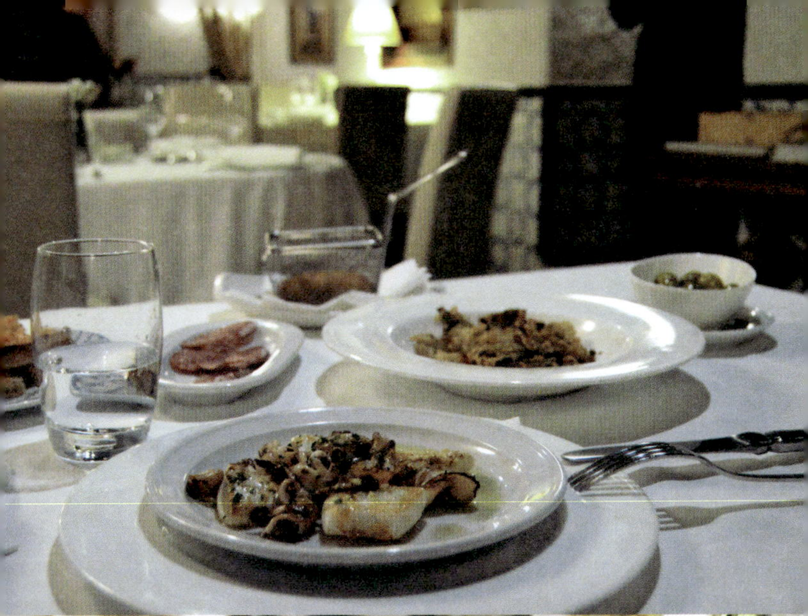

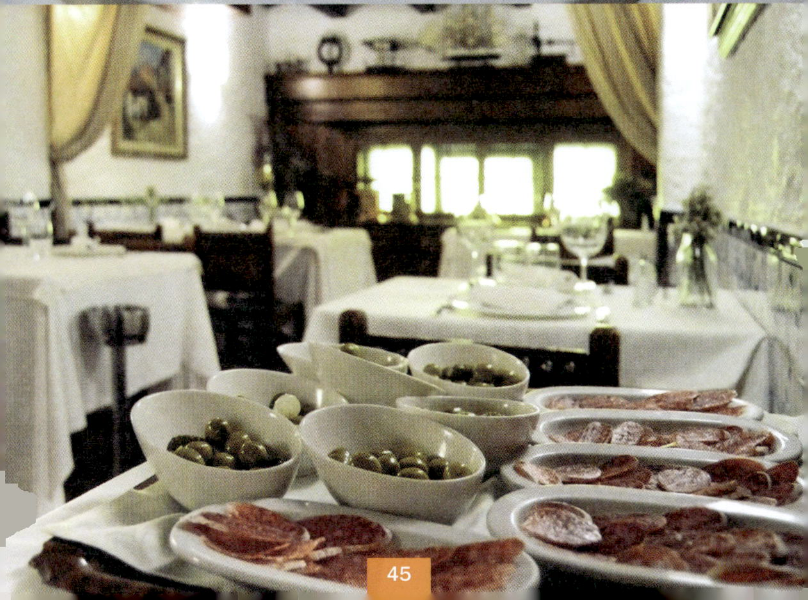

CASA TRAMPA

The Great Escape

Address: Plaça de Vallvidrera 3, Vallvidrera
Telephone: +34 93 406 8051
Hours: Sun.-Thurs. 7am-5pm (lunch from 1pm onwards); Fri.-Sat. 7am-5pm & 8pm-midnight; closed in August

Vallvidrera, a village at the entrance to Collserola National Park that offers gorgeous views of the surrounding forests and the city below, is just the place for a respite from Barcelona's bustling urban streets. And the place in Vallvidrera to go when hungry is without a doubt Antiga Casa Trampa. Founded in 1804, this small bar and restaurant has been in the same family for the past 80 years and the food hasn't changed much in all this time.

Casa Trampa is known for the quality of their *jamón*, which they get from a small village in Salamanca. The food is, to put it quite simply, *comida de abuela* (Spanish grandma food), and we mean that in the best possible way. There isn't anything fancy on the menu, nor is there a multitude of choices, just excellently prepared standbys like ham *croquetas, mandonguilles amb samfaina* (meatballs in a vegetable stew made of tomatoes, eggplants, peppers, garlic and olive oil) and chicken stuffed with cheese, plums, ground beef and onions. As with most home-cooked dishes throughout Spain, almost everything on the menu – from the stewed pigs' trotters served with baked *mongetes* (beans) to the *galtes de porc* (pork jowls, a fatty and flavorsome cut similar to bacon) served with baked potatoes and onions – starts with *sofregit,* a mass of tomatoes and onions that are slowly cooked together in order to form the base of the dish that will follow.

By the time dessert came around we felt like we could barely fit into our chairs but still tried the *Bunyols de nata* (whipped cream fritters) – essentially donut holes, only better, because they came dripping with honey and served with a few dollops of fresh whipped cream. In the end we hadn't eaten anything new (if you don't count the fancy donut holes) but then again, we weren't really looking for anything new. All we wanted was some home-cooked food that tasted as good as it smelled, and that's exactly what we got.

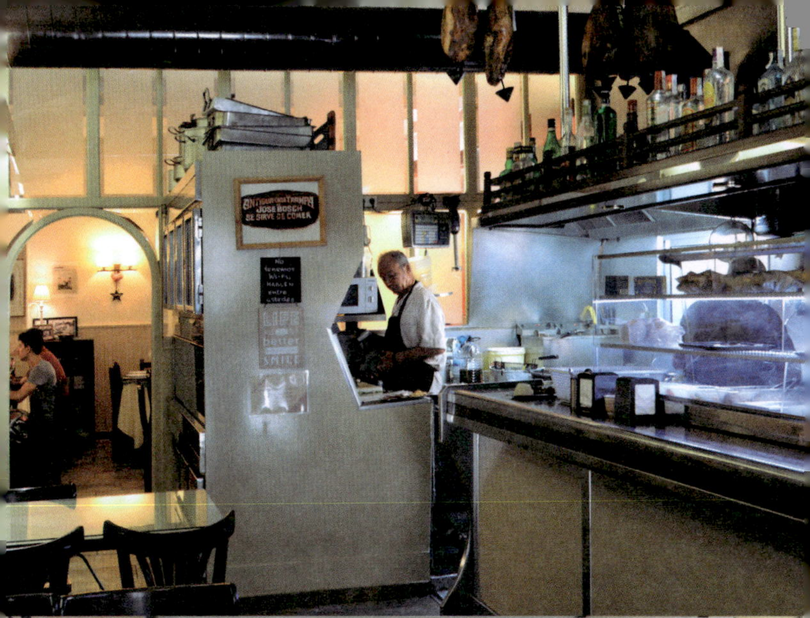
JOSE BOSCH
SE SIRVE DE COMER

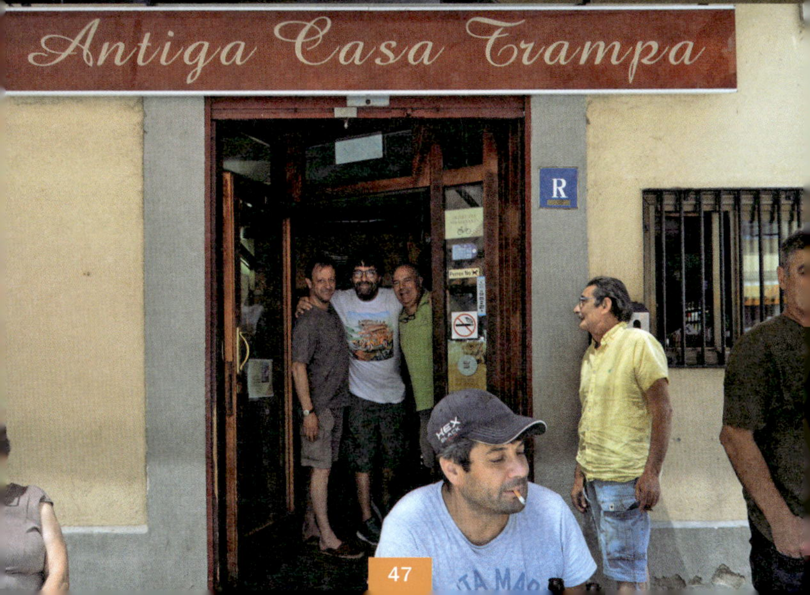
Antiga Casa Trampa
R

EL BISAURA

Fishmonger to Table

Address: Mercat de Les Corts
(from the main entry, on the right)
Travessera de les Corts 215, Les Corts
Telephone: +34 93 339 9362
Hours: Tues.-Sat. 6:30am-4:30pm

Inside Barcelona's lesser-known Mercat de Les Corts is a small, unassuming bar offering up the bounty of the Mediterranean.

El Bisaura opens up shop at 6:30 a.m., serving *esmorzars de forquilla* (hearty Catalan breakfasts like sausage and beans, tripe stew and grilled cuttlefish) to local workers. At lunch, it serves a more refined seafood menu composed of whatever owner Alfonso Puig gets from Peixateria Anna, the fish stand on the other side of the market. The fish and seafood of the day are always seasonal, local and impeccably fresh – which is no surprise, since Puig is also the owner of the fish stand.

Order a glass of wine and give free rein to your appetite: El Bisaura makes some of the best *calamares a la romana* (Roman-style fried squid) in Barcelona, prepared with pristinely fresh squid and a touch of Vichy sparkling water in the batter. And that's just the beginning.

The cuisine and recipes continue to be straightforward and simple. The fish come from the Mediterranean and are caught using sustainable methods. Only before lunchtime (around 1 p.m.) do some marine creatures appear behind the glass; most of the seafood is carried straight from the fishmonger to the kitchen in its ice-filled box. From time to time, you can see Puig bring more fresh fish from the other side of the market – no need to keep all the fish waiting under the counter lights, better to keep it fresh and in optimal conditions before it's prepared and served.

El Bisaura is, as its customers know well, the perfect respite from the surrounding office buildings and urban traffic. Once there, we recommend resting your feet and ordering a chilled Penedés or Albariño and enjoying a wonderful tapa of fried squid or grilled scorpion fish, some delicate yet highly flavorful *escamarlans* (langoustines) or some very special Noah's Ark shellfish.

You can rest assured knowing everything came straight from the source.

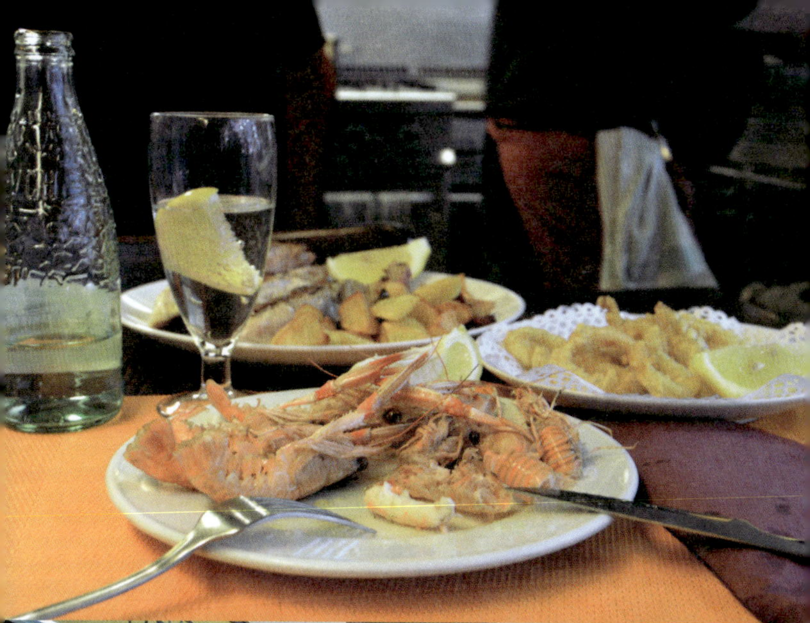

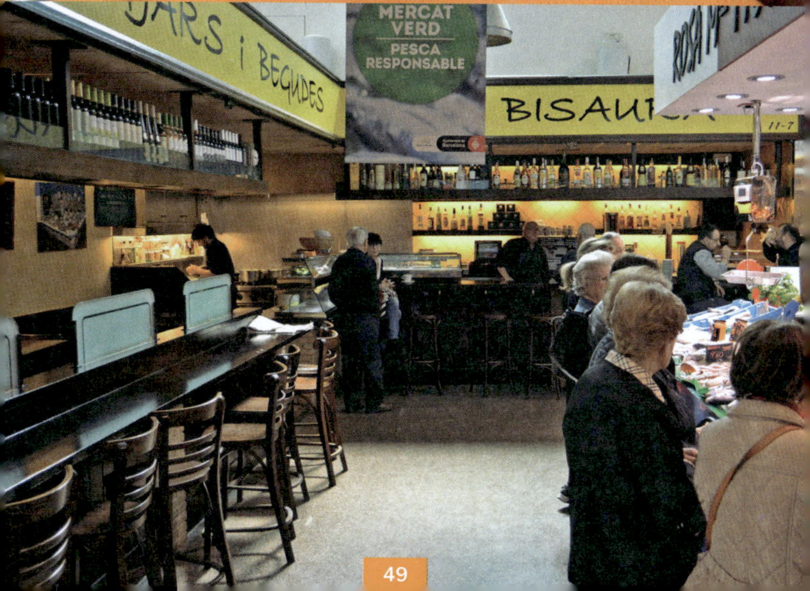
ARS i BEGUDES
MERCAT
VERD
PESCA
RESPONSABLE

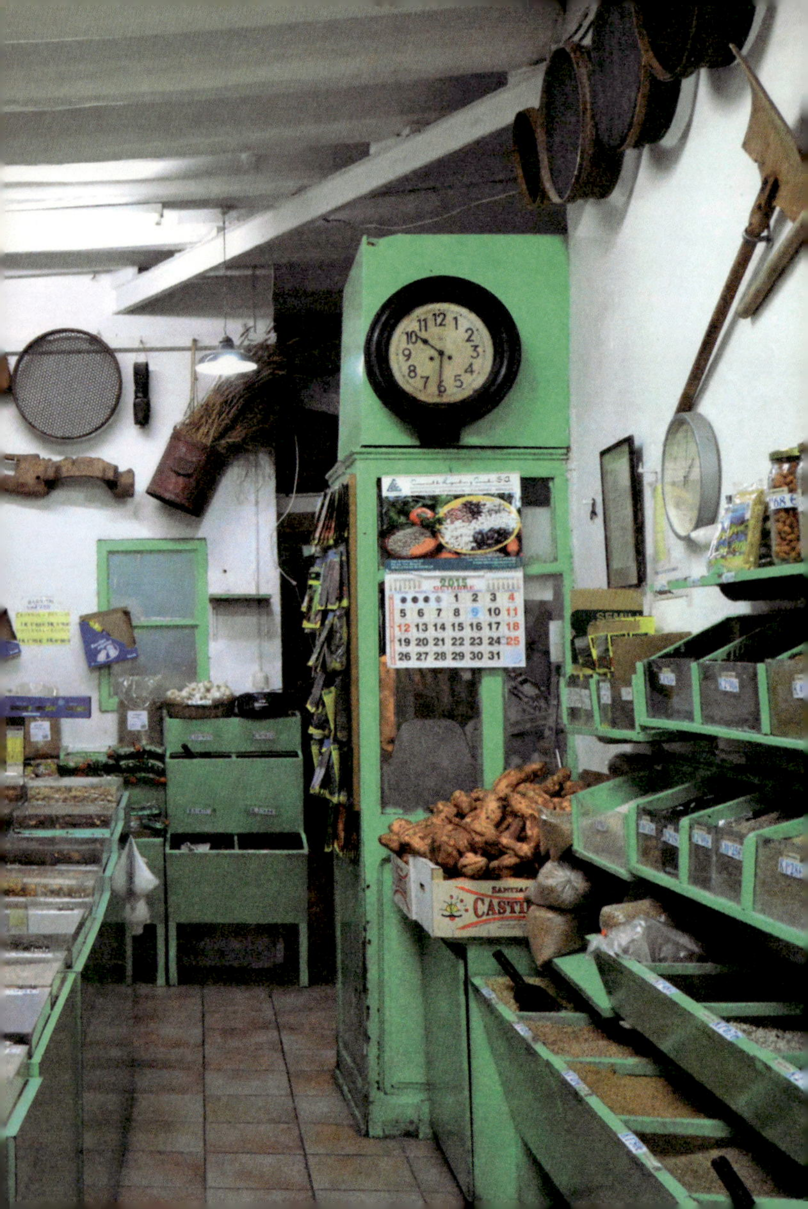
2015
OCTUBRE
1 2 3 4
5 6 7 8 9 10 11
12 13 14 15 16 17 18
19 20 21 22 23 24 25
26 27 28 29 30 31
CASTI

THE GRÀCIA DISTRICT

BILBAO

Address: Carrer Perill 33, Gràcia
Telephone: +34 93 458 9624
Hours: 1-4pm & 9-11pm;
closed Sunday, holidays
and in August

The Family Jewel

Pere Valls Isart is passionate about his restaurant, Bilbao, which his family bought in 1954. "This is the thing that I most love in the world," he told us. "This is my life!" Over the years, this old-school neighborhood restaurant has become one of Barcelona's culinary institutions, a bastion of traditional Catalan cooking.

When Valls took over Bilbao, he saw that times were changing, and he wanted to do something more and better. He sourced better ingredients and improved the contents of the dishes and the wine cellar, adding excellent Catalan and Spanish bottlings. He has updated the menu through the decades, bringing in eel, seafood, morels, oysters, Iberian ham – but at the same time always staying true to his roots.

The kitchen is now helmed by chef Jordi Olivet, who upholds Valls's legacy with his own contributions. To begin with, we love the amazing oxtail, which is marinated for 24 hours in a mixture of wine, orange and lemon peel, onion, garlic and carrots, then stewed for four hours and served with a delicate wine-poached pear. The beef has become luscious, velvety and melting, with the sweetness of the pear a perfect counterpoint to its rich, meaty flavors.

Another customer favorite is the risotto-style rice, and we also love the Palamós prawns, a huge local red variety, which are lightly grilled and seasoned with flaky Maldon sea salt. The black truffle *caneloni* with *bolets* and foie gras is one of Bilbao's greatest hits. And while it's in season, we recommend a dish of salted artichokes with fine shavings of ham, a well-balanced flavor pairing.

On our next visit, we plan on ordering the cod *morro* with garlic mousse and *cardinale* sauce – because, yes, Bilbao is that special kind of place where as soon as you've finished feasting like a king, you can't help but begin planning your next meal there.

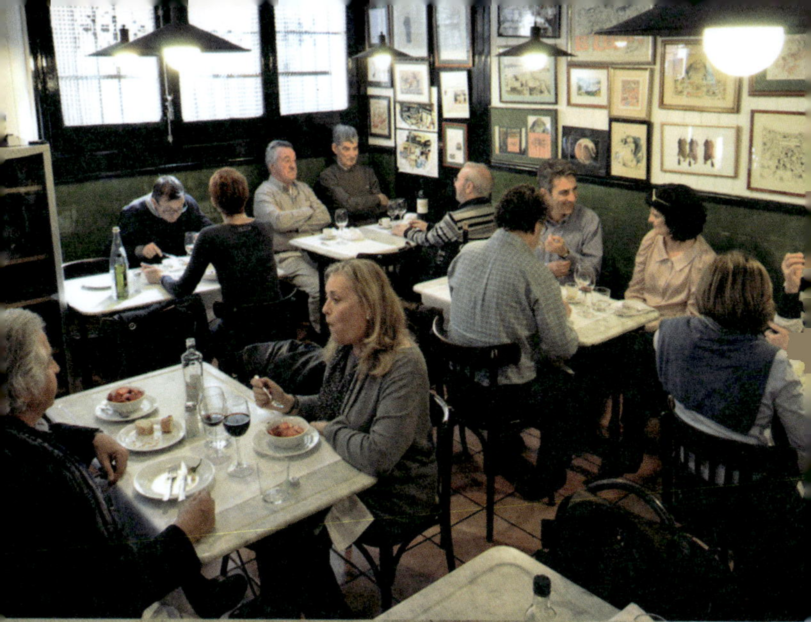

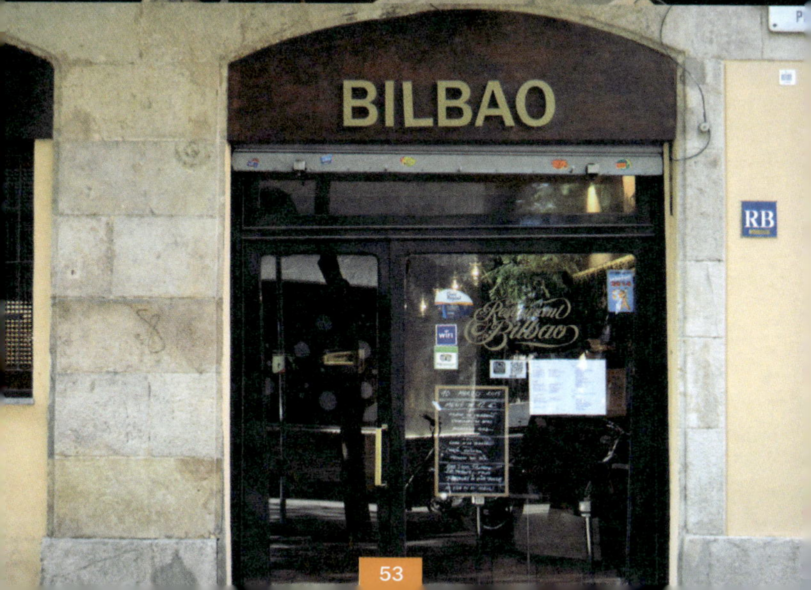
BILBAO
RB
Restaurant Bilbao

BODEGA LO PINYOL

Address: Torrent de l'Olla 7, Gràcia
Telephone: +34 93 217 6690
Hours: Tues.-Sat. noon-4pm & 7pm-midnight; Sun. noon-4pm; closed Monday

Book Club

La Bodega Lo Pinyol, which specializes in wine, *vermut* and books, is owned by Pau Raga, a Valencian librarian and literature devotee, and the Barcelona artist and curator Carles Poy. Two years ago, these longtime friends decided to find and resuscitate an old bodega (a wine shop with bar service), a traditional kind of venue that they both love and that is in danger of disappearing.

Bodega Piñol, a classic wine shop/bar in Gràcia, had been run by three generations of the Piñol family since 1943. When they bought it, Raga and Poy kept the old lamps, the original floor with its typical Barcelonan tiles, and the characteristic wooden bar, but reorganized the space and the details to bring more warmth and meaning to the atmosphere. They created a space for book swapping, with contributions from friends and customers, and also regularly organize cultural events. While they are still working with the same bulk vermut and wine purveyors as the original owners, they have improved the selection of bottled wine and cavas with interesting small Catalan producers, many of them organic and biodynamic.

Lo Pinyol feeds the body with the same care as it feeds the soul. There's an extensive menu of tapas, *pintxos, montaditos* (slices of bread with various toppings) and grilled sandwiches, all based on Catalan and Valencian traditions. A few special tapas offerings change with the seasons. Some of our favorite pintxos include the salted cod and roasted red pepper *esgarraet*, little *tartaletas* of gorgonzola, *mató* cheese and walnuts garnished with crispy fried onions, fresh sheep's milk cheese with anchovies – excellent with vermut – and the seasonal and very Balearic *sobrassada* and honey with Mahon cheese.

Many regulars of the bodega in its former life still visit its new incarnation, which offers an eclectic atmosphere for many book lovers, artists and students who come here to share a vermouth and write a new page in the book of Barcelona's traditional bodegas.

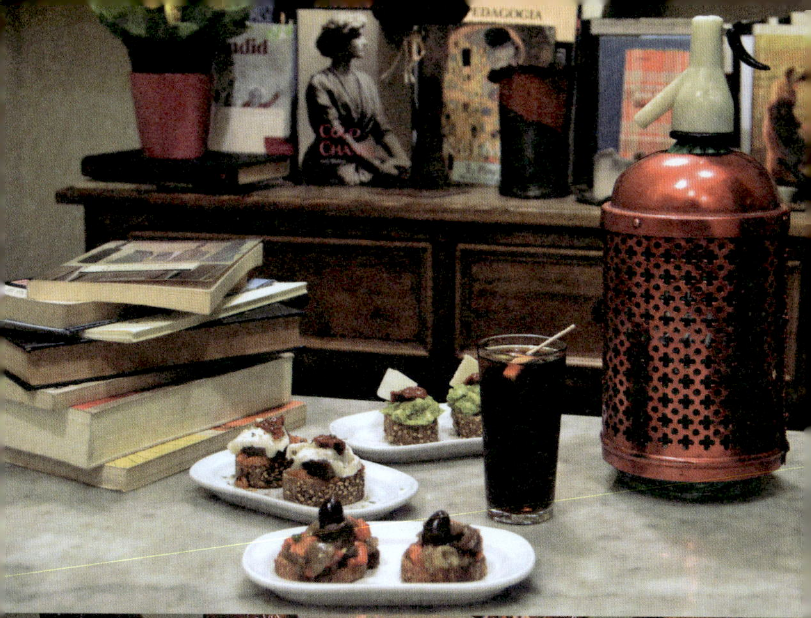

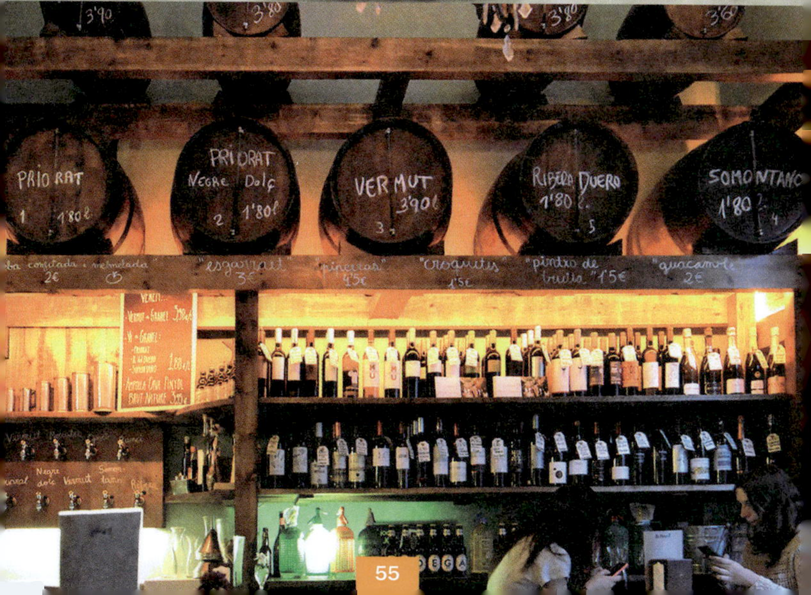

PRIORAT
1 1'80€
PRIORAT
Negre Dolç
2 1'80€
VERMUT
3'90€
3
Ribera Duero
1'80€
5
SOMONTANO
1'80
4

BODEGA MANOLO

Address: Torrent de les Flors 101, Gràcia
Telephone: +34 93 284 4377
Hours: Tues.-Sat. 1-4pm; Thurs.-Sat. 9-11pm; Sun. 12-3pm

More than Meets the Eye

At first glance, Bodega Manolo seems like the usual wine shop/tapas bar that Barcelona does so well: a solid place to replenish our wine stocks from the barrels, quench our thirst with a cold *caña* or satisfy our hunger pangs with a *vermut* and a tapa or two of oil-drenched anchovies. None of which sound too shabby. However, at dinnertime, the brilliant white tablecloths in the rear reveal the venue's greater ambitions.

Bodega Manolo is not for the fainthearted or the figure watcher. These are indulgent, rich, yet seriously delicious plates of food from the talented hand of owner Manolo, who learned his trade under Josep Lladonosa, head chef of iconic Barcelona restaurant 7 Portes, as well as during internships at other restaurants. He takes traditional, high-quality Catalan ingredients and serves them in gutsy, generous portions with a creative touch.

Who could resist ordering a plate of *patatas bravas*, here called "anarco bravas." Crispy, chunky sliced fried potatoes with a moreishly pungent garlic and squid ink sauce are drizzled with parsley oil, tomato sauce and a further daub of briny ink on the plate to scrape the spuds through. A purée of potatoes livened up with a poached egg yolk and a pork trifecta – *jamón* topped with *morcilla* (paprika-infused black pudding) and crispy bacon – goes by the winking name "Destroyer," perhaps for the potential effect it might have on the arteries. On a slightly lighter note, there's a dish of elegant, delicate white beans topped with meltingly tender octopus, peppery arugula leaves and more generous smears of that squid ink sauce which surprisingly never gets tiring.

Though vegetable dishes and accompaniments are few, the eggplants cooked on the *plancha* grill with a drizzle of honey and zesty piece of toasted goat's cheese are a delight. But it's the generous portion of pan-fried foie gras in a sweet and tangy sauce of port, braised apples and booze-soaked raisins that is really the star of the show.

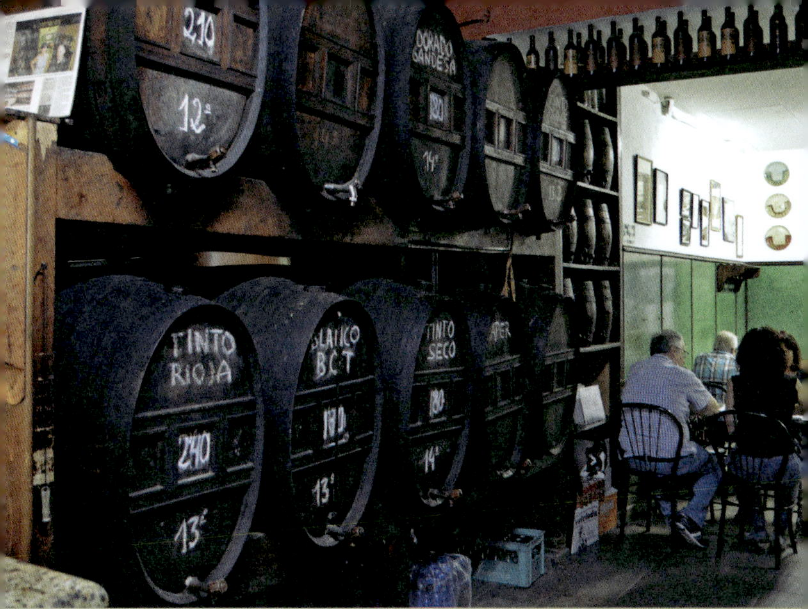
210
12º
DORADO GANDESA
180
14º
TINTO RIOJA
240
13º
180
13º
TINTO SECO
180
14º

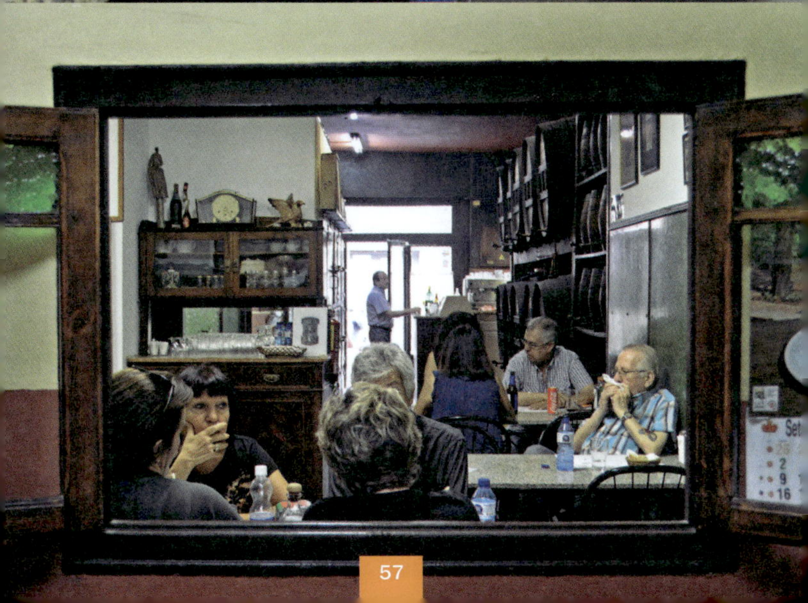

BODEGA QUIMET

Same As It Ever Was

Address: Carrer de Vic 23,
Gràcia
Telephone: +34 93 218 4189
Hours: Mon.-Wed. 10am-11:30pm;
Thurs.-Sat. 10am-12:30am;
closed Sunday

De toda la vida is a Spanish expression that basically means "It's been around forever," and it's a sure thing that the locals in Barcelona's Gràcia neighborhood will utter those words if you ask them about Bodega Quimet.

After brothers Carlos and David Montero brought the bodega from the Quimet family in 2010, they made the somewhat unusual decision to keep everything, from the low prices to the décor, pretty much the same as it always had been. In the early afternoon, you'll see many an *abuelo* (grandpa) popping in for a quick apéritif accompanied by the traditional *banderilla*, a variety of olives, artichoke hearts, *piquillo* peppers and sardines impaled on a long stick.

In the evening, the crowd is younger, filling the small space with the loud chatter of good friends sharing stories while sipping drinks and munching tapas. The venue is well known for their high-quality *embutidos* (sausages) and tinned foods, particularly seafood. *Conservas* are a huge part of the culinary culture in Spain and, even in regions where fresh seafood is widely available, they form a significant part of the menu in any self-respecting tapas bar.

We ordered the "Variado Vermut del Quimet," an array of tuna, cockles, razor clams, anchovies and olives accompanied by a basket of *pa amb tomàquet*, or peasant bread rubbed with tomato. Everything on the plate was excellent but the *atún* (tuna) in particular was high-quality stuff – certainly no "chicken of the sea." We also tried some tasty *papas arrugás* ("wrinkled potatoes"), a traditional dish from the Canary Islands that was served with a sumptuous *mojo* sauce made from olive oil, garlic, paprika and vinegar.

It may be a bit early to wonder if there are any little Monteros being groomed for the next generation, but we can't help but hope so. Like everyone else in Gràcia, we fully expect Quimet to always be *de toda la vida.*

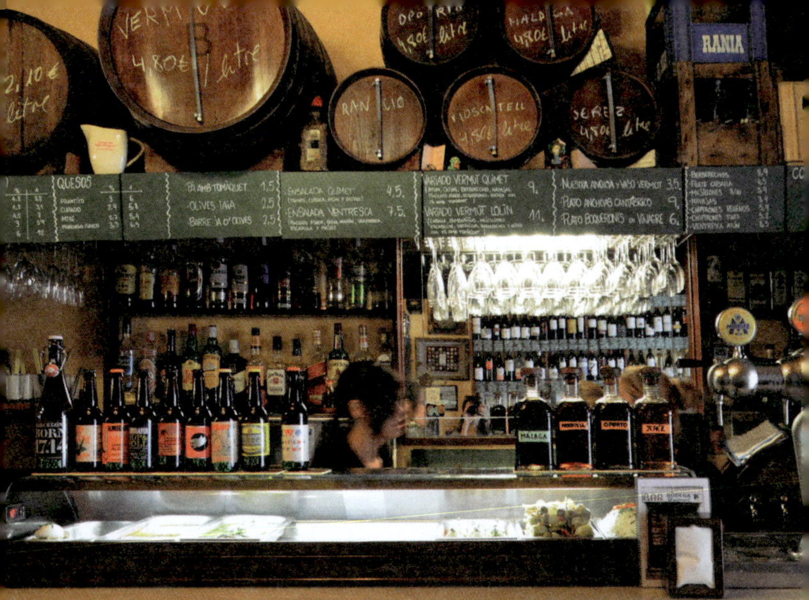
4,80€ / litre
RANCIO
MOSCATELL
JEREZ
RANIA
QUESOS
PA AMB TOMÀQUET 1,5
OLIVES 2,5
ENSALADA QUIMET 4,5
ENSALADA VENTRESCA 7,5
VARIADO VERMUT QUIMET 9
VARIADO VERMUT LOLÍN 11
PLATO ANCHOAS CANTÁBRICO 9
PLATO BOQUERONES en VINAGRE 6
MALAGA
OPORTO
JEREZ

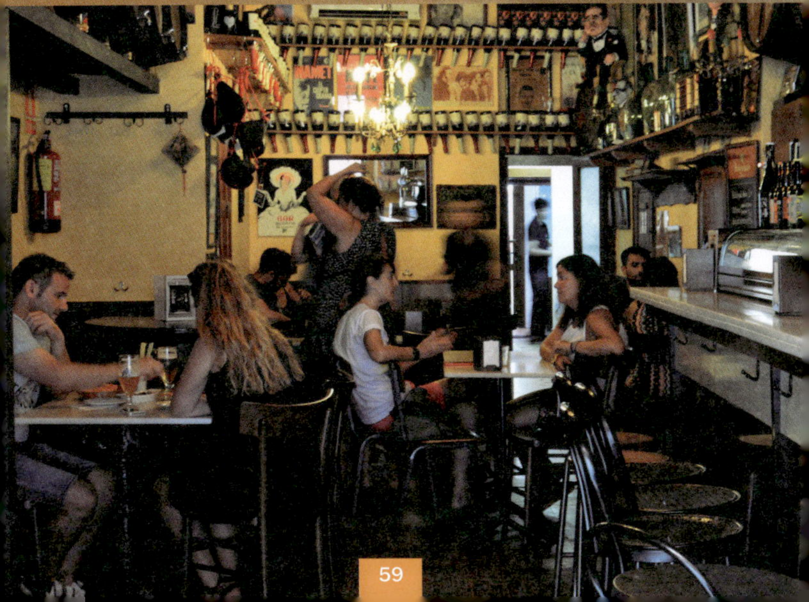

CAPET

Address: Carrer Benet Mercadé 21-23, Gràcia
Telephone: +34 93 115 5366
Hours: Tues.-Sat. 1-3:30pm & 8:30-11pm; closed Sunday and Monday

Small Wonder

The seeds of inspiration for chef Armando Álvarez's cooking at Capet can be found both in his homeland of Venezuela, where he began learning to cook, and in the restaurants of Catalonia, where he worked before striking off on his own.

Capet has a menu of small sharing plates – part modern tapas fare, part tasting menu at an ambitious high-end restaurant, but with more accessible prices – to be enjoyed by the lucky few who claim the limited number of tables or grab seats at the friendly bar in front of the kitchen. Capet's kitchen is also very small, and it's here that the staff choreographs their ballet in miniature according to what's fresh and in season and with a Venezuelan inflection that Álvarez picked up from his mother.

Beyond the must-try Iberian pork or salt cod dishes, one of our favorite *platillos* was the brilliant reinterpretation of the typical octopus tapa, sliced and with fried yucca – a stand-in for the usual potato, offering the perfect textural counterpoint – and served with a punchy green herb mayonnaise. The South American influence can also be felt in the platillo of tuna ceviche, with a little Spanish inflection from Galician Padrón pepper and red pepper, as well as the addition of trout eggs, an intense transoceanic bite that reminds us just how big and close the Hispano-American world is. The marinated sardine takes us back to Iberian traditions but then flips them with cucumber, celery, radish and green acid apple with yogurt and a touch of curry.

We recently got to taste the tender, aromatic *ternera gallega* (Galician veal) that Álvarez uses in his kitchen. The little dish of veal cheeks with potatoes *Parmentier* and Catalan summer truffle from the Pyrenees is a creamy, melting delight, incredibly fragrant and with a deep, rich, complex sauce.

Capet may be small, but Armando Álvarez has found a way to explore continents of flavor inside it.

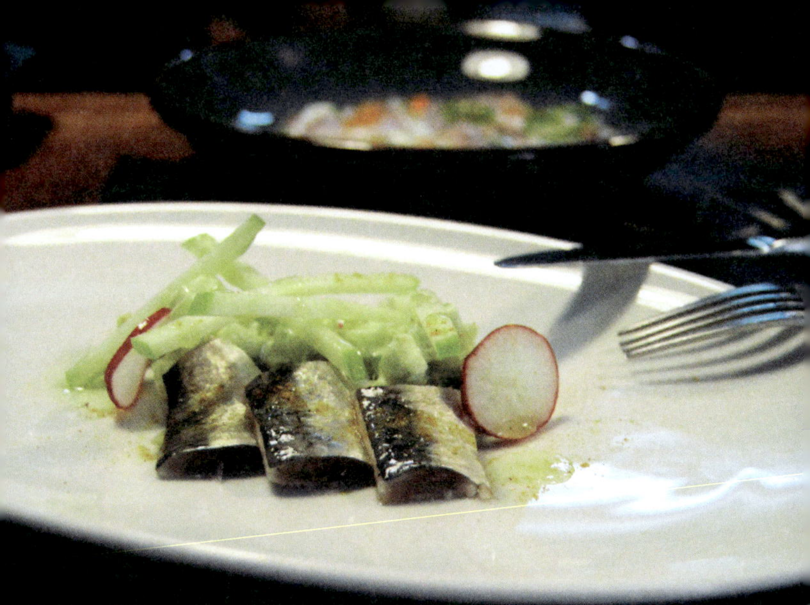

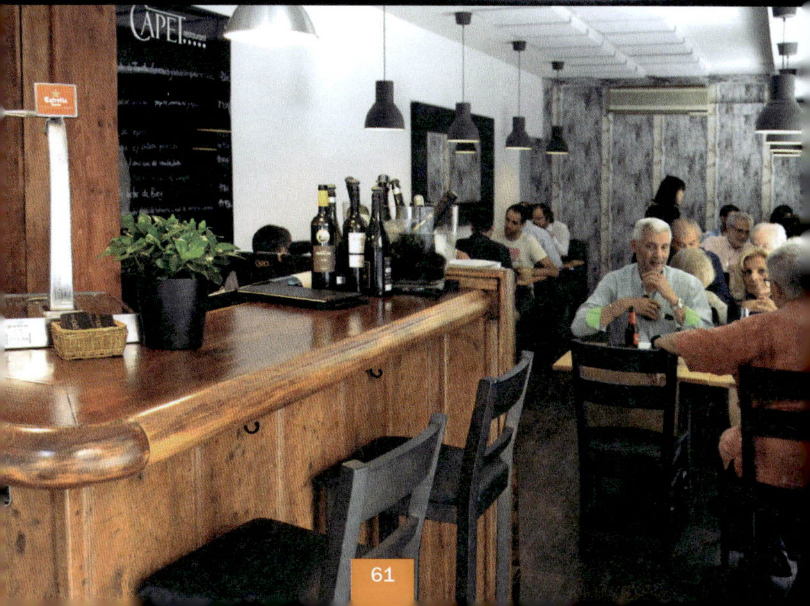
CAPET

EL TAST DE JOAN NOI

Sea-to-Table Dining

Mercat de la Llibertat, Stalls 117-125
Address: Plaça Llibertat 27, Gràcia
Telephone: +34 93 124 0106
Hours: Tues.-Fri. 8am-5pm;
Sat. 8am-3pm;
closed Sunday and in August

El Tast de Joan Noi, a fish and seafood restaurant situated in El Mercat de la Llibertat in Gràcia, offers diners the huge pleasure of discovering an eye-catching piece of tuna amongst the ice and then seeing how the expert chef cooks it in front of their very eyes.

That chef, Paco González, has 18 years' experience at Botafumeiro, one of the best-known (and most expensive) seafood restaurants in Barcelona. At El Tast de Joan Noi, he works with a menu based on the seasonal fish and seafood sold in the stall next to the bar, with most items served grilled. He says the simplicity of the setup – without a real kitchen or cold-storage facilities, but with a fish purveyor right next door – guarantees that everything at Joan Noi is always fresh, cooked right in front of diners and served in the moment. For us, two of the most appealing specialties are the baby scallops and the diced tuna, prepared with recipes created by González exclusively for Joan Noi. The delicate and tasty scallops, simultaneously soft and crunchy, are sprinkled with salt and pepper, placed on a toasted slice of bread with caramelized onions and some brandy, then topped with a cheese sauce and finally baked *au gratin* in the oven.

González also prepares special paella and rice dishes, which need to be ordered in advance; these include the *Arroz Caldoso con Bogavante* (lobster with a brothy rice stew) and the *Zarzuela de Pescado* (seafood casserole). But the simply amazing diced tuna is perhaps the venue's star dish. The tuna is perfectly grilled to the point where it has a thin, golden grilled layer on the outside, while the inside remains pink and as soft as butter. The whole dish is drizzled with a vinaigrette made with soy sauce, Jerez wine (sherry) and walnuts.

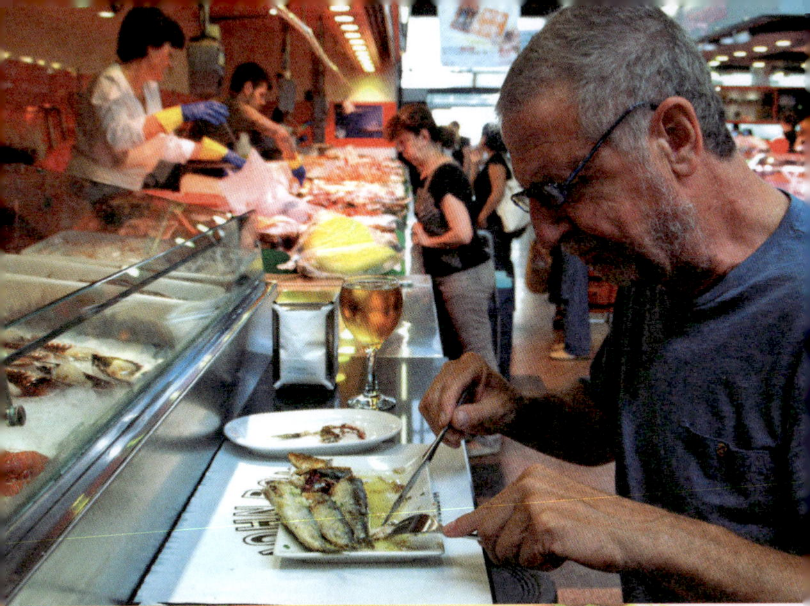

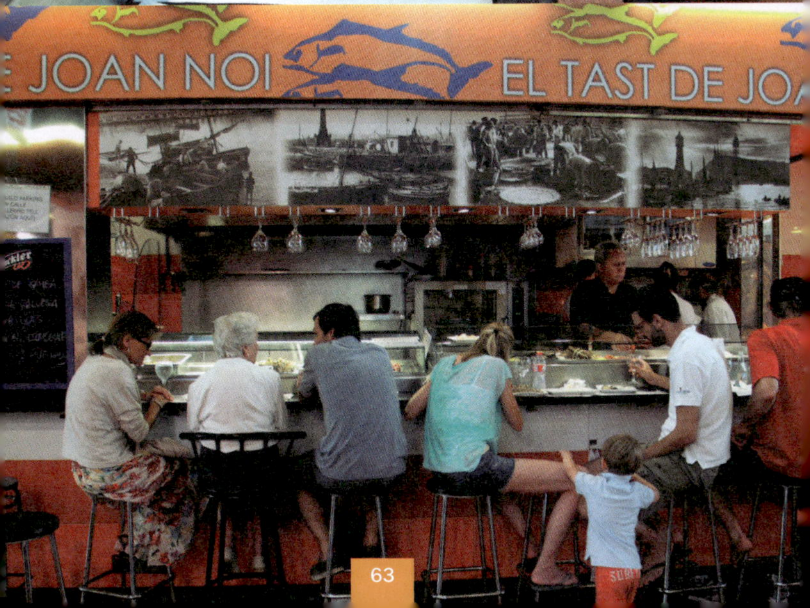
JOAN NOI
EL TAST DE JO

LA PANXA DEL BISBE

Mountain Man

Address: Carrer del Torrent de les Flors 15
Gràcia
Telephone: +34 93 213 7049
Hours: Tues.-Sat. 1:30-3:30pm
& 8:30pm-midnight;
closed Sunday and Monday

The Bishop's Belly, La Panxa del Bisbe, is not the midsection of a Catalan priest, but both a restaurant and a mountain. The latter is one of the peaks of the sacred Catalan mountain of Montserrat, so-called because its shape evokes a small head over a rotund, pronounced belly. Chef Xavi Codina loves the mountain so much, he named his restaurant in honor of the peak.

At La Panxa, Codina has created a menu of almost 30 tapas or *platillos* (small dishes) and four desserts, combining traditional Catalan cuisine with international influences. Much of the menu changes according to season and customers' tastes, but there are a few perennial favorites, such as the homey croquettes, with their generous quantity of chicken and carrots; duck liver with pears and wine; and the *cap i pota*, a traditional dish made from pork trotters and head that Codina varies all through the year.

La Panxa's seafood specialties are some of our favorites. Codina respects the unique flavors of his ingredients, coaxing out a delightful intensity in each – especially for such wonderful specimens as the Galician clams. He cooks these with El Prat artichoke hearts and very delicate, almost creamy *mongetes de Santa Pau* (a type of tiny white beans) and dresses the dish with a typical sauce from southern Catalonia, *picada* ("minced"), made with ground almonds and bread. The rockfish soup with clams and mussels is another highlight, a soul-comforting *cuenquecillo*, or "small bowl," enough to have an individual good dose of broth made from rockfish and pieces of monkfish, with a couple of bread slices luxuriating within.

When we're more interested in meat, we might order *picanya* (the Argentinian beef chop) with potato threads and *béarnaise* sauce or the succulent lamb neck with potato and red pepper *escalivado* (meaning "roasted" or "baked"), served with a *pensamiento* (literally "thought" but also the word for pansy), a pastoral touch that harkens back to the restaurant's mountain roots.

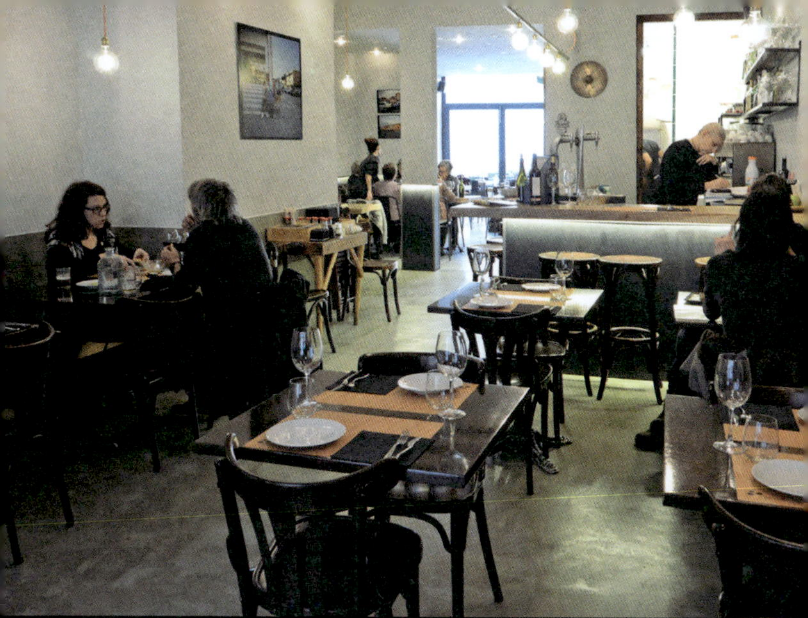

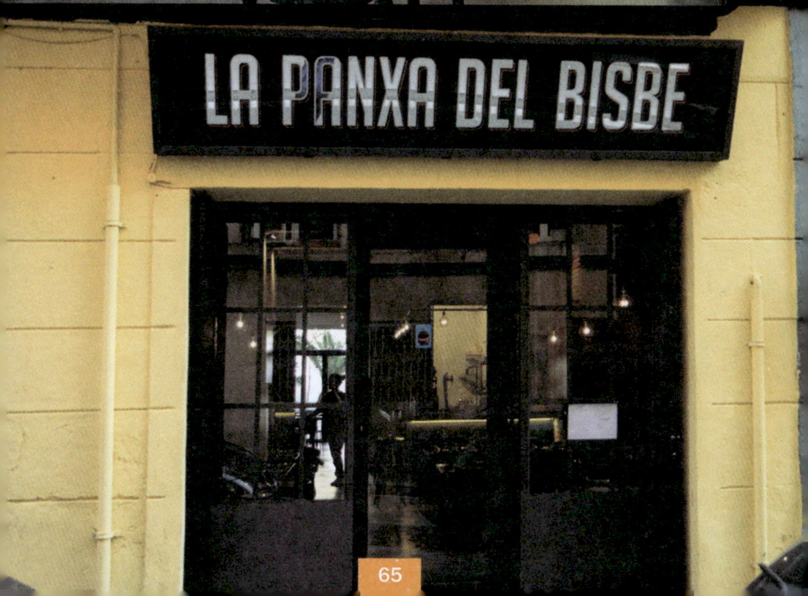
LA PANXA DEL BISBE

LA PUBILLA

Address: Plaça de la Llibertat 23, Gràcia
Telephone: +34 93 218 2994
Hours: 8:30am-5pm; closed Sunday

Destined for Greatness

When chef Alexis Peñalver was looking for a location for his restaurant, he found this gem adjacent to the Mercat de la Llibertat in Gràcia and decided to keep the name of the original establishment. *Pubilla* is a bygone word in Catalan for the eldest daughter destined to receive the family inheritance if there were no male heirs. Nowadays a pubilla (the prettiest girl in town) is named *reina de la fiesta* at many festivals in Catalonia.

Here you won't find a menu in Spanish or English, only Catalan. This was by design, not only to facilitate seating and ordering, but also to encourage patrons to have a tableside dialogue with the affable staff, commandeered by Dídac Pellicer. Pellicer used to work with Peñalver at Casa Juliana, where they first met. They decided to open a restaurant together whose focus would be authentic Catalan market cuisine.

Lunch at La Pubilla begins with Arbequina olives, hinting at more local ingredients to come. On one visit, we had *saltat de coliflor amb ibèric i alls tendres*, cauliflower delicately sautéed with bite-sized pieces of *jamón ibérico*, garlic and green onions – a dish that confirms that Peñalver is a master at preparing and proportioning ingredients. Raise your hand if you like meat dripping off the bone: *¡Si, señor!* Our second course, *galta de porc amb patates enmascarades*, was a simple yet spectacular combination of perfectly cooked pork cheek and potatoes. For dessert we grinned ear-to-ear while spooning a homemade *compota de poma i codony*, apple compote and quince jelly.

Lunch reservations are required during the week. On Saturday, the format changes from *menú* to *à la carte*, the atmosphere is more relaxed and the pace is slower. And in August, when many businesses shut down for extended vacation, La Pubilla is thankfully one that keeps its doors open.

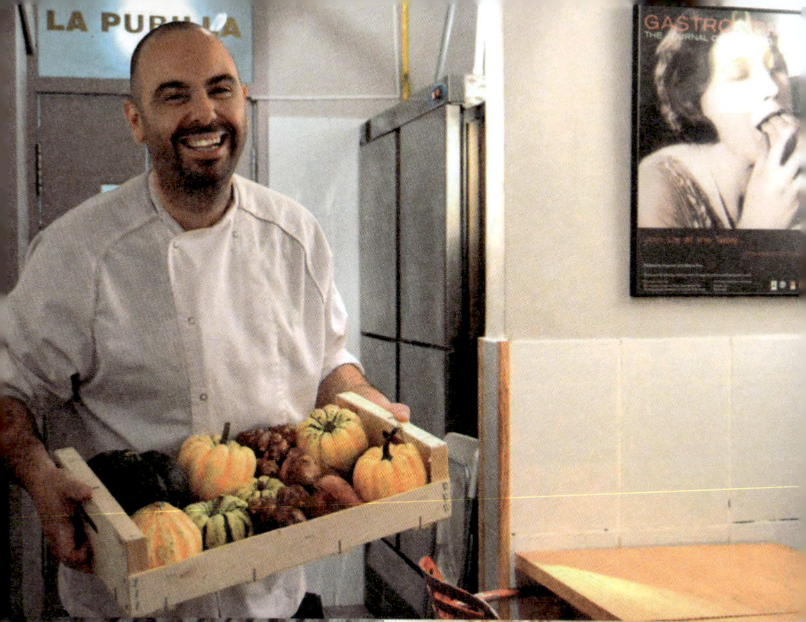

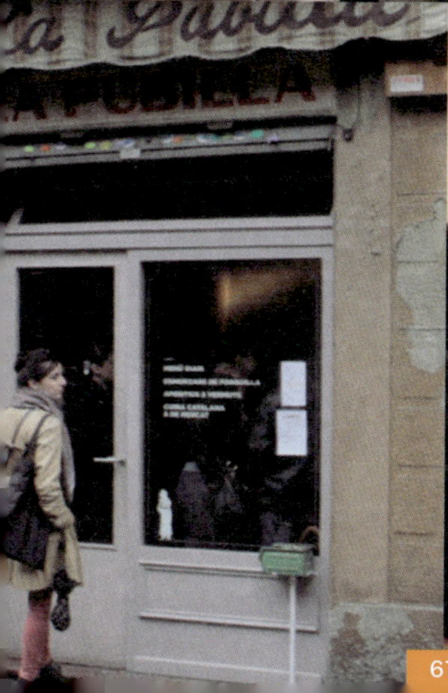

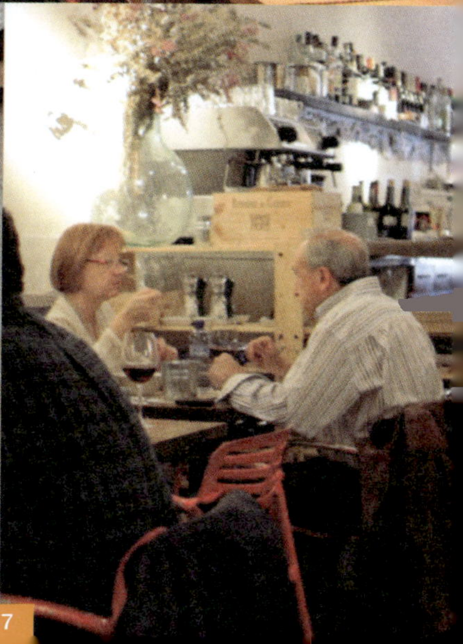

LATA BERNA

Address: Carrer Torrent de les Flors 53, Gràcia
Telephone +34 93 193 0288
Hours: 1pm-midnight; closed Monday

The Tin Man

The name of this appealing Gràcia eatery is a play on words, an amalgam of *la taberna*, or "tavern," and *lata,* or "tin." Owner and head chef Juanjo Martínez has dedicated his restaurant to the culture of canned food and other uncanned treasures that are linked to traditional Spanish *tapeo* and rituals like *vermut* hour, which always include preserved foods.

The concept here is *la lata y la tapa*. Conservas, canned foods, are intimately connected with the vermut tradition and the spirit of the traditional taverns – and thus a part of the Spanish culinary soul and nostalgia. At the same time, these products have a rising gourmet status. To consolidate this link, Martínez began working with one of the most beloved local brands of high-quality canned specialties, Espinaler. Using high-quality fresh ingredients, he created a repertoire of amazing hot and cold tapas that are often served in an evocative tin container.

His cooking style draws from many Spanish regional culinary traditions and is inflected with modern international influences and a little insouciant punk attitude to free the mind and palate. Among his many innovations are the *tortita de camarones de Triana*, a typical crispy Andalusian pancake of shrimp with an atypical Thai vinaigrette, and the delicate, delicious scallop ceviche with passion fruit caviar. We love the *patatas bravas encabronadas*, in which the "mischievous" potatoes are served in a tin with two bold sauces, a garlicky white and a spicy red one, as well as the creamy, savory mini *caneloni* (a traditional Catalan preparation with some Italian influence) of roasted meat or spinach, also served in a tin, with dried tomatoes and a hint of basil. But best of all is the soft-shell crab in black tempura (made with squid ink) with tartar sauce and yucca chips. It may look like a crustacean-shaped lump of coal, but the combination of flavors and textures is beyond brilliant.

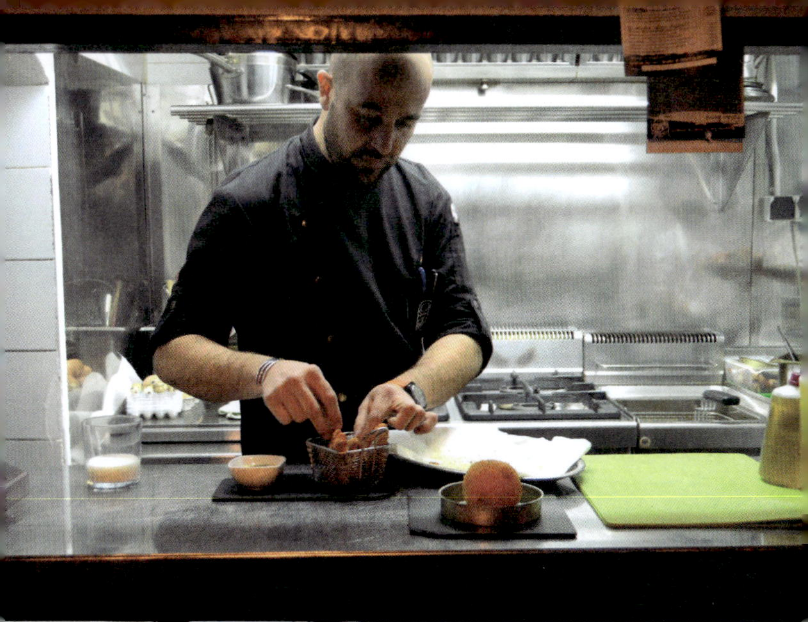

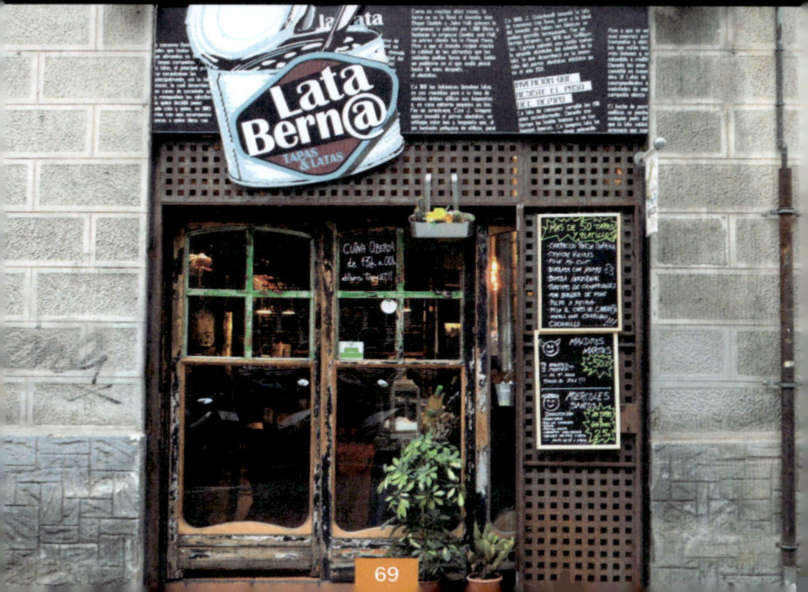
Lata Bern@
TAPAS & LATAS

SANTA GULA

Address: Plaça de Narcís Oller 3, Gràcia
Telephone: +34 93 185 7649
Hours: Sun.-Thurs. 1-4pm & 8-11pm; Fri.-Sat. 1-4pm & 8-11:30pm

Blessed Are the Gluttons

Halfway between a French bistro, a Nordic café and a Spanish *casa de comidas* (a traditional small family-run eatery where the menu changes according to season and the market), Santa Gula (Saint Gluttony) is the perfect place to sin – gastronomically speaking – in Gràcia.

This cozy restaurant with its wonderful outdoor terrace (set up in spring and summer) attracts a crowd of faithful customers who all flock to Santa Gula to enjoy traditional recipes made with a personal touch, as well as more internationally inflected dishes cooked with top-quality seasonal ingredients.

Santa Gula's menu offers very personal versions of classic dishes – all designed to be shared – such as El Prat artichoke hearts, which they preserve themselves rather than serving straight from a tin, homemade croquettes with squid ink filling instead of the usual ham or cod and Galician octopus *á feira*, the traditional boiled octopus with paprika, olive oil and salt, to which they add Iberian pork neck and black garlic *parmentier.*

The menu, which changes religiously every two weeks, also stands out for being an excellent Spanish regional product atlas, as some of the dishes are a mashup of products from Catalonia and other parts of Spain. One standout example is the sweet peas from Catalonia's Maresme region with fried eggs from Calaf, another Catalonian region, and *cecina* (the beef version of the traditional Spanish *jamón*) from northwestern Spain's León.

Old-style dishes with international twists are available here too, such as crispy batter-fried sardines with teriyaki sauce and grilled eggplant purée and oxtail cannelloni cooked in the meat's juices with truffled pecorino and béchamel sauce – both magnificent. Even bolder and more innovative combinations also have a place in Santa Gula's menu. Segovia boneless suckling pig with caramelized mango could easily sound like a real sin to an orthodox Spanish gourmand, but, as the owners of Santa Gula say, *"En cuestión de comer, todos hemos nacido pecadores."* ("When it comes to good food, we were all born sinners.")

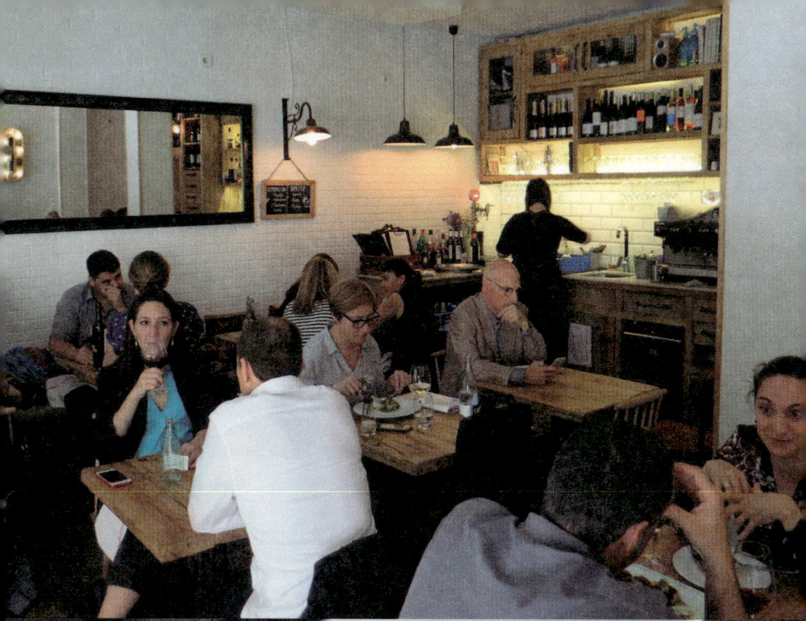

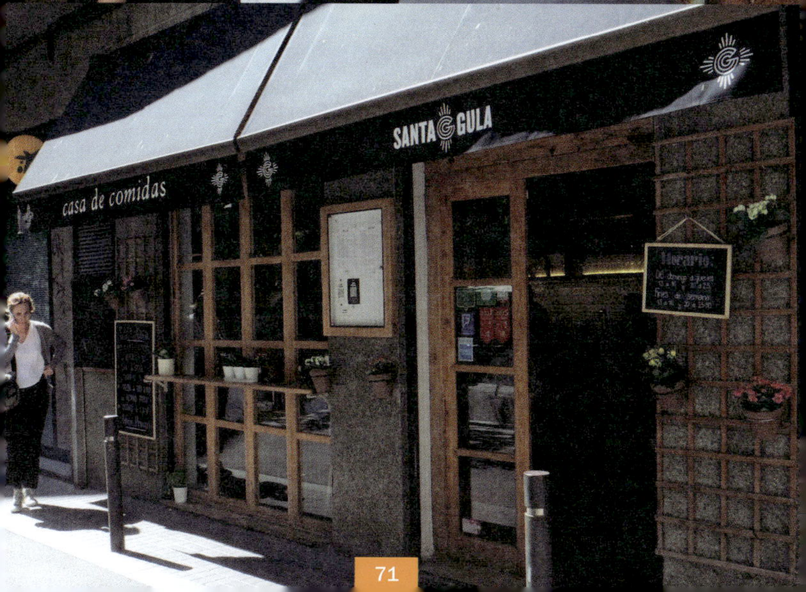
SANTA GULA
casa de comidas

VERMUTERÍA LOU

Address: Carrer de l'Escorial 3, Gràcia
Telephone: +34 93 285 5421
Hours: 8am-midnight; closed Sunday and holidays

Mistress of Croquettes

Located on busy Carrer de l'Escorial on the edge of Gràcia, Vermuteria Lou is a tiny, cozy venue that is exactly what we look for in a neighborhood place. Owner Lourdes Branco, a former butcher, has a talent for cooking that comes through in the venue's wide selection of traditional dishes that always manage to go beyond the basics, whether in their rich ingredients or their outstanding preparations.

Highlights include the fried eggs with foie gras and Iberian ham shavings, an elaborate cod stew, a clay pot with a tasty sauté of cuttlefish with mushrooms fried in olive oil and onion sauce, and the *esqueixada*, a traditional salad of dried cod with fresh onions and red peppers. There is also *carpaccio* of beef and even cod, a potato omelet featuring Iberian ham, and a homemade Russian salad made with fresh vegetables. Lourdes' potato bomb is a real winner, both delicate in flavor and packing an explosive punch. The large ball of creamy mashed potatoes contains tasty veal cheek and foie gras inside, and is topped with a spicy sauce of tomato, nuts, black pepper and cayenne.

But what we enjoy the most – and so, it would seem, do other customers – are Vermuteria Loú's 20 or so different kinds of delicious *croquetas*, all lovingly prepared by hand by Lourdes, who makes three or four varieties per day and rotates the selection throughout the week. Fillings range from Iberian ham, *ceps* mushrooms with foie gras, or black Catalan sausage with parmesan cheese to prawns and monkfish, spinach with goat cheese and pine nuts, or cod, among others. On our visit, Lourdes offered us freshly made croquetas with ceps: creamy, oblong balls, thoroughly crunchy on the outside and perfectly soft inside, in which we could really appreciate the homemade *béchamel* sauce dressing the ceps, a very well-loved Catalan mushroom because of its intense flavor.

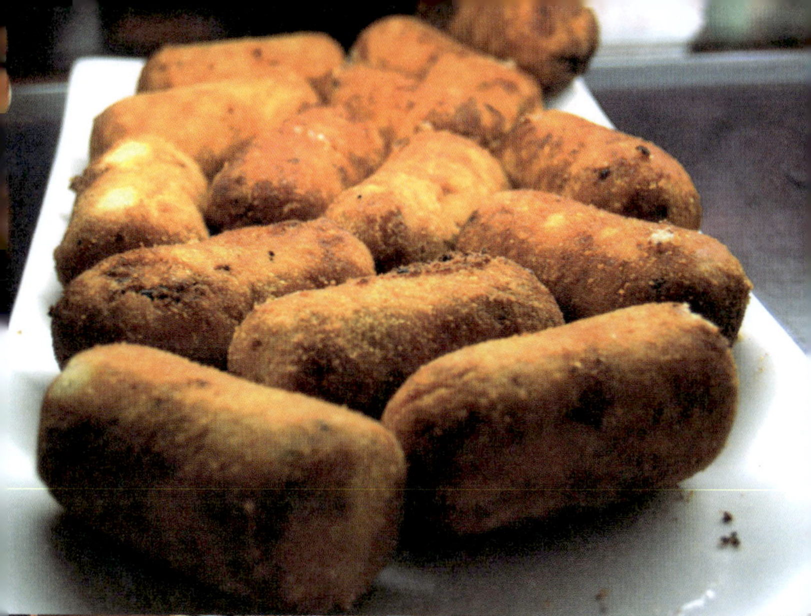

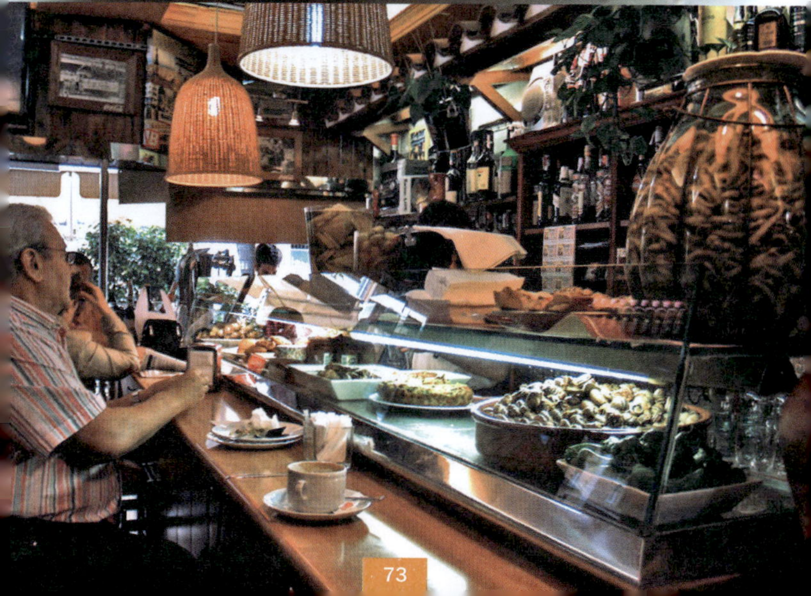

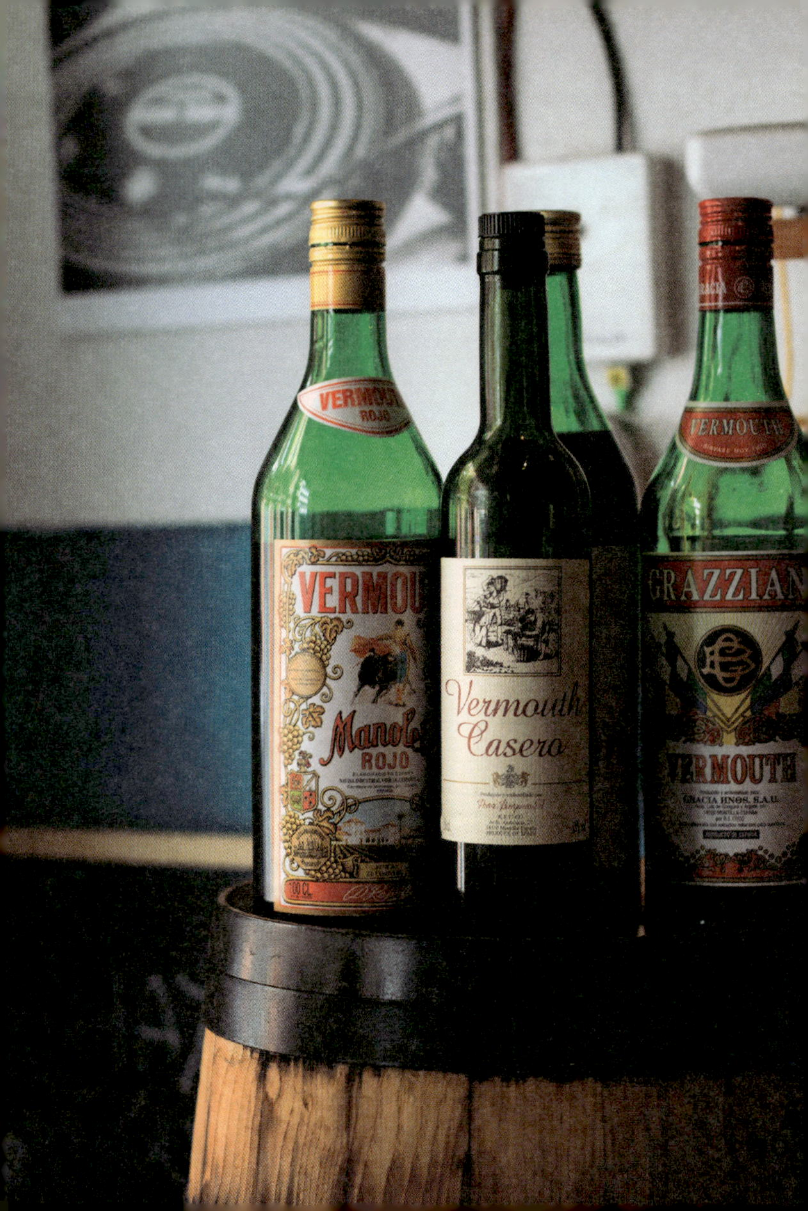

VERMOU
ROJO
VERMOU
Manol
ROJO
100 CL.
Vermouth
Casero
VERMOUTH
GRAZZIAN
GRACIA HNOS. S.A.U.

BEYOND THE CENTER (SOUTH)

BAR BODEGA SALVAT

Home Sweet Bar

Address: Carrer d'Andalusía 2, (corner Carrer Sagunt), Sants-Montjuïc
Telephone: +34 93 481 2360
Hours: Mon.-Sun. 9am-10pm

Some sociologists say that Spanish society and culture can't be properly understood without spending time in its bars. In Barcelona, there are as many bars as taxis and ten times more bars than bookshops. Bar Bodega Salvat in the *barrio* of La Bordeta is a perfect example of a bar that's not only a simple hospitality business, but also a second home for its loyal clientele.

Depending on the time of the day, you might spot housewives sipping coffee before visiting the local food market, workers reading the paper during their break, seniors playing dominos, students doing their homework or Barça football supporters watching a televised live match. On Sundays, the pavement outside the bar is the most crowded in the neighborhood.

However, it's Bodega Salvat's famous anchovy dish that attracts people from all over the city. The

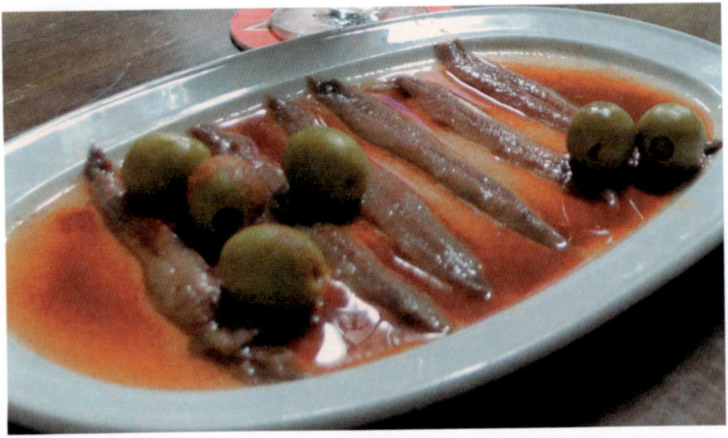

tasty and fleshy fish, straight from the Cantabrian Sea, is seasoned with a homemade sauce of wine vinegar, black pepper and paprika. Legend has it that in the 1950s, three of Club Barcelona's most famous football players, the Hungarians Kubala, Kocsis and Csibor – the Messi, Iniesta and Suárez of their time – used to go to Bodega Salvat after training for anchovies and alcohol.

The current menu is short but well-balanced, with a variety of vegetarian, seafood and meat tapas. Grilled artichokes and onions as well as *piparras* (green pickled chilies) are good vegetarian options. Meat tapas highlights include *torreznos* (strips of crispy fried bacon), chorizo and *cecina de León* (cured beef). Apart from the much-celebrated anchovies, *moixama* (cured tuna loins) and *xipirons farcits* (stuffed baby squid) are also worth trying. Croquette lovers make short shrift of the fried breaded pouches filled with cod, *botifarró* (pork black sausage), beef or Cabrales (an Asturian blue cheese). Drinking options vary from lager to dark beer on tap and house wine from Priorat, but it's the house vermouth from Reus that matches perfectly with a plate of anchovies.

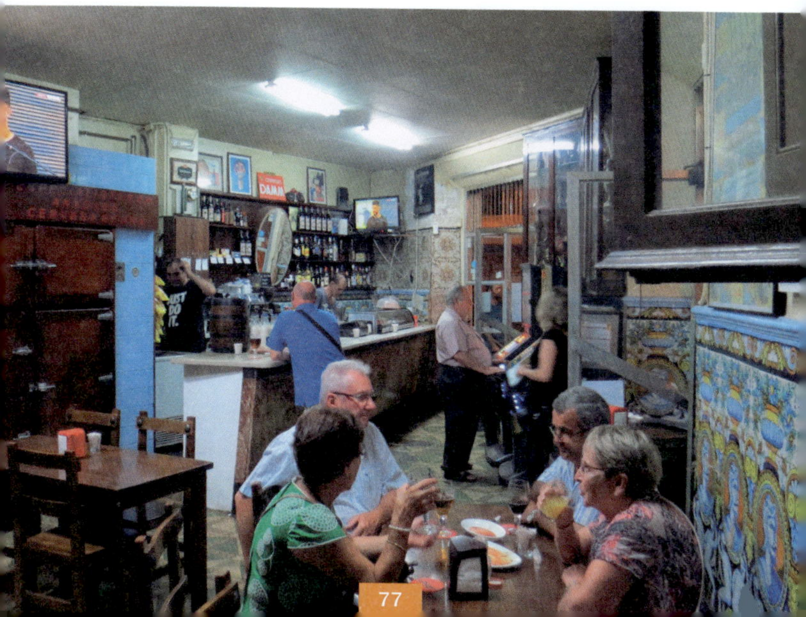

GRANJA ELENA

Address: Passeig Zona Franca 228,
Sants-Montjuïc
Telephone: +34 93 332 0241
Hours: Mon.-Fri. 7am-4pm;
Sat. 7am-1pm

From Farm to 'Farm'

Granja Elena, a family business now run by the third generation in the same *barrio* in which it was founded in 1974, was originally a small granja (farm), a kind of typical Catalan shop-bar where one can eat breakfast and supper and buy farm products such as milk, cold cuts for *bocadillos*, coffee and hot chocolate. Significant change really came to Granja Elena with the mother of the sibling trio who now own the place: She started cooking dishes at home to sell at the shop, a move that was such a success that the family decided to put in a new kitchen so that these traditional dishes could be prepared in the shop itself.

Today, Granja Elena serves dishes in the Catalan-Spanish tradition, but with a bit of sophistication. These include *cap i pota amb samfaina* (beef head and leg stew with ratatouille) and a delicious and potent *callos* (spiced tripe stew with chorizo and *morcilla,* often also with beef leg and sometimes also with chickpeas), which is tender but substantial and served in a thick marble bowl.

One seasonal specialty we enjoyed recently was a great first course of red mullet cured in salt and marinated in Kalamata olive oil and served with chive and dill in a granite dish. Each bite evoked a Mediterranean forest – a bit of surf and turf that transported us, if only for a moment, far from the concrete and asphalt just outside the restaurant. Another taste of the ocean came from a bowl of tuna and egg yolk with soy sauce and Galician sea urchin. The salmon eggs on top offered a little splash of the sea as they popped in our mouth.

Best of all, however, was the roasted tuna *galete* (jowl) with *piquillo* peppers. The galete was like butter, pleasantly gelatinous and refined, and the pepper purée complemented it with a subtle, earthy sweetness.

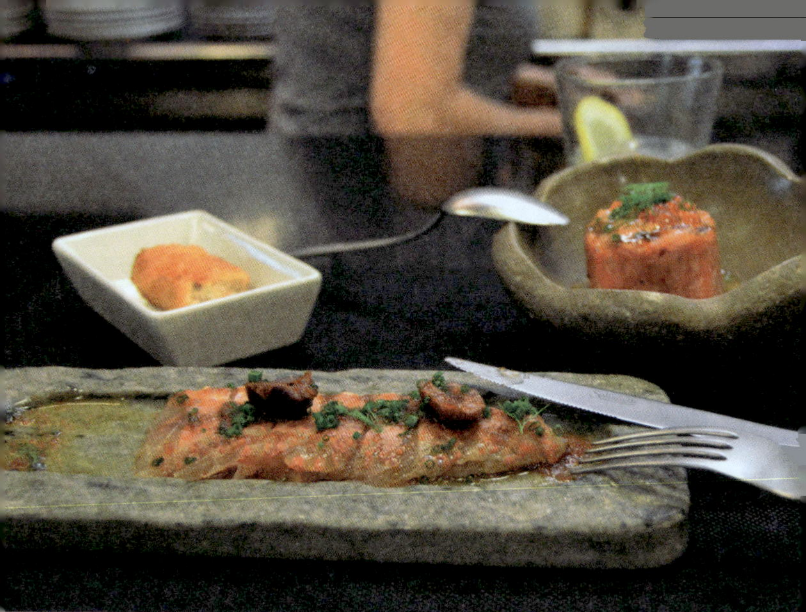

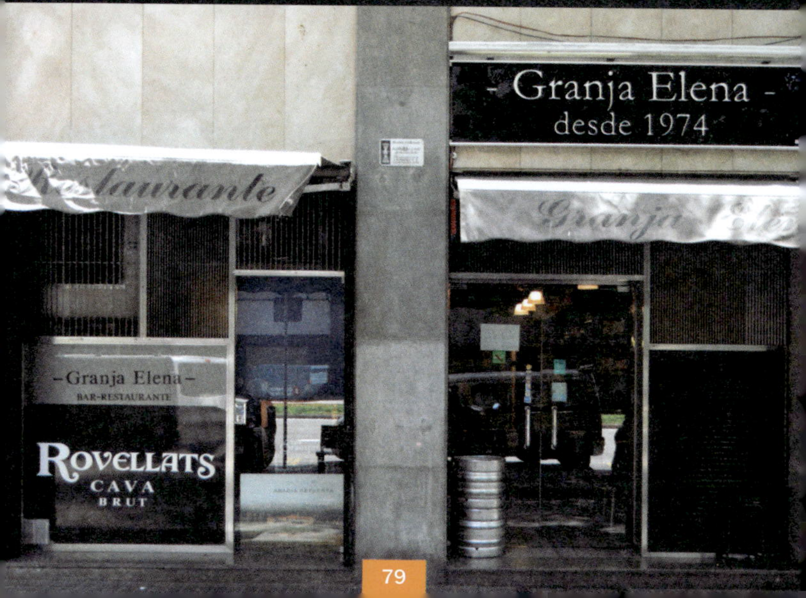
- Granja Elena -
desde 1974
Granja
- Granja Elena -
BAR-RESTAURANTE
ROVELLATS
CAVA
BRUT

TERRA D'ESCUDELLA

Homage to Catalonia

Address: Carrer Premià 20, Sants-Montjuïc
Telephone: +34 93 422 1613
Hours: 9am-midnight; closed Sunday

In *Homage to Catalonia*, his diary of fighting with a leftist militia during the Spanish Civil War, George Orwell wrote about craving food at the front. But if he had come to Catalonia in peacetime with no food shortage, he may have eaten at a place like Terra d'Escudella.

Located in Sants, a district with a historically very strong working-class identity, Terra d'Escudella's traditional, seasonal Catalan cooking is made with only fresh, local ingredients, at very affordable prices. The set lunch menu changes daily and offers the kind of old-school dishes that Catalan grandmothers used to make: *escudella* (a slow-cooked meat stock with vegetables, meatballs and bones), meatballs with cuttlefish, assorted sausages, cod with romesco sauce and pork feet with almonds.

There's also a highly recommended evening tapas menu with platters of artisanal *charcutería* and cheese, *patatas bravas* with aioli sauce and homemade croquettes among other old-style dishes. A list of sandwiches with traditional cured meats such as *donja* (pork sausage) is also available.

Desserts are not an afterthought here: *crema catalana* foam, Marcona toasted almonds covered with caramel, hazelnuts with white chocolate and a shot of ratafia, honey and the ricotta-like *brossat* cheese, sheep's milk yogurt, curd pudding with almond cookies and nougat ice cream are just a few examples.

Wines come from all over the Catalan-speaking areas, and the list changes monthly. Each week, the restaurant highlights a different wine sold by the glass. Catalan craft beers such as the celebrated Cervesa del Montseny have an important presence here too. Even the soft drinks and distilled spirits are Catalan.

In short, Terra d'Escudella is a gastronomical homage to Catalonia, an ode to Catalan popular cuisine and a little trip back to the 19th-century *fondes dels sisos* (humble inns frequented by workers, artisans and travelers). The restaurant's walls are covered with posters that resemble old Anarcho-syndicalist, Bolshevik, feminist and labor union propaganda – Orwell's politics would have been right at home here too.

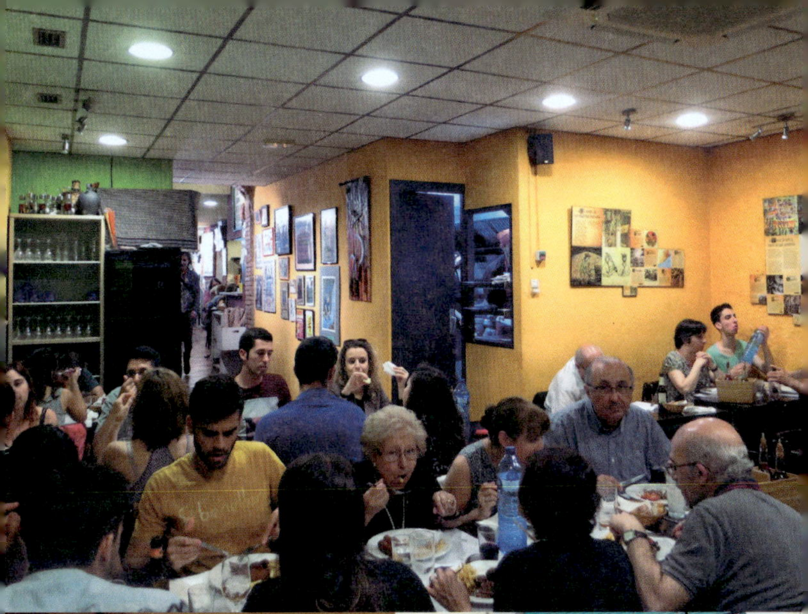

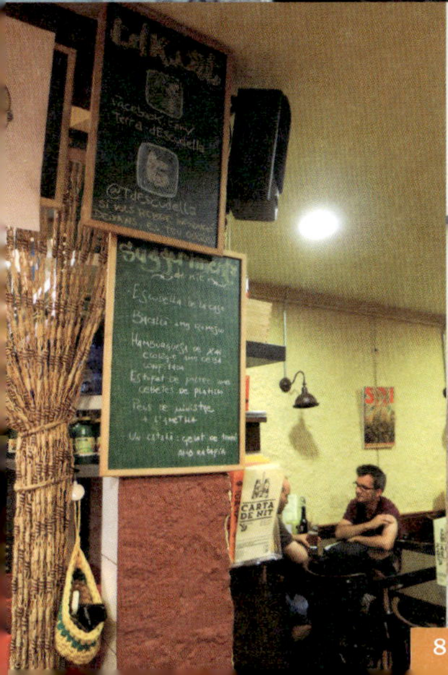
@Tdescudella
CARTA DE NIT

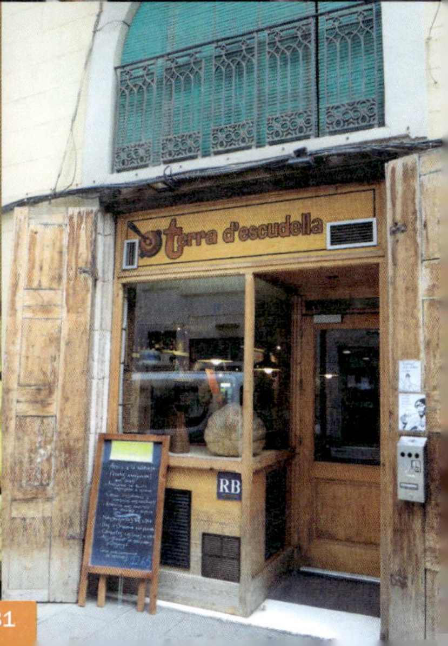
terra d'escudella
RB

LA CHANA

Andalusian Flavors, Hold the Flamenco

Address: Carrer del Poeta Cabanyes 8, Sants-Montjuïc
Telephone: +34 93 016 1843
Hours: Tues.-Sat. 12:30-4:30pm & 7pm-midnight; Sun. 12:30-4:30pm; closed Monday

Owner Natalia García, who grew up in Cádiz, has made her tiny bar La Chana into a gastronomic community center of sorts for other *gaditanos* and *sevillanos* living in Barcelona who long for a taste of authentic southern specialties. She and her small staff serve up dishes rarely found in this part of Spain, as well as a variety of cheeses, sausages, cured meats and wines from Spain's southwest.

In Andalusia – and most other parts of Spain – fried food is a way of life, so we began in typical fashion with an assortment of crispy bites of seafood. The *chocos* (cuttlefish), *boquerones* (fried anchovies), *cazón en adobo* (fried dogfish marinated in vinegar) and *ortiguillas* (sea anemone) were all fresh and tasty, served on small plates with a little pile of breadsticks as accompaniment. While the fried dishes are good, La Chana's truly special offering is its list of imported products from the South. This section of the menu, *De Barbate al Poble Sec,* is chock-full of unique, delectable treasures.

Barbate, a fishing village located an hour south of Cádiz at the mouth of the Strait of Gibraltar, is world-famous for its tuna, mostly eaten domestically in the form of salt-cured tuna, or *mojama de Barbate*. Good mojama isn't dry and tough like jerky, but supple and delicate, with a slight, iron-rich tuna flavor. Sliced thin and dressed with olive oil (and perhaps scattered with a few *marcona* almonds as garnish), this is a must-try at La Chana.

Along with the mojama, we passed around a dish of *hueva de maruca*, the bright orange salted and pressed roe sack of the ling fish, which had an interesting, slightly waxy texture and bold flavor. We absolutely loved the *chicharrones de Chiclana*, rich pork belly that had been slowly cooked in pork fat and spices, then sliced thin and served at room temperature with a sprinkling of black pepper.

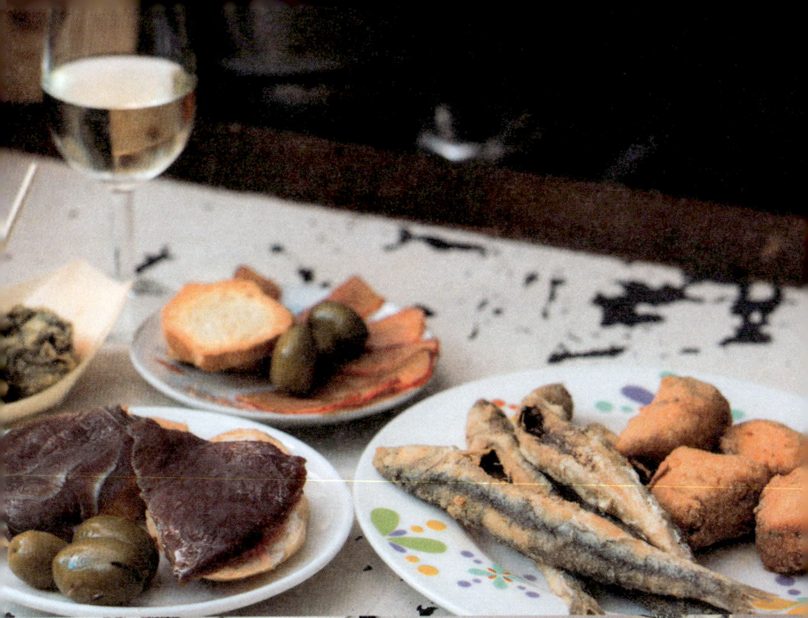

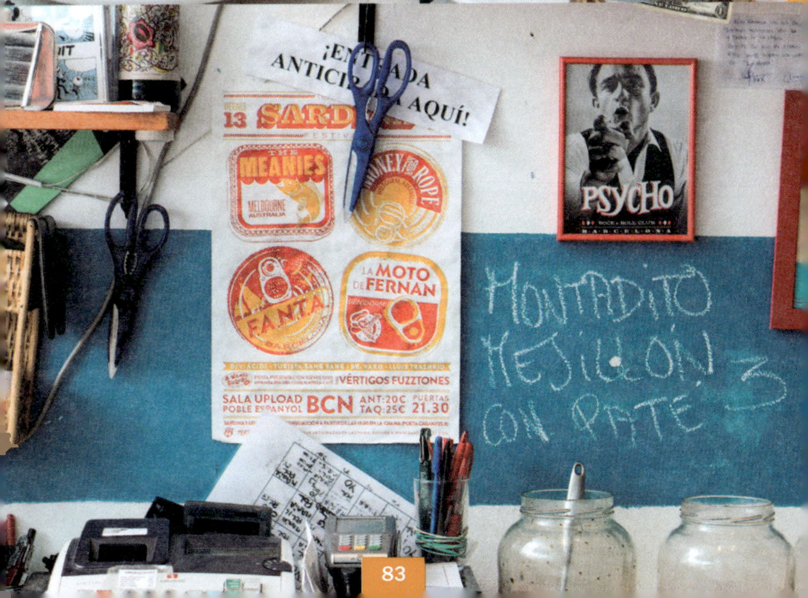
¡ENT ADA
ANTICI A AQUÍ!
13 SARD
THE MEANIES
MELBOURNE AUSTRALIA
MONEY FOR ROPE
FANTA
LA MOTO DE FERNAN
VÉRTIGOS FUZZTONES
SALA UPLOAD POBLE ESPANYOL
BCN
ANT:20€ TAQ:25€
PUERTAS 21.30
PSYCHO
ROCK & ROLL CLUB
BARCELONA
MONTADITO
MEJILLÓN
CON PATÉ 3

O MEU LAR

Galician Surf y Turf

Address: Carrer Margarit 24, Sants-Montjuïc
Telephone: +34 93 329 7074
Hours: Mon.-Sat. 1:30-4:30pm & 8:30pm-12:30am; Sun. 1:30-4:30pm; closed Sunday evening and Tuesday (except holidays)

Galicia, the autonomous region in northwest Spain, is famous for its extraordinary beef and an abundance of spectacular seafood. Like many Galicians, chef Antonio Rodríguez has a strong culinary connection with his homeland, and this serves as the foundation of his *brasería* (restaurant-grill) in Poble Sec.

Almost all the ingredients Rodríguez uses at O Meu Lar – its name means "my home" in Galician – are Galician, potatoes included. Here, you can get a *tapa* or half tapa of Padrón peppers (during the two months they're in season) as well as great Galician *tetilla* (cheese that looks like its name, "teat"). We love their mouthwateringly fragrant sautéed clams with smashed garlic, parsley, lemon and white wine – they're so tasty that we're compelled to mop up every last drop with bread.

O Meu Lar's specialty is Galician beef grilled over coals, known as *ternera Gallega*. The highly aromatic, tender beef needs special care in cooking in order for its best qualities to shine. Rodríguez offers several cuts, such as a 400 gram *entrecôte* or an enormous *chuletón*, or chop, weighing in at nearly 1 kilo – perfect for sharing – which is served in a smoking-hot clay dish so that the meat finishes cooking at the table.

O Meu Lar's bevy of seafood options also includes barnacles, crab, razor clams, cockles and scallops. We like the *polbo á feira,* or "festival-style" octopus, in which the cephalopod is cooked, sliced, dressed with paprika and served with some boiled potatoes, as was traditionally done at fairs in rural Galician villages.

We like to cap off our feast with Galician digestifs or a top-notch black coffee with a few drops of orujo, Galician white grappa. And whenever we go, we note that this is the kind of place where the owner makes the rounds to tables full of friends and regulars – all of whom undoubtedly call O Meu Lar their home away from home.

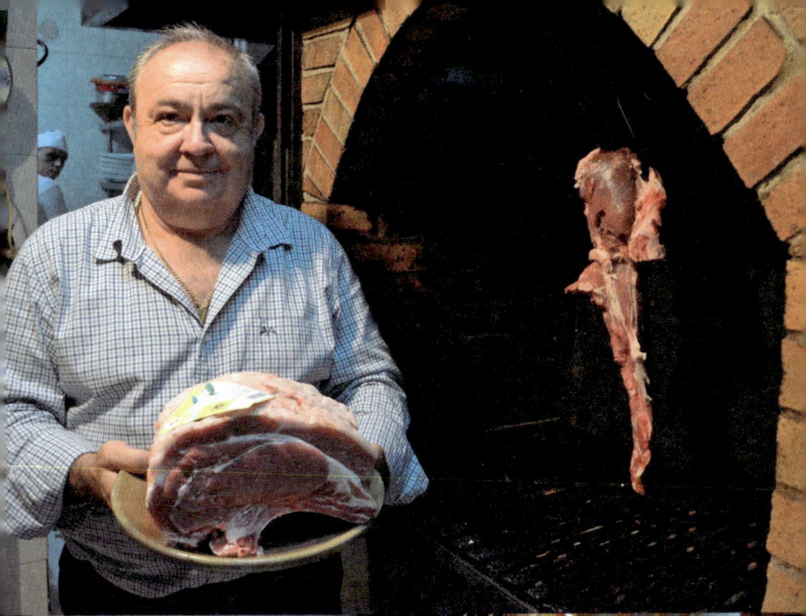

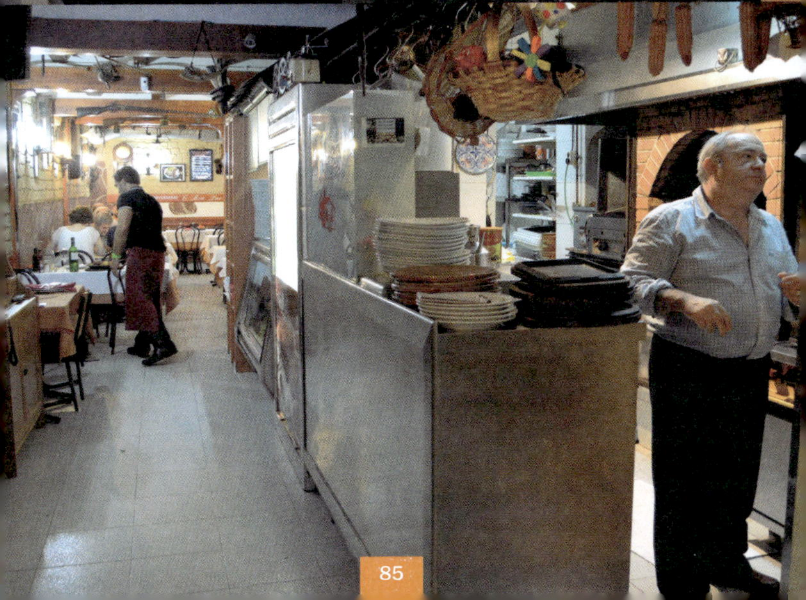

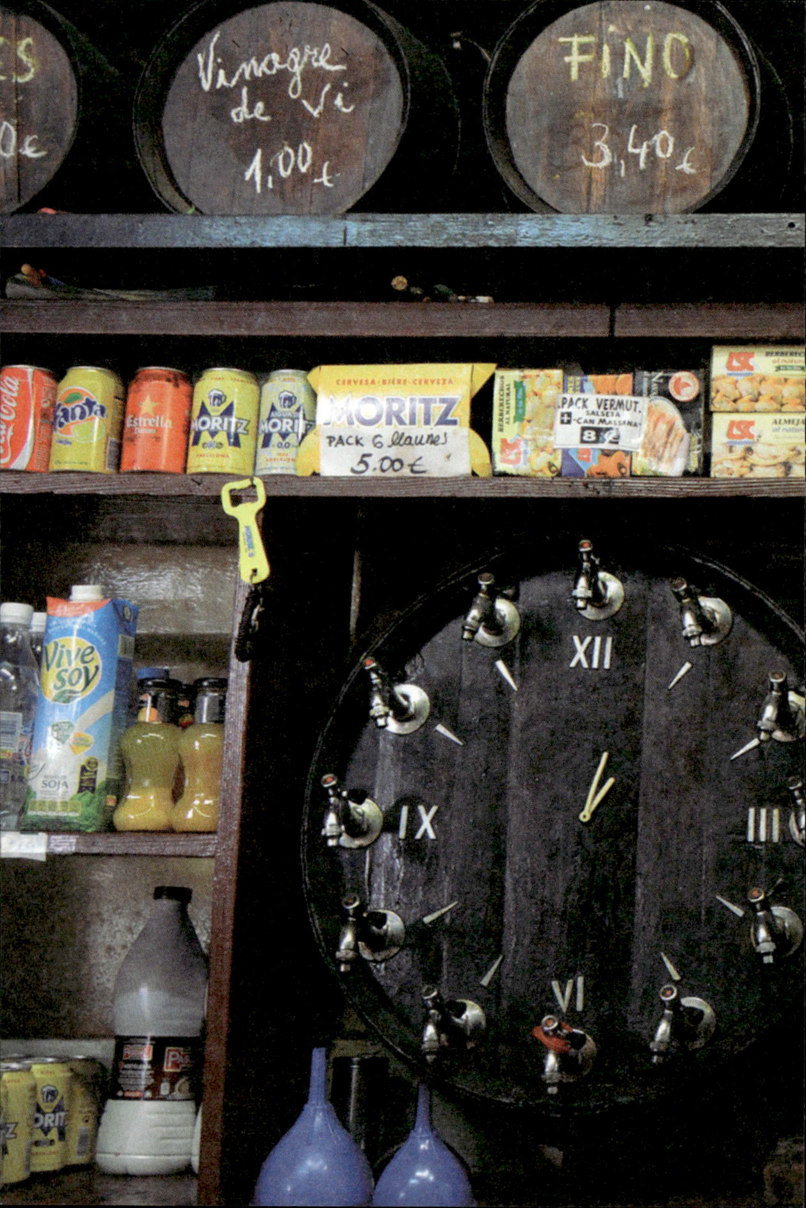
Vinagre de Vi
1,00 €
FINO
3,40 €
Coca-Cola
Fanta
Estrella
MORITZ
MORITZ
CERVESA · BIÈRE · CERVEZA
MORITZ
PACK 6 llaunes
5.00 €
PACK VERMUT
+ SALSETA
+ CAN MASSANA
8 €
Vive soy
SOJA
XII
IX
III
VI

BEYOND THE CENTER (NORTH)

CAN PINEDA

Address: Carrer de Sant Joan de Malta 55,
Sant Martí
Telephone: +34 93 308 3081
Hours: Tues.-Sat. 1-4pm & 9-11pm;
closed Sunday, Monday and holidays

A Workers' Canteen Grows Up

The rustic family favorite Can Pineda has been holding down this corner of Barcelona's El Clot neighborhood since 1904. It was not a restaurant originally, but a typical wine shop and canteen, where local factory workers would come for a glass of wine to go with a simple meal or to drink while warming up their lunch boxes.

Partners and brothers-in-law Paco Cuenca (front of the house) and Jaume Jovells (head chef) have run Can Pineda since the 1970s. Since then, dish by dish, they have gone from a simple bar to a more ambitious restaurant, turning excellent seasonal and local ingredients into carefully prepared dishes with a Catalan foundation and Spanish, French and Italian influences. The sardine *coca* (a traditional flatbread) highlights the deeply savory qualities of the fish with caramelized onion, tomato and *olivada* (tapenade), and the crispy coca offers a delightful contrast to the fleshy fish. We also like the homey meatballs (pork and beef), which are paired with delicious *xipirons*, or baby squid, in a satisfyingly earthy Catalan rendition of surf and turf.

In winter, the stew of artichokes and *mongetas del ganxet* (Catalan white beans) also combines flavors from land and sea with a few big, briny clams from Carril, a village on the Atlantic coast. The white truffles from Italy's Piedmont region bring their beguiling perfume to a few of the restaurant's Italo-French dishes, like the creamy, delicate fresh pasta or the *pochè* eggs with foie gras. Our all-time favorite, however, is the *guisantes lágrima*, sweet, tender and juicy peas, cooked with bits of ham and bacon, garlic and mint leaves, which imbue the dish with a subtle yet thoroughly enticing aroma.

We always make sure to save room for dessert – perhaps the praline biscuit with broiled yolk or the Roquefort cheese with pear and pepper. But most likely, we'll ask for the house specialty: *bombetas*, small bites of crispy phyllo that gush forth warm cream or chocolate when bitten into.

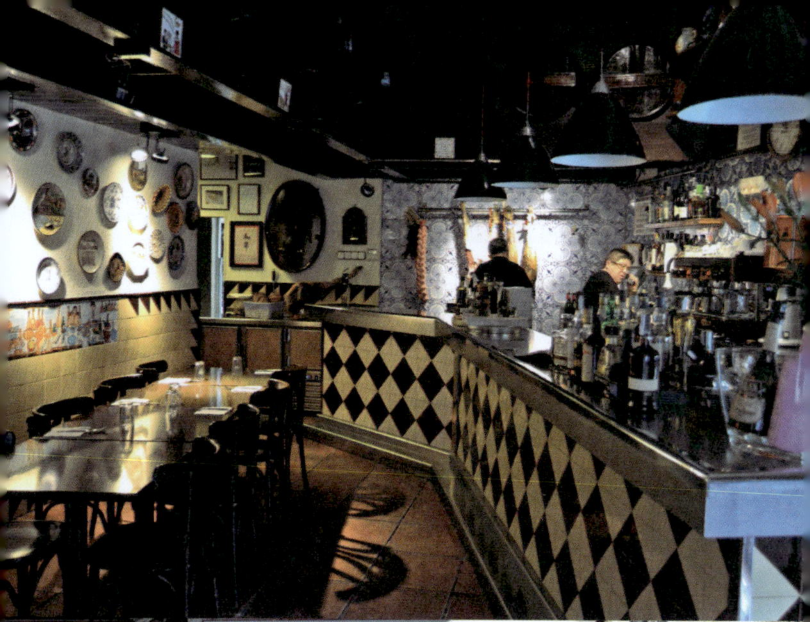

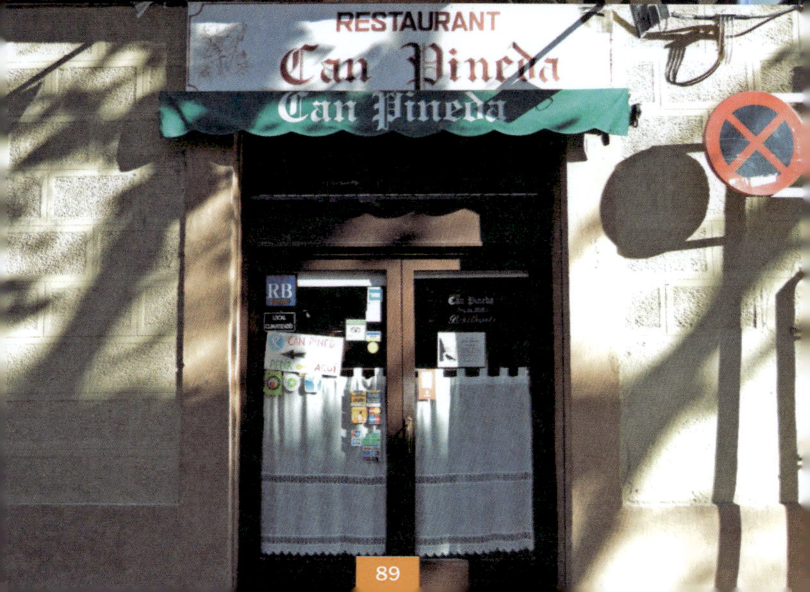
RESTAURANT
Can Pineda
Can Pineda
RB

CUINA DEL GUINARDÓ

Refinement, To Go

Address: Carrer Varsòvia 148,
El Guinardó
Telephone: +34 93 436 0919
Hours:
Restaurant: Tues.-Sun. 1:15-3:30pm;
Shop: Tues.-Fri. 9am-8pm;
Sat., Sun. and
holidays 9am-4pm;
closed Monday (excluding holidays)

Up in the high streets of the Horta-Guinardó hills, there is a restaurant with a big concentration of culinary talent but just eight tables. To make things worse, they are only available during two hours for lunch. Fortunately for those who can't snag one of those precious tables, La Cuina del Guinardó ("Guinardo's Kitchen"), a Catalan traditional market-cuisine restaurant, is also a store selling cooked food to take away from morning to evening and a great wine shop, with a tasting area (open lunchtime only) on the upper level.

This "kitchen," which opened in 1994, is run by Santi Velasco – a chef with 40 years of experience in three restaurants under his belt – along with his wife and their daughter, a noted sommelier. The variety of traditional dishes here are based entirely on seasonal Catalan recipes and carefully prepared with high-quality ingredients. In winter, the spoon is the queen of the table, for dishes such as the emblematic *callos* (tripe stew with spices), or the pig's feet with chickpeas (they have kept the same supplier for decades), with the addition of a bit of shredded black *butifarra* (a Catalan sausage) to give more flavor, cooked for a very long time until the meat detaches super-easily from the bones. Another standout dish is the rich, intense rich slow-cooked oxtail with red wine and chocolate.

We also love the delicious simplicity and local personality of the *fesolets d'ull negre*, a kind of black-eyed pea with caramelized onion and some beautiful 00-size anchovies (large cured anchovies preserved in olive oil) to take away. Always a pleasure is the monkfish and prawns *suquet* (fish stew with seafood broth) enhanced by a sauce made with rockfish and seafood broth, crab and mantis shrimp that fill the mouth with flavor. Tasty but lighter, perhaps ideal as a starter, are great *piquillo* red peppers stuffed with tuna and Basque chili vinaigrette, with the combination of two different olive oils and a Pedro Ximénez wine reduction.

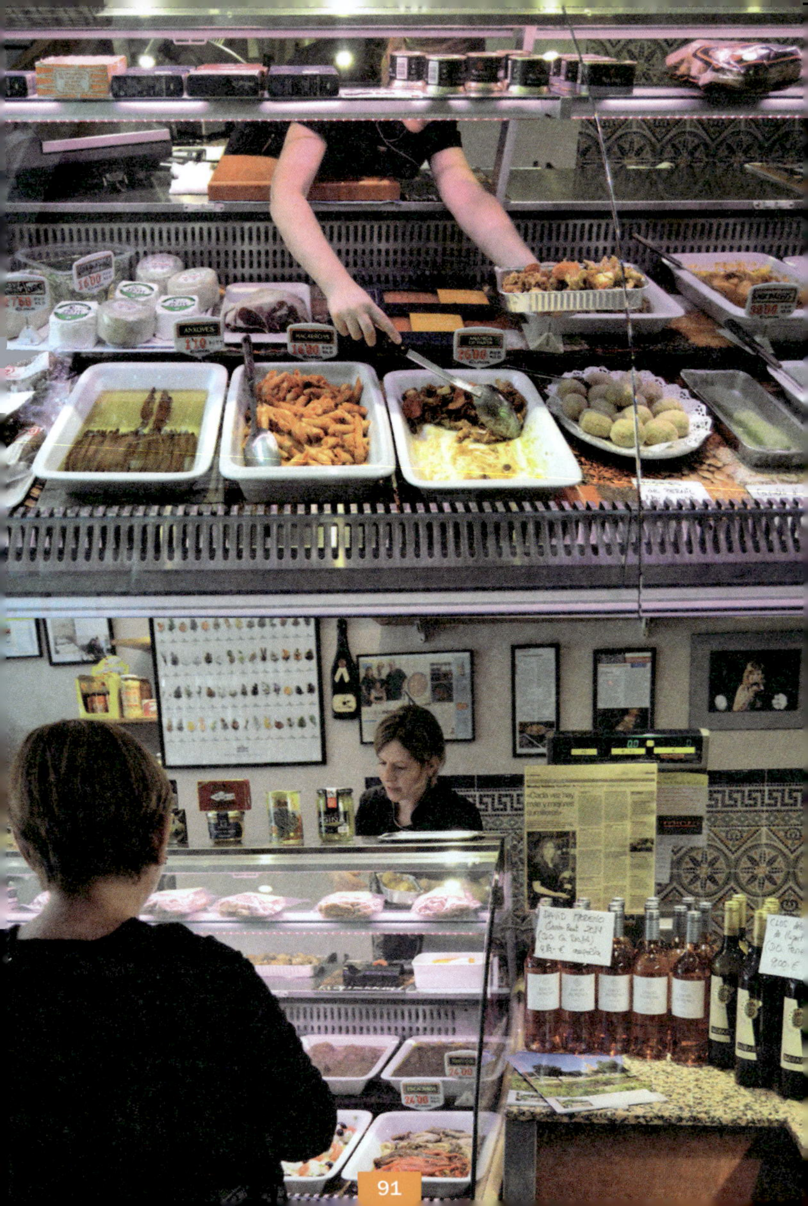
ANXOVES
MACARRONS

ELS PESCADORS

Address: Plaça de Prim 1,
El Poblenou
Telephone: +34 93 225 2018
Hours: 1-3:45pm & 8-11:30pm

A Fine Kettle of Fish

Anchoring one end of Poblenou's quiet and lovely Prim Square, Els Pescadors sits surrounded by the white houses that once belonged to the fishermen for which it's named. The old tavern opened in 1848, and through the 19th century, it was frequented by those fishermen, as well as workers from the numerous textile factories in the area.

Current owners Josep Maria Maulini and his wife, Toia Durán, created the restaurant as it is today, complete with an elegant, expansive terrace. They serve traditional Catalan seafood preparations, with all the Andalusian, Basque and Galician influences inherent in that cuisine. (Many fishermen came – and still come – from those coastal areas to work in Catalonia.) Everything is made with the utmost care, with a clean, direct and unembellished cooking style – the better to let the ingredients speak for themselves.

On a recent visit, we ate some *caixetes* ("little boxes"), local shellfish that are like something in between mussels and barnacles. They were full-flavored and very firm, a bit sweeter than expected and perfect just as they were, served warm and unadorned. We also enjoyed the Basque delicacy of *kokotxas,* soft, creamy and very juicy cod cheeks, which came with some green beans and chopped leeks enrobed in a foamy *pil pil* sauce. But our favorite may very well have been the *suquet*, a Catalan fish soup traditionally served in taverns or on boats as a communal meal. Fish heads and bones are used to make the broth, to which are added meatier chunks of fish, as in French *bouillabaisse*. This restaurant's exquisite version of *suquet* included Catalan *buffet negre* potatoes and a concentrated soup of fish and vegetables with a succulent piece of *escórpora,* red scorpion fish.

Els Pescadors has seen many changes through the years, but we like to think that the fishermen who once lived in those white houses around this tavern would feel very much at home in the tavern today. We certainly do.

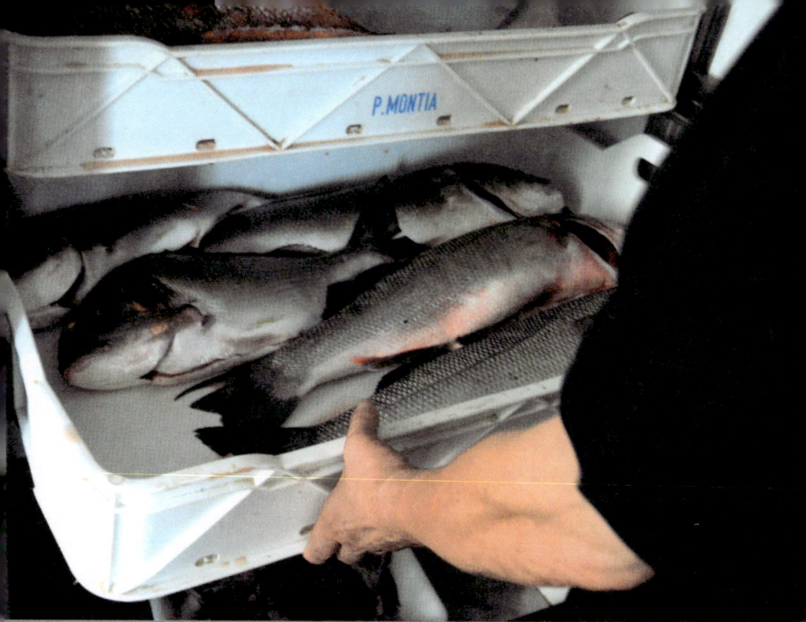
P. MONTIA
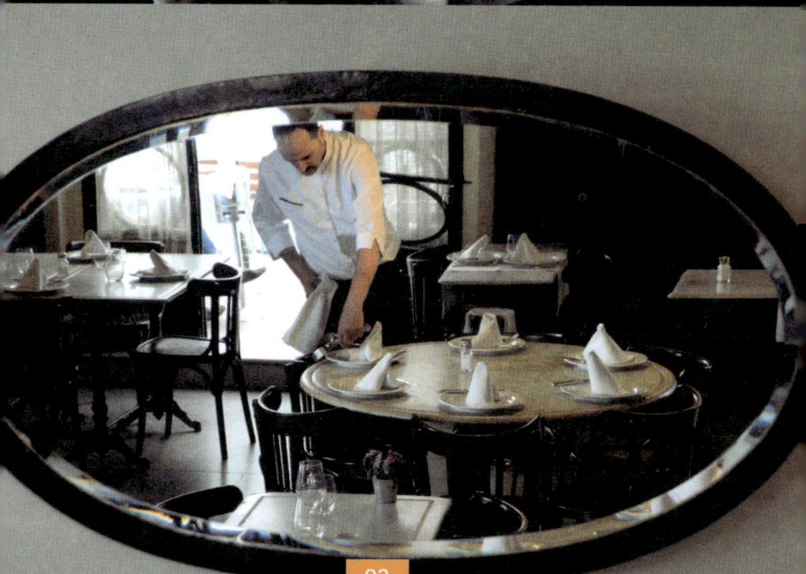

EL RACÓ DEL MARINER

Sole Survivor

Address: Port Fórum,
Carrer Port Esportiu, Local 1
Telephone: +34 64 559 3096
Hours: Tues.-Sat. 8am-4pm
(breakfast and lunch only)
closed Sunday & Monday

At El Racó del Mariner (The Sailor's Corner), everything and nothing has changed. For 40 years, the beloved seafood restaurant catered to fishermen, port workers and later the public at the old fishermen's dock in the port of La Barceloneta. But in 2016, during the final stages of the port's transformation into a marina for luxury yachts, El Racó del Mariner was forced to move.

Despite its new address in the modern Port Fórum area, there's still a sense of continuity. Inside, you can see the same faces – waiters Samba and Mamen and owner Jenifer Santana – stationed near the wooden boat-like bar, as if they were at the helm of a brand new ship amidst a sea of tables. Much of the décor from the previous location has been relocated to the restaurant's new home, such as the ship's wheel, the fishing nets and photos of boats.

But, of course, it's the food that provides the real constant here. There are the iconic grilled and fried fisherman's tapas of prawns, langoustines, clams, razor clams, squid, octopus, sardines and anchovies. Perhaps the most classic dish is the *morralla*, or fried fish, but the most in demand are their great fish and seafood stews, soups, seafood casseroles of lobster, hake or monkfish and the exquisite rice dishes. All continue to be made with the same impeccably fresh raw materials, mostly local (some even sourced by Santana's husband, a fisherman), and the same traditional preparations as before. Many of the habitués of the old venue come to the new location, six or seven kilometers up the road, because the food is just that good – it's worth the trip.

Like many others, undoubtedly, we are thrilled that El Racó del Mariner has managed to hold on to its authenticity and excellent cuisine. It's a tribute to themselves and a gift to the rest of us. And if the new location requires us to walk a little bit more, then all the better for us to arrive a little hungrier.

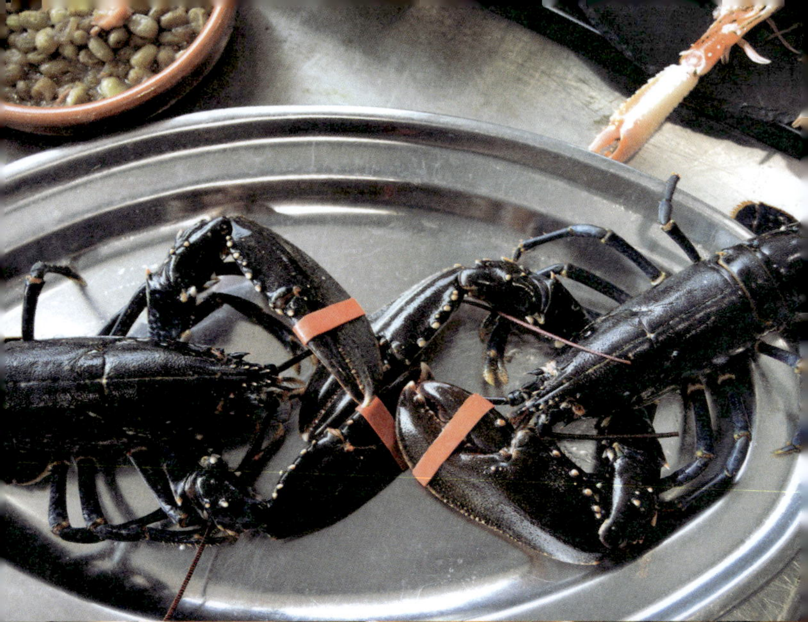

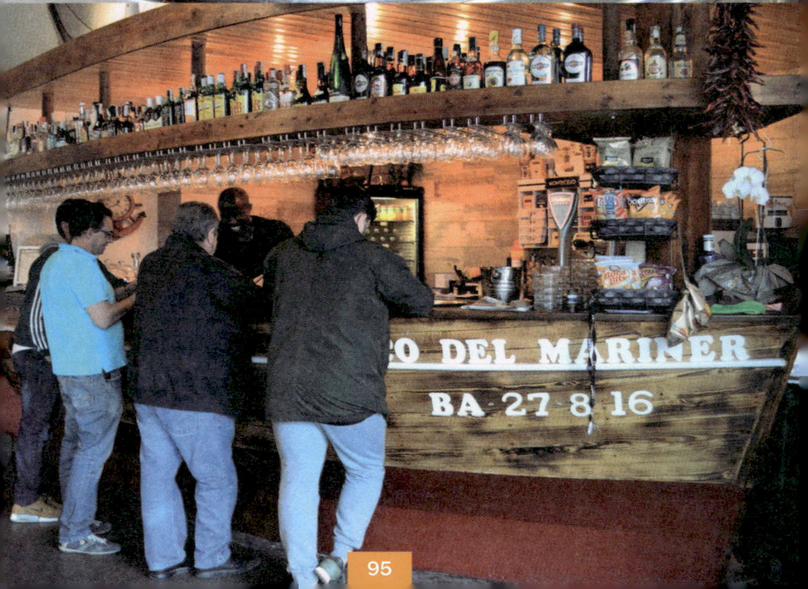
O DEL MARINER
BA 27 8 16

LAS DELICIAS

Tapas with a View

Address: Carretera del Carme
Carrer de Mühlberg :
El Carmel
Telephone: +34 93 429 2202
Hours: Tues.-Sat. 10am-4pm
& 7pm-10:30pm;
Sun. 10am-4pm;
closed Monday

Manolo, the protagonist of Juan Marsé's 1965 novel, *Last Evenings with Teresa*, possibly the saddest Spanish love novel ever written, spends a great deal of his time drinking and playing cards with the local elders in Las Delicias.

This bar was founded in the mid-1920s using a natural cave that was turned into a bomb shelter during the Spanish Civil War. El Carmel, a working-class neighborhood on Rovira hill with spectacular views over the city, was home to the Andalusian, Galician, Aragonese, Castilian and Extremaduran immigrants who moved to Barcelona looking for brighter futures during the postwar years. Las Delicias soon became their favorite local eatery, as portions were larger than usual.

Decades later, portions are still very generous, the bar is still a neighborhood institution and the menu still reflects the origins of those who once settled down here. There are Andalucian specialties such as *calamares a la andaluza* (deep-fried squid), *morcilla de Jaén* (pork blood sausage) and *pincho moruno* (marinated chicken on a skewer); Galician specialties like *pimientos de Padrón, lacón con cachelos* (boiled pork shank) and *pulpo a la gallega* (boiled octopus); *Aragonese longaniza* (pork sausage) and Castilian *callos* (beef tripe stew).

But if there is a tapa that makes it worth the trek – El Carmel is renowned for its steep streets and the lack of access to public transport – it's the *patatas suizas*, Las Delicias' own version of *patatas bravas*, the quintessential Spanish tapa: fried potatoes served warm with spicy tomato sauce and aioli. What makes Las Delicias' version so special is that its *allioli* sauce is less garlicky than usual and its tomato sauce is actually romesco (made from almonds and red pepper); the result is milder than the classic brava sauce but equally yummy.

A good way to burn off the calories inevitably gained with Las Delicias' tapas is to go for a stroll to the El Carmel bunkers, which offer arguably the best viewpoint in Barcelona.

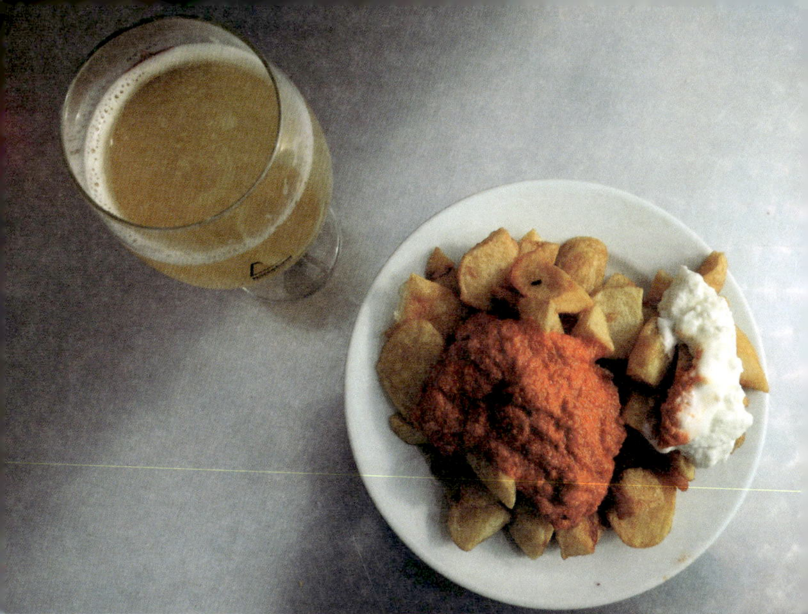

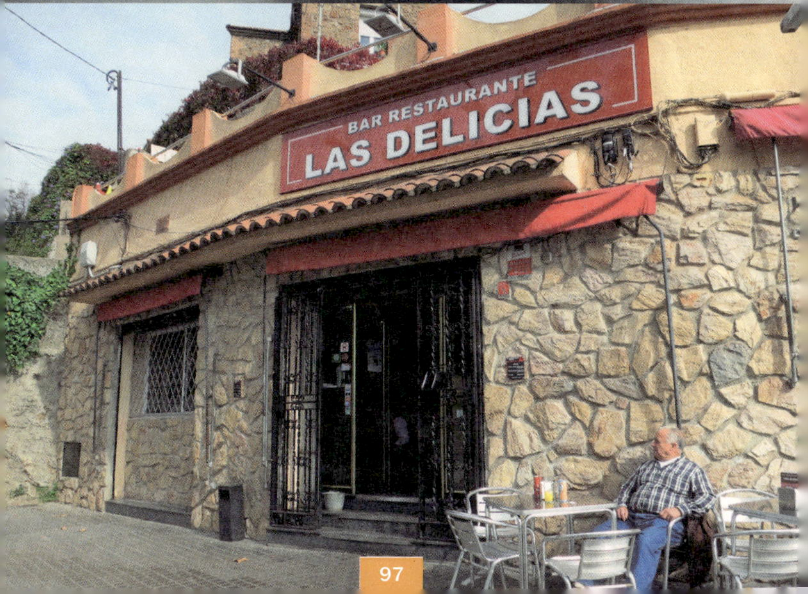
BAR RESTAURANTE
LAS DELICIAS

TAVERNA CAN ROCA

Gustatory Eye Openers

Address: Gran de Sant Andreu 209, Sant Andreu
Telephone: +34 93 346 5701
Hours: Mon.-Fri. 9am-5:30pm; Sat. 9am-5pm; closed Sunday

In the neighborhood of Sant Andreu we encounter very few city visitors wandering the cobbled streets or peering at the 19th-century two-story houses that pepper this district. Through the doors of Taverna Can Roca, we find even fewer. This is a place that can be considered *muy del barrio*.

What hit us when we stepped inside on a recent Saturday morning were the exuberance and noise of the busy throng sipping red wine and enthusiastically tucking into huge baguettes and Can Roca's famed Catalan *esmorzars de forquilla*. These "fork breakfasts" are a departure from the usual coffee and pastry that Barcelonans grab to start the day.

Offal may not be our first thought for breakfast but the braised tripe with chickpeas, bathed in paprika sauce, would convince the most skeptical eater and is really worth giving a try. We devoured our pork meatballs, lightly caramelized and sitting with miniature pieces of soft, stewed cuttlefish on a mound of tender, creamy baby white beans. The tomato sauce was sharpened and soured with a hint of vinegar, flecked with tiny peas and earthy saffron milk cap mushrooms, *rovellons*. The whole dish was brought together by a dash of deep green extra-virgin olive oil and a smattering of raw garlic and parsley.

If our stomachs need easing into the morning, there's always the half baguette sandwiches brimming with French omelet and bacon or sausages topped with a pickled green pepper or two or drizzled with parsley oil and blanketed by a generous helping of pungent Grana Padano cheese.

The wine we ordered came in a carafe, and groups might get a *porrón*, the traditional glass vessel with the narrow spout that can be passed round the table to ensure everyone gets a drink but no one's lips touch the bottle. (Invariably more will end up down our clothes than in our mouths.) Yet you don't have to finish it all; you pay only for the amount you drink.

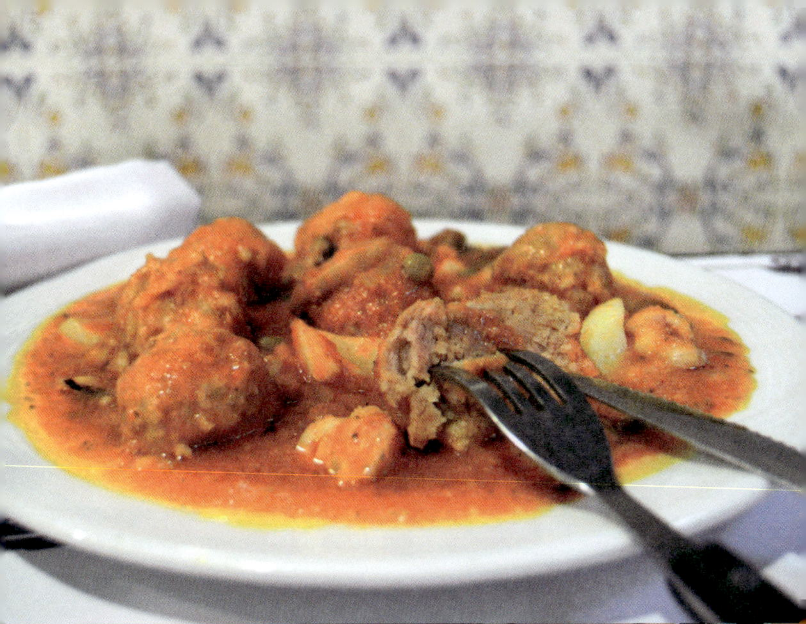

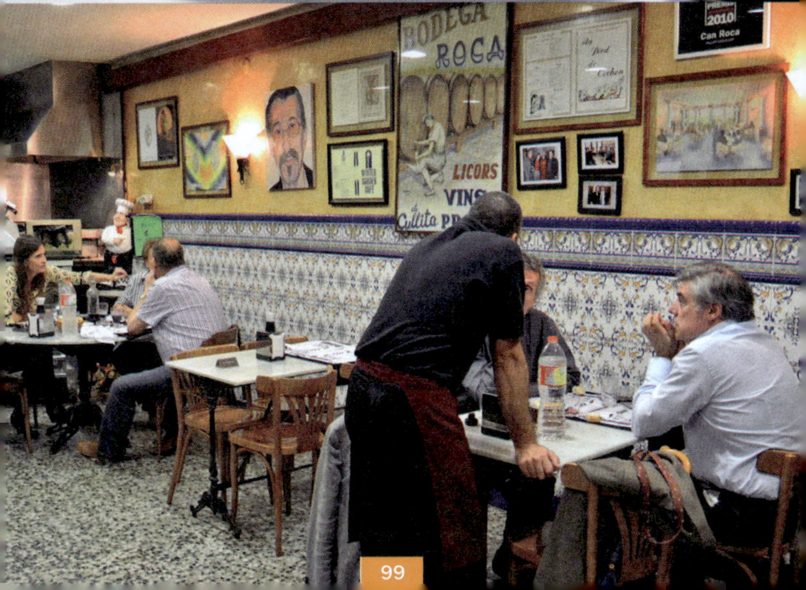
BODEGA
ROCA
LICORS
VINS
2010
Can Roca

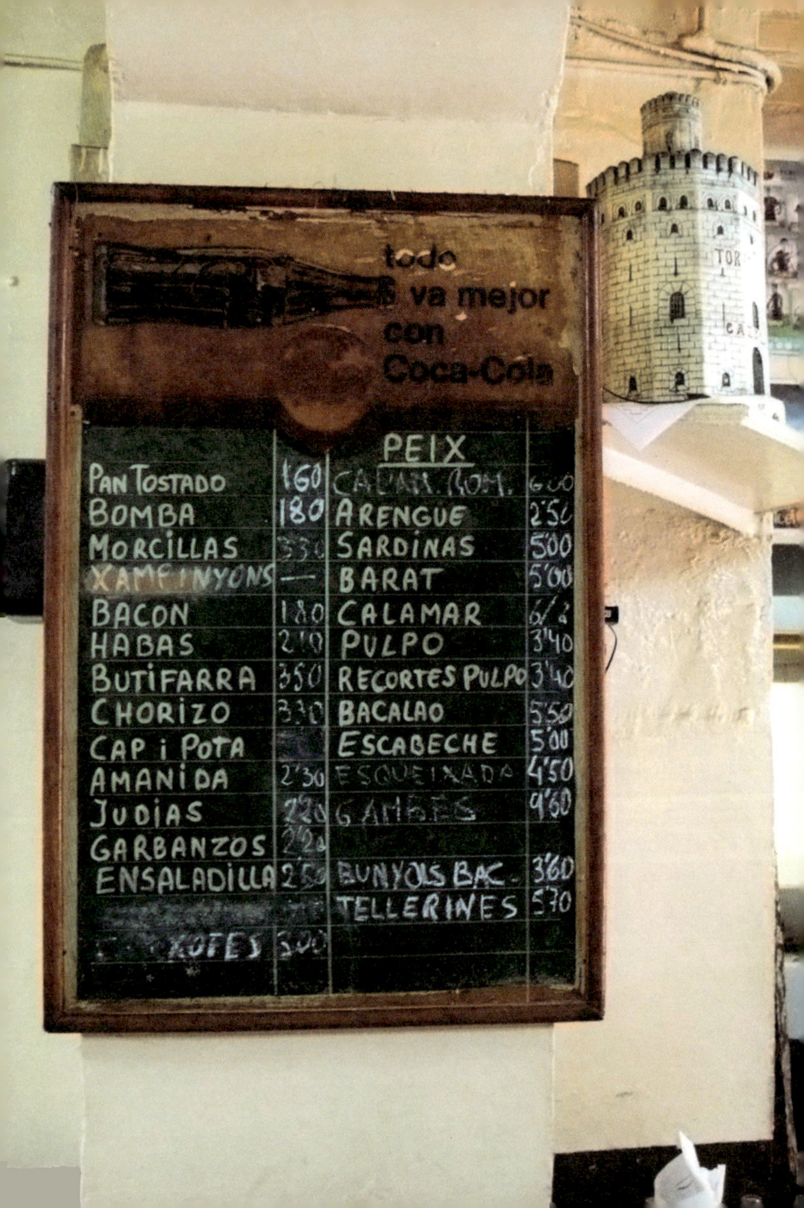

todo
va mejor
con
Coca-Cola
PEIX
PAN TOSTADO 160
BOMBA 180
MORCILLAS
XAMPINYONS
BACON 180
HABAS
BUTIFARRA 350
CHORIZO
CAP i POTA
AMANIDA 2'30
JUDIAS
GARBANZOS
ENSALADILLA
ARENGUE
SARDINAS 5'00
BARAT 5'00
CALAMAR
PULPO 3'40
RECORTES PULPO
BACALAO 5'50
ESCABECHE 5'00
ESQUEIXADA 4'50
GAMBES 9'60
BUNYOLS BAC. 3'60
TELLERINES 5'70

SPECIALS

BEYOND THE BOQUERÍA

Barcelona's Local Food Markets

Any guidebook to Barcelona is sure to sing the praises of the famous Boquería market, but although it's certainly worth a visit, you can avoid the swarms of tourists by heading to one of the city's smaller, more local food markets.

One of our favorites is the **Mercat de la Llibertat** in Gràcia. Designed in 1888 by Miguel Pascual, the brick and iron structure is an impressive example of Modernist architecture. With more than 40 stalls – a few of which have been in the same families for over 80 years – selling a variety of delicious-looking food products, the market can seem overwhelming at first. We can recommend *xarcuteria* Bragulat for *jamón* and sausages, Bordas for top-notch meats, Peix Fresc Esther for fish, and La Grana for *frutos secos*, including toasted hazelnuts, almonds, desiccated coconut, dried fruit, chocolate and delicious *torró* (nougat).

Not far away, in Barcelona's upscale Sarrià-Sant Gervasi neighborhood, is **El Mercat de Galvany**, considered by many to be one of the most outstanding structures in Barcelona. The food stalls inside are also attractive but, since the market tends to be a bit on the pricey side, visitors might do just as well to remain outside and let the gorgeous façade serve as a feast for the eyes.

For take-home food shopping, head to the **Mercat de Santa Caterina** in the El Born–La Ribera neighborhood. Originally built in 1848, on the site of the previous Sant Caterina Convent, it was completely refurbished in 2005 by architects Enric Miralles and Benedetta Tagliabue.

Inside the market you'll find more than 70 stalls with high quality products and several bars and restaurants. The food stalls include groceries, butcheries, charcuteries specializing in ham and cured sausages and cheeses, olives and conservas stalls, codfish stalls (*bacallaneries*), fresh fish, nuts, spices and much more. For olives, try "Olives i Conservas Torres." For honey, head to "Manantial de Salud,"

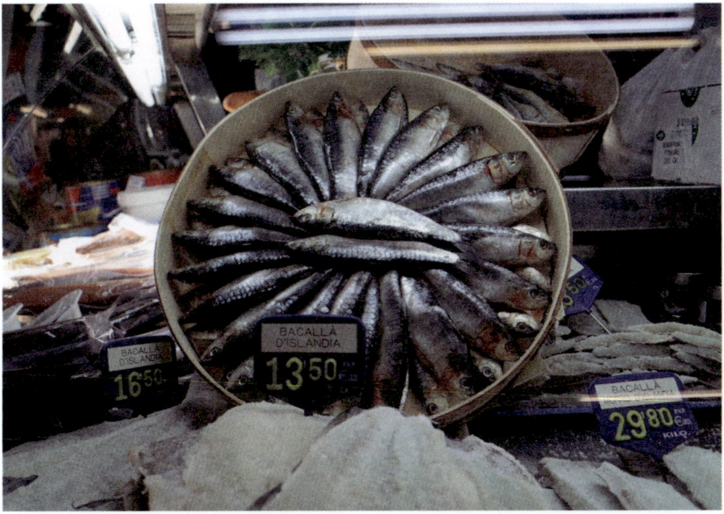
BACALLÀ
D'ISLANDIA
13'50
16'50
BACALLÀ
29'80
KILO

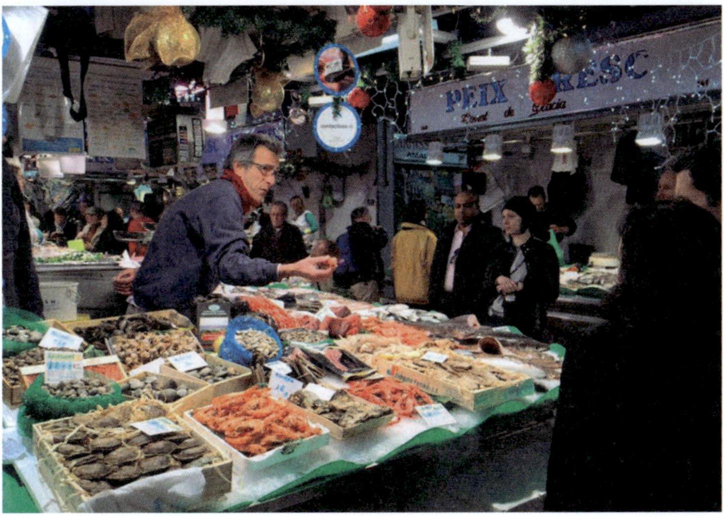
PEIX

who carry a range of artisanal honeys produced from different flowers like thyme, rosemary or orange blossom. Also look out for the "LaMiel" stall, for good honey, nuts and a cornucopia of spices.

In the L'Eixample district, the updated **El Mercat del Ninot** ("Doll Market") now includes tasting bars and restaurants among the market stalls. Fish shops like La Medusa 73 or La Barra offer fresh oysters, clams, mussels, barnacles and prawns for eating on-site accompanied by a chilled glass of wine or cava, as well as daily specials like homey seafood rice and *ortiguillas* (battered and fried anemones). There's confited tuna at Peixateria Ribera, and many of the fishmongers will even cook to order whatever fish you purchase – which you can then eat there with some wine or beer, of course. Perello, a classic (open since 1898) cod and *conserves* stall, serves the excellent Casa Mariol *vermut* alongside traditional dishes like *esqueixada*, a kind of Catalan ceviche made from salt cod and dressed with tomato, fresh pepper, onions, olive oil and vinegar; *rocs*, cod *brandada* battered and fried in

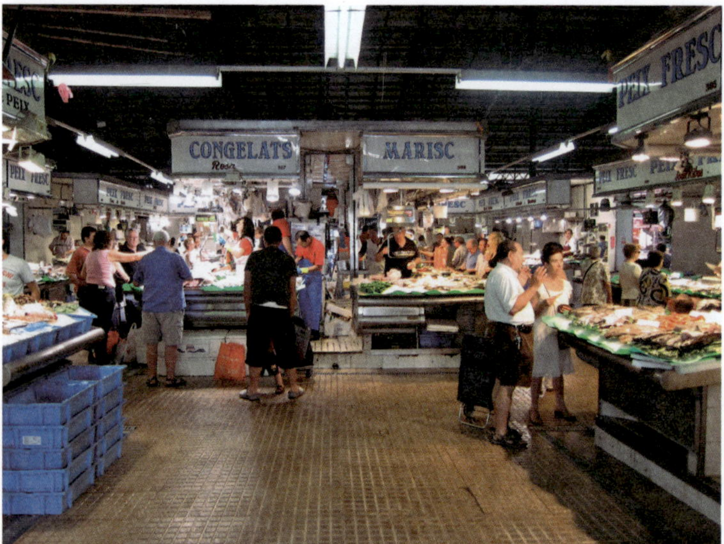

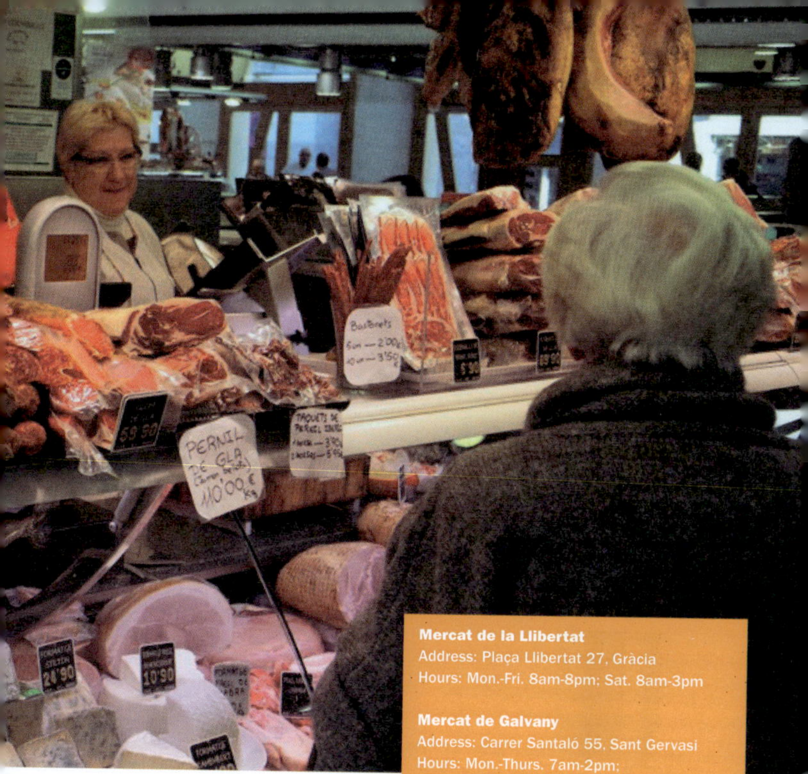

crispy pieces and served with *allioli* and romesco sauce; and smoked salmon and cod chops.

Another update that has made the Mercat del Ninot more accessible is to the open hours, which now run from 8 a.m. to 9 p.m. (it was previously open only in the morning). That's plenty of time to spend eating and drinking your way around the market.

Mercat de la Llibertat
Address: Plaça Llibertat 27, Gràcia
Hours: Mon.-Fri. 8am-8pm; Sat. 8am-3pm

Mercat de Galvany
Address: Carrer Santaló 55, Sant Gervasi
Hours: Mon.-Thurs. 7am-2pm;
Fri.-Sat. 7am-2:30pm

Mercat de Santa Caterina
Address: Avinguda de Francesc Cambó 16,
El Born-La Ribera
Telephone: +34 933 19 57 40
Hours: Mon.,Wed. & Sat. 7:30am-3:30pm;
Tues.-Thurs. 7:30am-8:30pm

Mercat del Ninot
Address: Carrer del Mallorca 133-157,
Eixample
Telephone: +34 93 323 4909
Hours: Mon.-Sat. 8am-9pm

CALÇOTS

Not Your Average Onion

We don't mind winter in Catalonia because it means the return of *calçots*, our beloved spring onions, and *calçotades*, the wonderful celebrations that bring people together to eat them. As the legend goes, a 19th-century Catalan farmer was out experimenting in his fields when he came up with a new kind of longer, juicier green onion, the *calçot*. In creating the onion, the farmer also paved the way for the rise of a distinctly Catalan cultural event.

Why are people in Barcelona so crazy about getting together and eating *calçots*, which are really nothing more than scorched green onions? Because they are a good excuse to meet up with friends; because eating calçots requires a certain skill, and people love showing off; because it's funny how you end up with dirty hands and reeking of onions; and, last but not least, because they're delicious. When it comes to *calçots*, you always want to eat just one more.

The most popular way to cook calçots is to grill them over an open barbecue. Rather than fully cleaning the onions, it's best to leave some soil on their surface, which protects their outer skin. The *calçots* are grilled directly over the flames until they became completely black on the outside. (Don't worry; the best part – the inside – will be still white and clean). They are typically served wrapped in newspaper to keep them warm and eaten off curved terracotta roof tiles. *Calçots* must be eaten directly with the fingers; the trick is to hold them by the green leaves with one hand and pull off the burned and blackened outer layer of skin with the other hand. The tender and juicy inner bulb is then dipped in *salsa romesco*, a special sauce made from dried red peppers, nuts, garlic, vinegar and olive oil that is typical of Tarragona. Finally, the *calçot* is ready to be eaten!

Calçotades typically take place between January and March in public barbecues in the countryside, known as *merenderos*; at rural Catalan restaurants called *masias*; or in peoples' homes. In Barcelona, many restaurants offering grilled dishes

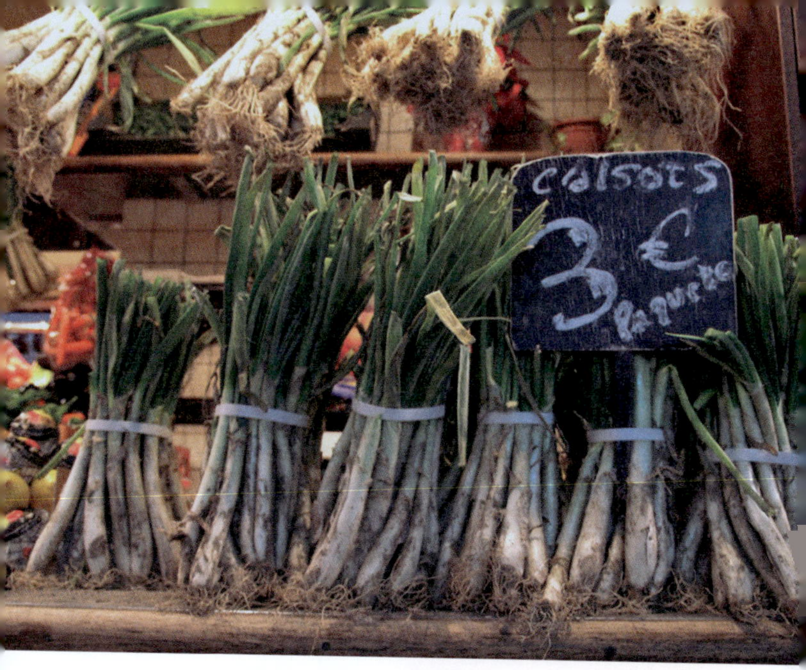

include *calçots* in their menus during the season. In the spirit of traditional *calçotades*, the rustic restaurant **Carmen** in the Sants neighborhood prepares a great lunch for a group (these onion feasts are not the kind of thing you do solo). If you want to taste prized calçots from the Valls region, **Can Xurradas** in L'Eixample, a more upscale grill spot known for its meats, is great option. For a *masía* experience inside the city, **Can Travi Nou** (see p. 116) – located inside is a beautiful and rustic 17th-century house – offers two special Calçotada menus.

Restaurante Carmen
Address: Carrer de Valladolid 44, Sants
Telephone: +34 93 330 3688
Hours: Tues. & Wed. 1-4pm; Thurs.-Sun. 1-4pm & 8pm-midnight; closed Mon.

Can Xurrades
Address: Carrer de Casanova 212, Eixample
Telephone: +34 93 217 3097
+34 68 756 6667
Hours: Mon.-Sat. 1pm-midnight; Sun. 1-4pm

Can Travi Nou
Address: Carrer Jorge Manrique s/n, Horta
Telephone: +34 93 428 0434
Hours: 1:30-4pm & 8:30-11pm

CATALAN ICE CREAM

The Real Scoop

As you might expect from a city whose weather forecast tends to be sunny, Barcelona has plenty of excellent ice-cream options, even as summer fades into fall. And, sure, like most of the world's food-loving metropolises, this town has its share of internationally loved, Italian-style *gelateries* – many even run by real, live Italians. Places like Vioko, DelaCrem, Gelaaati di Marco and Amorino sell gelato that is licked and loved by the most discerning tongues in the city. But if you want a frozen treat with more local flavor, we suggest licking – ahem, looking – beyond the Italian stuff.

Torronerías have a Valencian origin and are so called because they dedicate themselves to making artisanal nougat or *torró* (in Catalan) in the winter. That leaves summertime for making refreshing and energizing *orxata*, plus their popular artisanal ice cream and slushes (though you can still get turrón in summer and ice cream in winter). The popular *torronería* **La Valenciana** offers wonderful ice creams with flavors like Xixona-style Marcona almond nougat and *leche merengada* (meringue milk). But you'll probably find even longer lines snaking into the door at **Sirvent**, in Sant Antoni, and in front of **Tío Che**, in Poblenou.

Open since 1920 and 1912, respectively, Sirvent and Tío Che are old classics that continue to deliver, but there are (relative) newcomers on the frozen treats scene, too. **Bodevici**, in Gràcia, is a small chain (there are three shops in Catalonia) that specializes in organic ice cream, frozen yogurt, slushes and cold drinks. The cream they use comes fresh from cows or goats in Extremadura, the westernmost region of Spain. You can customize your flavor selection with many combinations and toppings of various grains or fruit, as well as with traditional temptations like *crema catalana* (similar to *crème brûlée*) and the bestseller, dark chocolate. All their products are completely natural and certified organic, without artificial colors, flavors or preservatives.

Not far from Bodevici, in La Plaça de la Vila de Gràcia, you'll find **Pyreneum**, a shop with strong ties to Catalan

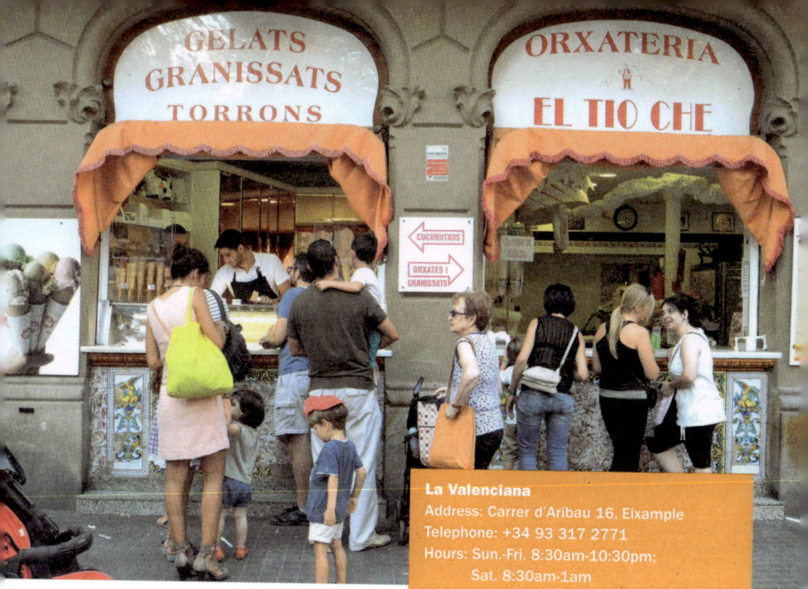

terroir that offers profoundly flavorful, lusciously rich ice cream. Pyreneum's owner, Stephane Orsoni, a Corsican, lives in the Catalan Pyrenees, in the beautiful area of La Cerdanya, which is where many of his ingredients come from. A farming cooperative there produces superb, incredibly fragrant and sweet cream, made from milk that is just half-pasteurized to better retain those aromas. Orsoni also sources cheese, apples, pears, figs, berries, herbs, honey and even olive oil and balsamic vinegar from the mountains.

Of course, all the shops we've mentioned offer your more basic flavors in addition to the unusual ones (blue cheese, anyone?). Fortunately, Barcelona's surfeit of sunny days means there's plenty of opportunities to try them all.

La Valenciana
Address: Carrer d'Aribau 16, Eixample
Telephone: +34 93 317 2771
Hours: Sun.-Fri. 8:30am-10:30pm;
Sat. 8:30am-1am

Sirvent
Address: Carrer del Parlament de Catalunya 56, Eixample
Telephone: +34 93 441 2720
Hours: 9am-10:30pm

Tío Che
Address: Rambla del Poblenou 44-46, Sant Martí
Telephone: +34 93 309 1872
Hours: summer 10am-10pm (sometimes until midnight); winter 10am-2pm & 5-10pm; closed Wednesday

Bodevici
Address: Carrer Torrijos 21, Gràcia
Hours: Mon.-Fri. 4-9pm;
Sat. 12:30-9pm; Sun. 5-9pm

Pyreneum
Address: Plaça de Vila 5, Gràcia
Hours: 2-8pm

CATALAN CHEESE

From Old Traditions to New Wave

Catalonia produces the greatest variety of artisan cheeses of all the regions in Spain, with more than 150 kinds at last count, many of them made by small producers or in milk cooperatives in the mountains using both pasteurized and raw milk from cows, sheep or goats.

The oldest documented Catalan cheeses are *mató, serrat* and the *singular tupí*. Soft, spreadable, ricotta-like mató is very easy to make and is usually made from cow's milk but occasionally also goat's milk. In medieval times, it was served with honey in the dessert called *mel i mató,* and this preparation is still commonly offered today in cheese shops and traditional restaurants throughout Catalonia.

Serrat is an intensely flavored, round, compact (its name derives from the word *cerrado*, or "closed," for its structure), washed-rind sheep's milk cheese with an exterior that is traditionally decorated with various drawings and shapes. It's aged like Manchego and is similar in taste and texture but smaller.

The pungent, spicy and creamy tupí has origins as old as those of serrat and was made by the same shepherds and farmers in the Pyrenees mountains. They put leftover and overly mature bits of serrat in a clay vessel known as a tupí and mixed them with a strong liquor like *orujo* (grappa), *anis* or *ratafía*.

Catalan cheesemaking in the 21st century has flourished dramatically, with a new generation of cheesemakers who are internationally influenced, yet also grounded in local traditions and interested in improving the national market with new cheeses.

Biologist Paula Fonollà manages cheese production at Mas Reixagó, whose raw cow's milk Sant Ignasi has a soft rind and paste, with an almost liquid center, intense barnyard flavor, grassy notes and a lengthy finish. Mas Reixagó is also known for Blau de Jutglar, a creamy, spicy blue cheese also made from raw cow's milk.

Former agronomic engineer Salvador Maura I Rajó of Mas d'Eroles makes the wonderful raw cow's milk

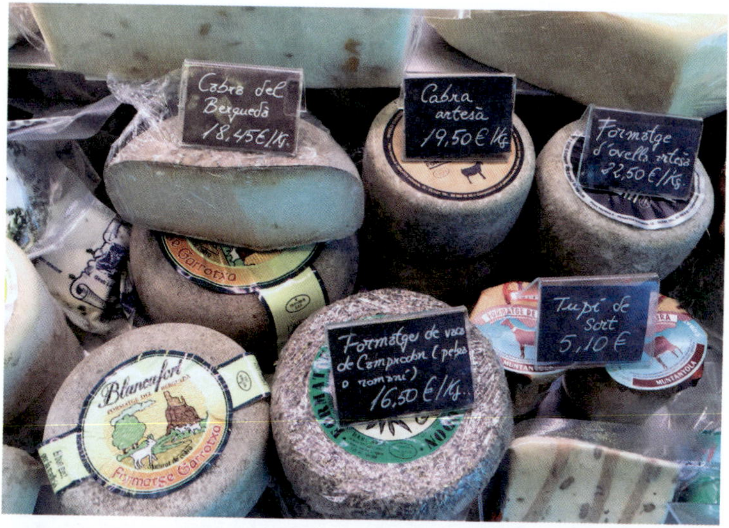
Cabra del Berguedà 18,45€/Kg.
Cabra artesà 19,50€/Kg
Formatge d'ovella artesà 22,50 €/Kg.
Garrotxa
Tupí de Sort 5,10 €
Blancafort
Formatge Garrotxa
Formatge de vaca de Camprodon (pebre o romaní) 16,50 €/Kg.
MUNTANYOLA

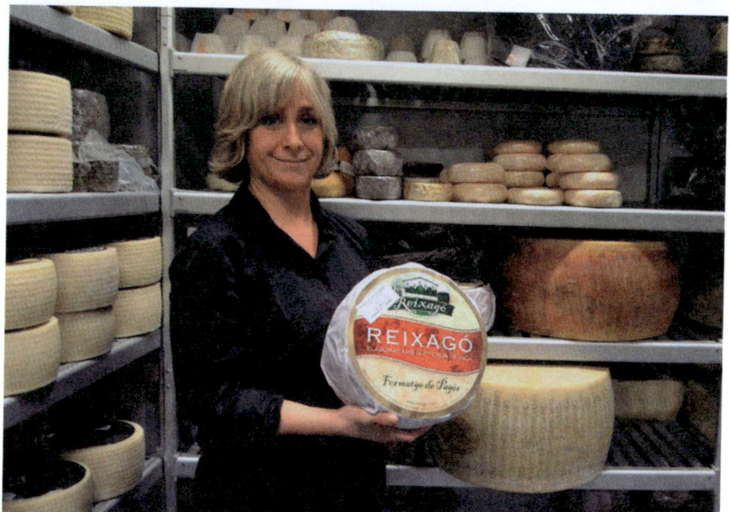
Reixagó
REIXAGÓ
Formatge de Pagès

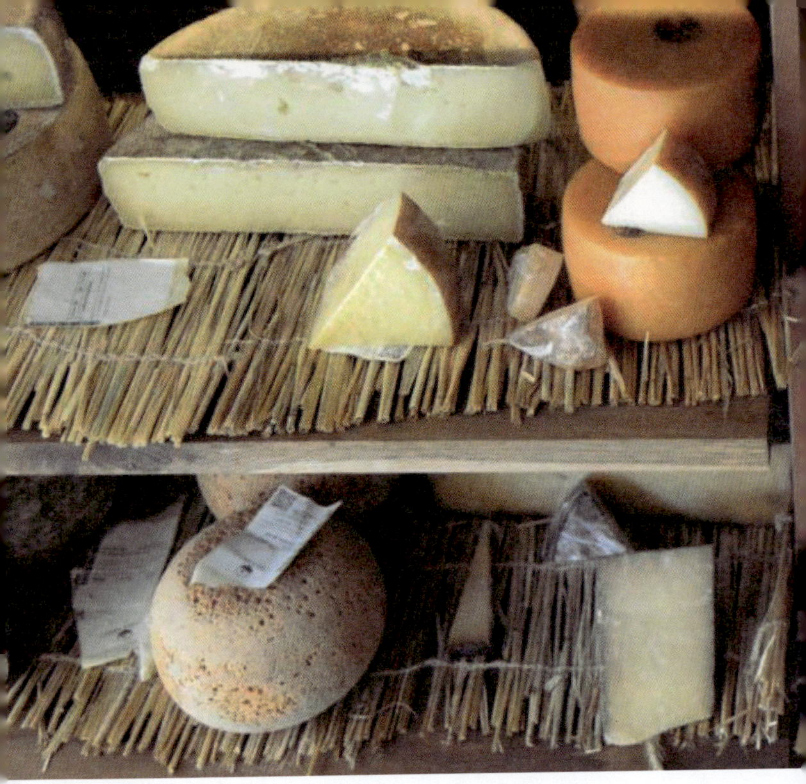

Castellot, which has a brushed rind, compact interior and gentle persistence. We especially love his Brisat, also made from raw cow's milk, whose grape pomace-covered rind lends it a subtle hint of wine and fruit.

Pablo García of La Balda turns fresh milk from his neighbors in and around Sant Martin de Llémena into a simple soft cheese, Fermió, that is elegant, full-bodied and delicious.

The raw cow's milk Puigpedrós from Molí de Ger has a firm interior and concentrated nuttiness with floral notes. Washed with brine, Puigpedrós has a distinctive orange rind.

Manel Marcè of Mas Marcè produces Llanut, which means "woolly." Each piece of cheese is covered in a bit of sheep's wool for preservation and presentation and must be very carefully cleaned before being

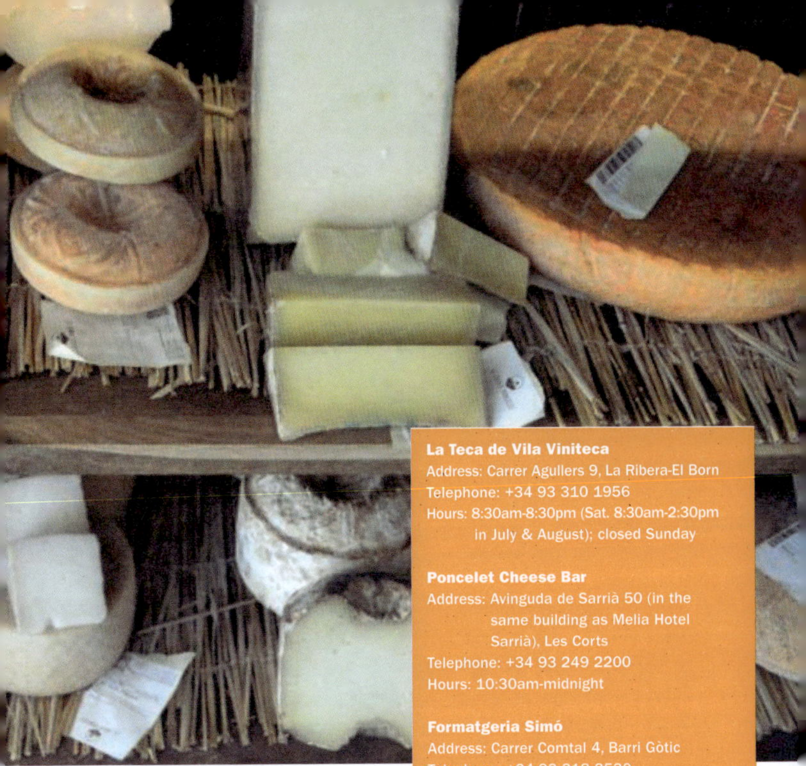

served. This cheese is made from the raw milk of Mas Marcè's own sheep, as well as vegetable rennet, which results in a fresh, milky, barnyard flavor.

You can taste these and other artisan cheeses at markets, specialized shops, restaurants and bars in Barcelona, including those listed in the accompanying box.

La Teca de Vila Viniteca
Address: Carrer Agullers 9, La Ribera-El Born
Telephone: +34 93 310 1956
Hours: 8:30am-8:30pm (Sat. 8:30am-2:30pm in July & August); closed Sunday

Poncelet Cheese Bar
Address: Avinguda de Sarrià 50 (in the same building as Melia Hotel Sarrià), Les Corts
Telephone: +34 93 249 2200
Hours: 10:30am-midnight

Formatgeria Simó
Address: Carrer Comtal 4, Barri Gòtic
Telephone: +34 93 318 3530
Hours: Mon.-Fri. 10am-3pm & 5-8:30pm; Sat. 10am-2:30pm & 5-8:30pm; closed Sunday (closed Saturday from June 24 to September)

Formatgeria La Seu
Address: Carrer de la Daguería 16, Barri Gòtic
Telephone: +34 93 412 6548
Hours: Tues.-Thurs 10am-2pm & 5-8pm; Fri.-Sat. 10am-3:30pm & 5-8pm; closed Sunday and Monday

CAVA

Spain's All-Day Sparkler

While cava is produced in many areas of Spain, most production takes place in Catalonia, and especially Penedès, an area of historical importance for this type of wine. The word "cava," in fact, means "cellar" or "cave" in Catalan. In the 18th century, Catalonians began learning about sparkling wine when they became the cork suppliers to the first French wineries that were making champagne. In fact, cava is produced using the same *méthode traditionnelle* that is used for champagne: after the base wine is fermented from the pressing, it's bottled, usually with a mixture of sugar and yeast, to undergo a second fermentation to produce that festive fizz. The typical white grape varieties of xarel-lo, parellada and macabeo produce sparkling wines with fresh citrus flavors and bright notes of fruit and white flowers.

There are several types of cava available in wine shops: the classic white, the enigmatic *blanc de noirs*, with a base white wine made from red grapes, and the glamorous rosé. Levels of aging are identified with specific stamps on the top of the bottle: white guarantees a minimum of nine months of fermentation inside the bottle, green indicates a minimum 15 months for Cava Reserva and black, denoting a minimum of 30 months, is for Cava Gran Reserva. The last two designations can offer especially interesting, complex aromas of toast, nuts and vanilla.

The wines are also categorized by sweetness level, from Dulce, the sweetest, containing at least 50 grams of sugar per liter, to Semiseco, with 35 to 50 grams, all the way down to Brut (3 to 12 grams), Extra Brut (under 3 grams of sugar) and Brut Nature, which has no added sugar and reveals perhaps the most of the original wine's character.

Cava goes particularly well with a traditional hearty Catalan breakfast, but it can also be enjoyed as a light apéritif with some salad, olives or pickles. We love it with a typical Sunday lunch of roast chicken and with every kind of cured or cooked

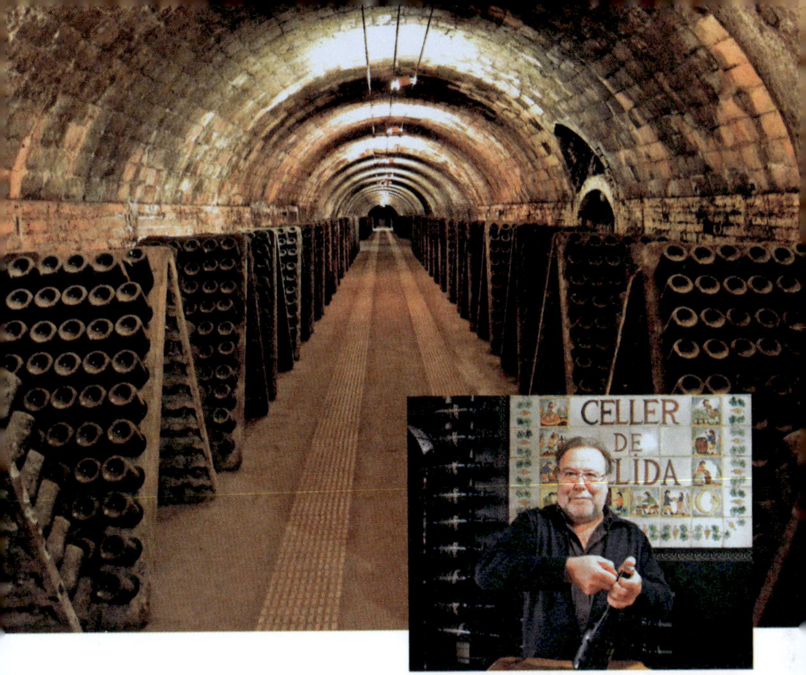

meat. Cava has enough body to stand up to these kinds of dishes, while its bubbles and touch of acidity cut through the fat. It's also refreshing paired with paella at a *chiringuito* (snack bar) on the beach and is a natural accompaniment to birthday cake. In the Catalan workplace, it's common practice to keep a bottle at the ready in the fridge to celebrate an accomplishment – or to soften the blow of a setback. Whatever the occasion, the bottle should be kept cold, preferably around 6 degrees C (43 degrees F).

Two of our favorite places to shop for cava:

Celler de Gelida
Address: Carrer Vallespir 65, Sants
Telephone: +34 93 339 2641
Hours: Mon.-Fri. 9am-2pm & 5-8:30pm;
Sat. 9:30am-2:30pm & 5-8:30pm;
closed Sunday, holidays, August, and Saturday afternoons in July and September

Vila Viniteca
Address: Carrer Agullers 7, El Born
Telephone: +34 90 232 7777
Hours: 8:30am-8:30pm
(Sat. 8:30am-2:30pm in July & August); closed Sunday

COUNTRY DINING

The Catalan Masía

As in many other rural parts of Europe, the Catalonian countryside is dotted with large, old farmhouses, legacies of feudalism that have since been converted into hotels, bed-and-breakfasts and restaurants. The origins of these masías, as they're known in Catalan, go back to the 11th-century, but it was not until the end of feudalism in the 16th-century that the former serfs turned masías into their own self-run farm holdings and homes. The buildings that survive today may be of a more recent vintage, built perhaps a century ago, sometimes older. Masías were usually named after the family who owned them; "Can Josep," for example, means "house of Josep."

The masía-restaurant is usually a rustic, down-to-earth eatery where local families and groups of friends gather together, especially during the weekends, to enjoy traditional and seasonal Catalan food at very affordable prices. (A few, however, currently hold Michelin stars: Bo. TiC, Fonda Xesc and Mas de Torrent in the Girona region and Els Casals and Can Jubany in the Barcelona region.) Foods visitors might tuck into include *mongetes amb botifarra* (beans and pork sausages), *escalivada* (grilled vegetables), *canelons* (cannelloni), *bacallà a la llauna* (fried and baked cod), *cargols* (cooked snails), *escudella* (stew), *embotits i pa amb tomàquet* (tomato spread on bread served with cured meats), *carn a la brasa amb allioli* (barbecued meats with garlic mayonnaise) or *calçots* (grilled green onions).

While masías were generally built far from towns and villages, there are a few that have been converted into restaurants in Barcelona. **Can Travi Nou** is an 18th-century masía with a spectacular flower-covered façade as well as a charming outdoor dining area where the fare is classic Catalan with a twist – such as sautéed lobster with chickpeas. The service is very attentive and the ambiance cozy. **Can Cortada**, an impressive building of Roman and medieval origins surrounded by peaceful gardens, serves fine Mediterranean cuisine and top-quality meats at higher prices. The restaurant is divided into different spacious lounges and private dining rooms, perfect for large groups. The Soler Ribatallada family, which has been in the hospitality business for decades, owns both restaurants. (They also have two more restaurants in other emblematic spots of the city: El Pintor, in the Gothic quarter, and Xalet de Montjuïc, in Montjuïc's gardens). Can Travi Nou and Can Cortada are both in the Horta neighborhood (walking distance from Mundet metro) and are the ideal way to get the rural masía experience without having to leave the city.

Can Travi Nou
Address: Carrer Jorge Manrique s/n, Horta
Telephone: +34 93 428 0434
Hours: 1:30-4pm & 8:30-11pm

Can Cortada
Address: Avinguda de l'Estatut de Catalunya s/n, Horta
Telephone: +34 93 427 2315
Hours: 1-4pm & 8-11:30pm

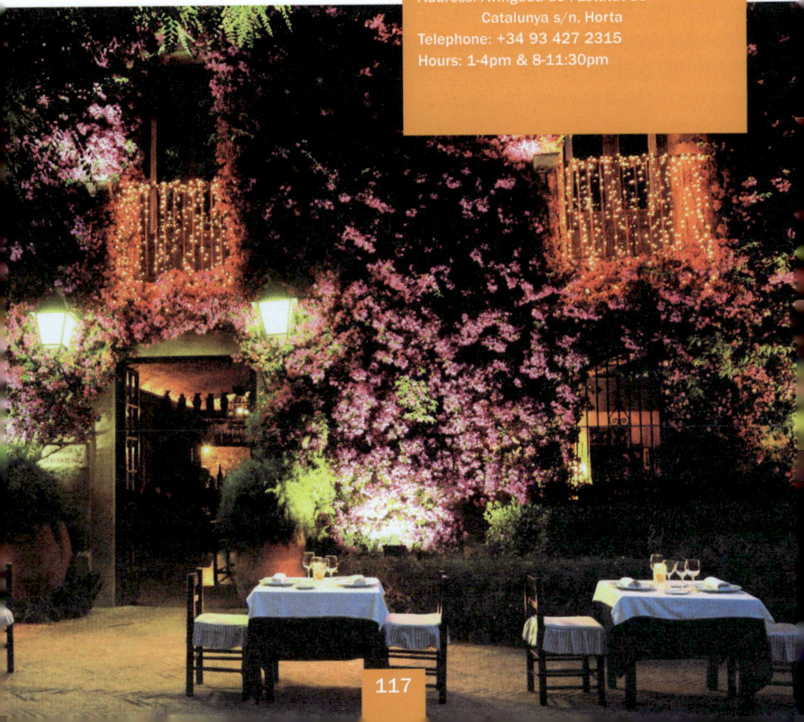

EDIBLE ART

Barcelona's Chocolate Artisans

In the weeks leading up to Easter, the best confectioners in Barcelona erect astonishing and fantastical chocolate constructions, known as monas, and display them in shop windows. Some of these wonderful visual confections – reproductions of monuments, scenes taken from classical history and abstract original creations – are on display at the **Museu de la Xocolata** in El Born, where you can also satisfy your craving for sweets in the museum shop. The practice has extended beyond the Easter season to become a professional expression of the local chocolate-making industry.

The chocolate artisans of **Bombonería Fargas** have been in business since 1827 and though they've had to move from their original location, the same intoxicating chocolate fragrance greets you at the door. Fargas's artisans continue to hand-grind their cacao and turn it into a wide-ranging assortment of wonderful chocolates.

The author of three books about "sweet cuisine," Oriol Balaguer is one of the best modern pastry chefs and chocolatiers of Barcelona, with a sophisticated style. He has two shops in Les Corts as well as the cafeteria **Xocolatería Oriol Balaguer**, which is the place to taste his hot chocolate along with a few churros, or some of his great chocolate candies.

Award-winning chocolatier Venancio Pallarés is famous in Spain for his large chocolate sculptures, including replicas of train engines and Olympic stadiums. Nowadays, his sons Jordi and Eduard **Pallarés** run the two Pallarés patisseries, offering mostly traditional creations with some contemporary touches.

Chocolatiers Ramón Morató and Quim Capdevila have created an excellent brand of Catalan chocolates, **Cacao Sampaka**. In their single shop in Barcelona, you'll find a whole world of cocoa: chocolate pastries and candies from different selected origins, hot chocolate, books on chocolate and some chocolate-making tools, along with a cozy cafeteria space.

The large shop/cafeteria **Chocolates Brescó** specializes in

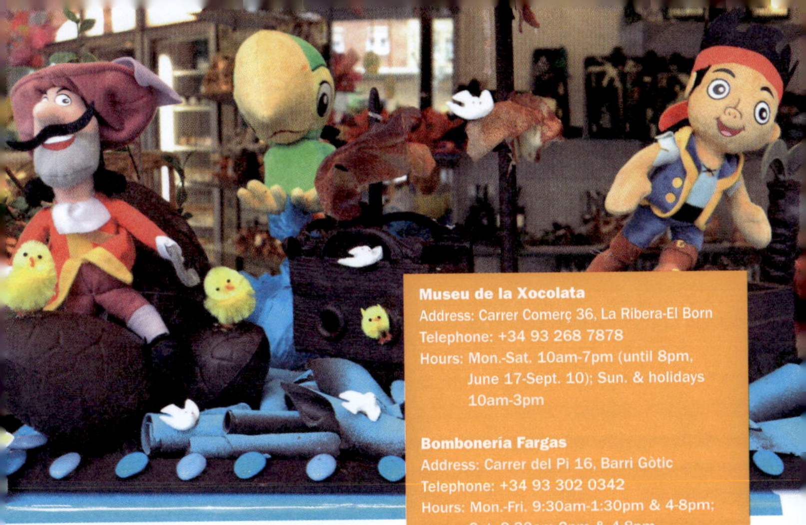

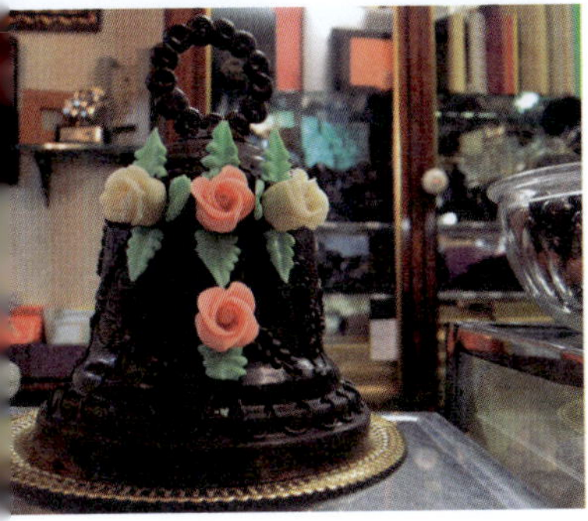

high-quality artisan chocolate, made since 1830 by the Brescó family. The products on offer range from traditional chocolates made from stone-milled cacao to modern curiosities such as chocolate dressing with olive oil or a chocolate massage cream.

Museu de la Xocolata
Address: Carrer Comerç 36, La Ribera-El Born
Telephone: +34 93 268 7878
Hours: Mon.-Sat. 10am-7pm (until 8pm, June 17-Sept. 10); Sun. & holidays 10am-3pm

Bombonería Fargas
Address: Carrer del Pi 16, Barri Gòtic
Telephone: +34 93 302 0342
Hours: Mon.-Fri. 9:30am-1:30pm & 4-8pm; Sat. 9:30am-2pm & 4-8pm

Xocolateria Oriol Balaguer
Address: Carrer Fusina 5, La Ribera-El Born
Telephone: +34 93 348 5267
Hours: Mon.-Sat. 9am-9pm

Pallarés
Address: Carrer del Comte d'Urgell 169, Eixample
Telephone: +34 93 453 2622
Hours: Mon.-Sat. 8am-8:30pm; Sun. 8am-3pm

Cacao Sampaka
Address: Carrer del Consell de Cent 292, Eixample
Telephone: +34 93 272 0833
Hours: Mon.-Sat. 9am-9pm; closed Sunday

Chocolates Brescó
Address: Carrer de Casp 48, Eixample
Telephone: +34 93 481 6591
Hours: Mon.-Fri. 9am-8:30pm; Sat. 9am-2pm & 5-8:30pm; closed Sunday

JAMÓN IBÉRICO

Spain's Leg-endary Ham

Ham is one of Spain's best-known culinary treasures, and different types of the cured meat offer their own flavors and characteristics, depending on the breed of pig, how the animal has been fed and raised, and how its meat has been processed and cured. The two major categories of Spanish ham are *jamón serrano* and *jamón ibérico*. The former comes from white or pink pigs normally raised on farms and fattened on grain, while the latter comes from the Iberian breed and is made according to very specific practices, yielding a special and often costly product.

The Iberian pig is an ancient breed of (usually) black pig that requires much more time to reach maturity and the right weight for slaughter than conventional breeds. Spain's best pork products – not just cured ham but also fresh cuts – come from pigs raised this way. The ham made from the black pig, *pata negra* ("black foot"), is easy to recognize by the black hoof, the distinctive shape of the leg and the intense maroon color of the meat.

The word "jamón" generally refers to the back leg, but the front legs are cured or cooked in the same way. When cured, the front leg is called the *paleta* or *paletilla* in Spanish and *espatlla* in Catalan. These tend to be smaller, less tender and juicy, often sold without the bone and less expensive than the other kind.

Jamón ibérico is produced mostly in the western-central and southern parts of Spain, with protected designations of origin guaranteeing the quality of the hams and the expertise that went into making them. Iberian pigs can be reared using industrial methods, but for the best meat, the pigs are raised in *dehesas*, or oak forests, where the animals can roam among the trees and forage for wild fruit, acorns and grass.

Jamón ibérico de cebo is the lowest subcategory and comes from grain-fed pigs. *Jamón ibérico de recebo* comes from animals fed a mixture of grain, pasture and acorns, while *jamón ibérico de bellota*, the most prized of all, comes from

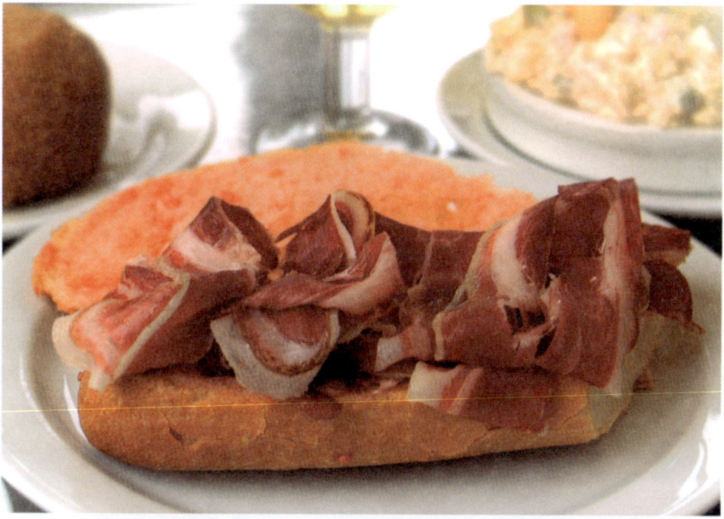

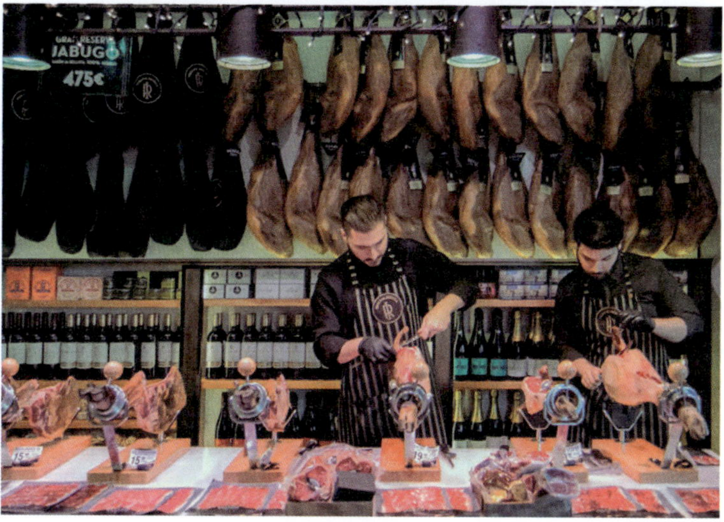
475€

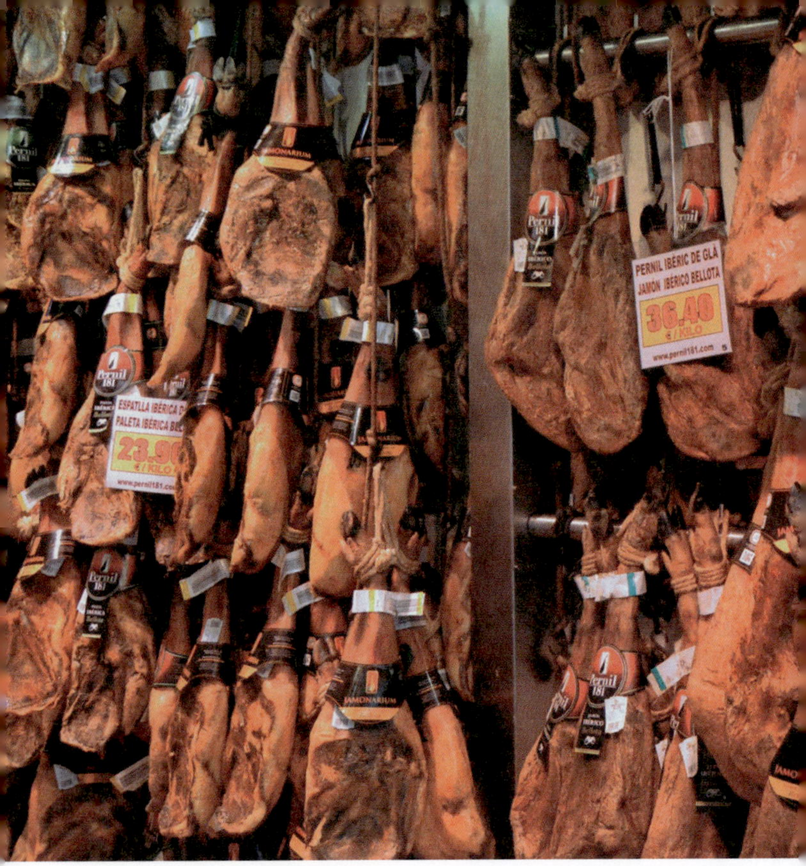

dehesa-raised pigs (*bellota* means "acorn") and boasts a luxurious amount of fat, an incredibly silky, melting texture and uniquely sweet-salty flavors. The definitive official code to recognize the best acorn Iberian ham is a series of colored seals: black (100% Iberian acorn-fed), red (75% or 50% Iberian purity and 100% acorn-fed), green (75% or 50% Iberian and free-range-fodder-fattened) and white (intensively fodder-fattened).

You can find jamón ibérico in bars, restaurants and food shops all over Barcelona (and Spain, for that matter), but the shops listed in the accompanying box are our favorite

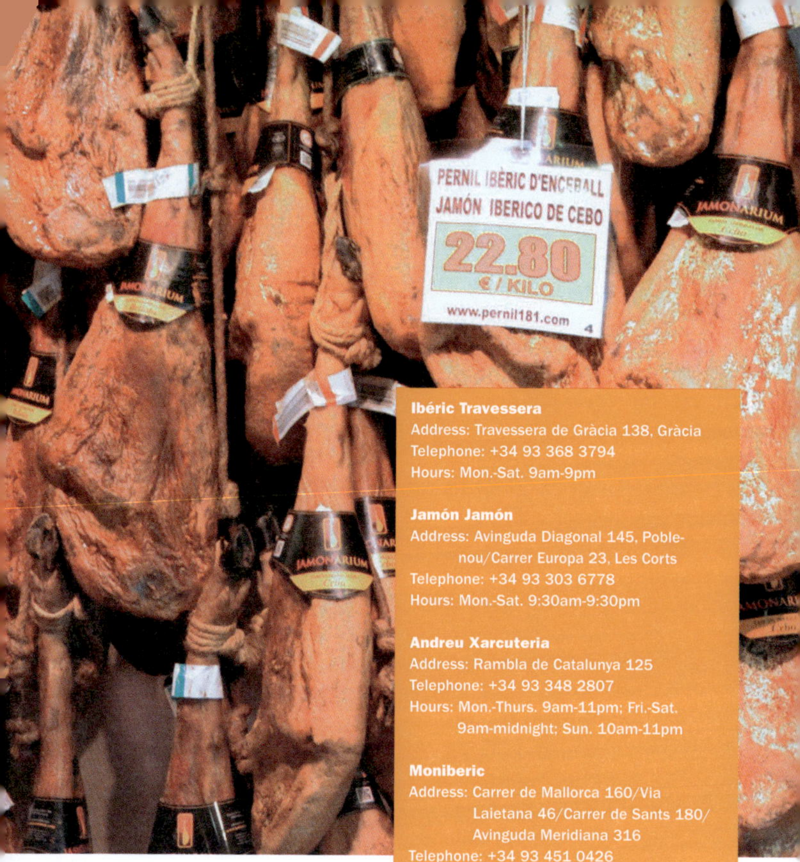

places in the city to get it. For jamón ibérico de bellota, look to specialized stalls in the markets, such as "Aroma Ibèric," stalls 183-5 in the Boqueria market, or "Can Marti Carles," stalls 5-7 in the Santa Caterina market, as well as Enrique Tomás or Reserva Ibérica, both big chains with numerous shops across the city.

Ibéric Travessera
Address: Travessera de Gràcia 138, Gràcia
Telephone: +34 93 368 3794
Hours: Mon.-Sat. 9am-9pm

Jamón Jamón
Address: Avinguda Diagonal 145, Poble-nou/Carrer Europa 23, Les Corts
Telephone: +34 93 303 6778
Hours: Mon.-Sat. 9:30am-9:30pm

Andreu Xarcuteria
Address: Rambla de Catalunya 125
Telephone: +34 93 348 2807
Hours: Mon.-Thurs. 9am-11pm; Fri.-Sat. 9am-midnight; Sun. 10am-11pm

Moniberic
Address: Carrer de Mallorca 160/Via Laietana 46/Carrer de Sants 180/Avinguda Meridiana 316
Telephone: +34 93 451 0426
Hours: 9am-9pm; closed Sunday

Germans Gracia Xarcuters
Address: Carrer de Gran de Sant Andreu 297/Enric Granados 22
Telephone: +34 93 274 3445/+34 93 453 1953
Hours: Mon.-Sat. 8:30am-2pm & 5-8:30pm

OLIVE OIL

Spain's Liquid Gold

Olives arrived in the southern part of the Iberian Peninsula around 9th century B.C.E. with the Phoenicians, and Spain leads production of olive oil to this day, with 45 percent of the global total. In recent decades, the Spanish olive oil industry has become part of the wonderful culinary flowering the country is experiencing. It's a new golden (or, perhaps, greenish) age for Spanish olive oil.

Of the 260 different olive varieties in Spain, only about 20 are used for the best olive oil production. As with wine, the characteristics of an oil depend on raw materials, *terroir* and harvesting and production methods. The trend in Spain right now is to produce greener and fresher single-variety extra-virgin olive oil and more organic ones. Olives harvested early, when they are still a bit green, make oils with live polyphenols, intense, fresh herbal and fruity aromas, some bitterness and a peppery bite. These oils are best enjoyed raw, with bread or vegetables or as a finishing touch to point up the flavors of cooked dishes. More mature olives generally produce oil with more golden tones, a nuttier and sweeter flavor and less bitterness and spiciness. This oil is less delicate, more stable and thus better for cooking.

Alongside the rise of excellent extra-virgin is the increasing number of specialty olive oil shops that have an important role as distributors, educators and curators of market trends, connecting consumers and producers.

Ana Segovia opened **Oro Líquido** in Barcelona's Barrio Gòtico in 2005, when she decided to change careers and reconnect with her grandparents' land through olive oil. Segovia was born in France after her grandfather and parents left their native Andalucía to flee the civil war and Franco's dictatorship. Located in the former antique shop that Segovia's father opened after returning to Spain, Oro Líquido sells some of the country's most prized and interesting extra-virgin olive oils,

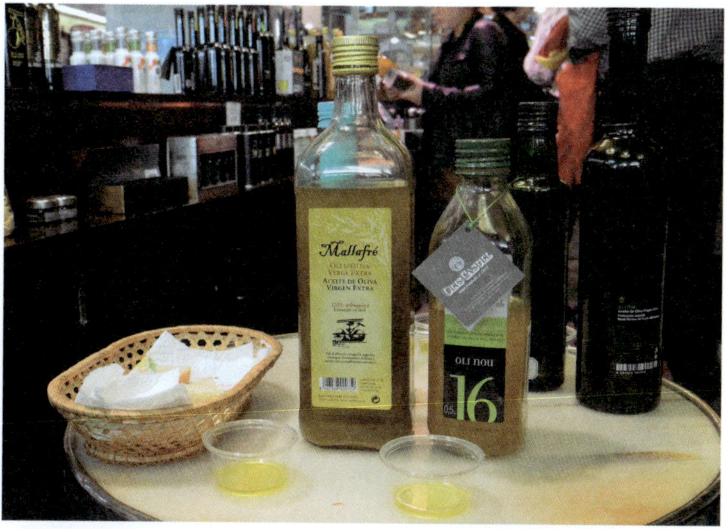
Mallafré
Aceite de Oliva
Virgen Extra
oli nou
16

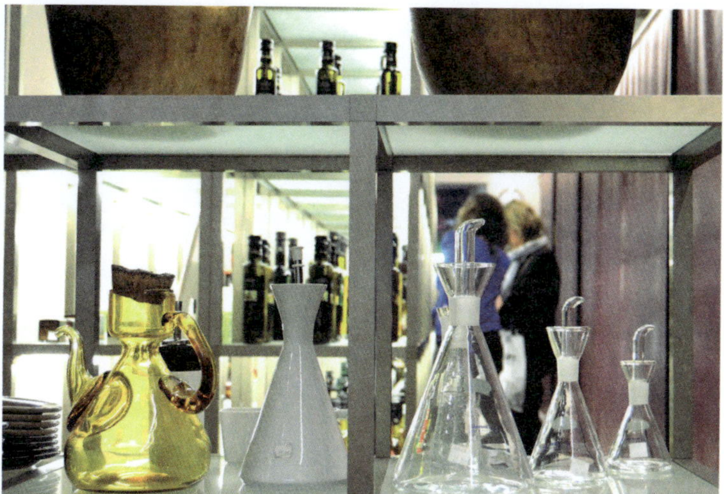

along with a top-notch selection of those made by Catalan producers and a range of olive oil-based cosmetics.

Inspired by the wine shops, Sandra Stefani opened **Oli Sal** in Gràcia nine years ago, with the idea of elevating Spanish extra-virgin olive oil to the gourmet level it deserves. The oils range from the most precious bottles to economy-sized *garrafas* and cans, and she carries a variety of salts and vinegars as well. She also told us that the shop's best customers, besides chefs and food lovers, are many of the elderly women in the neighborhood.

Inside Santa Caterina market, there's **Olis Oliva**, a busy little shop that has also been around since 2005 and is managed by Ana María García Webermann whose half-Spanish, half-French family comes from Alsace. Olis Oliva sells wonderful, high-quality Spanish extra-virgin olive oil in premium packaging, small bottles that are easy to transport and also big plastic *garrafas* and tins. The shop also carries excellent Spanish vinegars, a few carefully selected Italian and French products and some wine – it's the perfect place to buy an edible or quaffable present (whether for others or yourself).

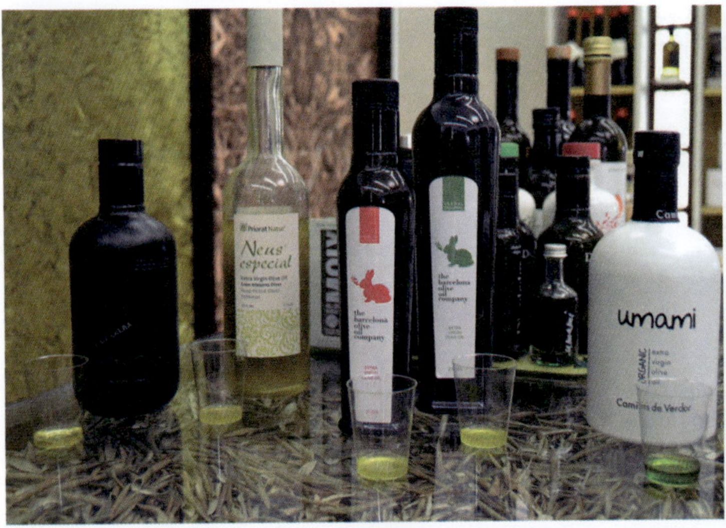

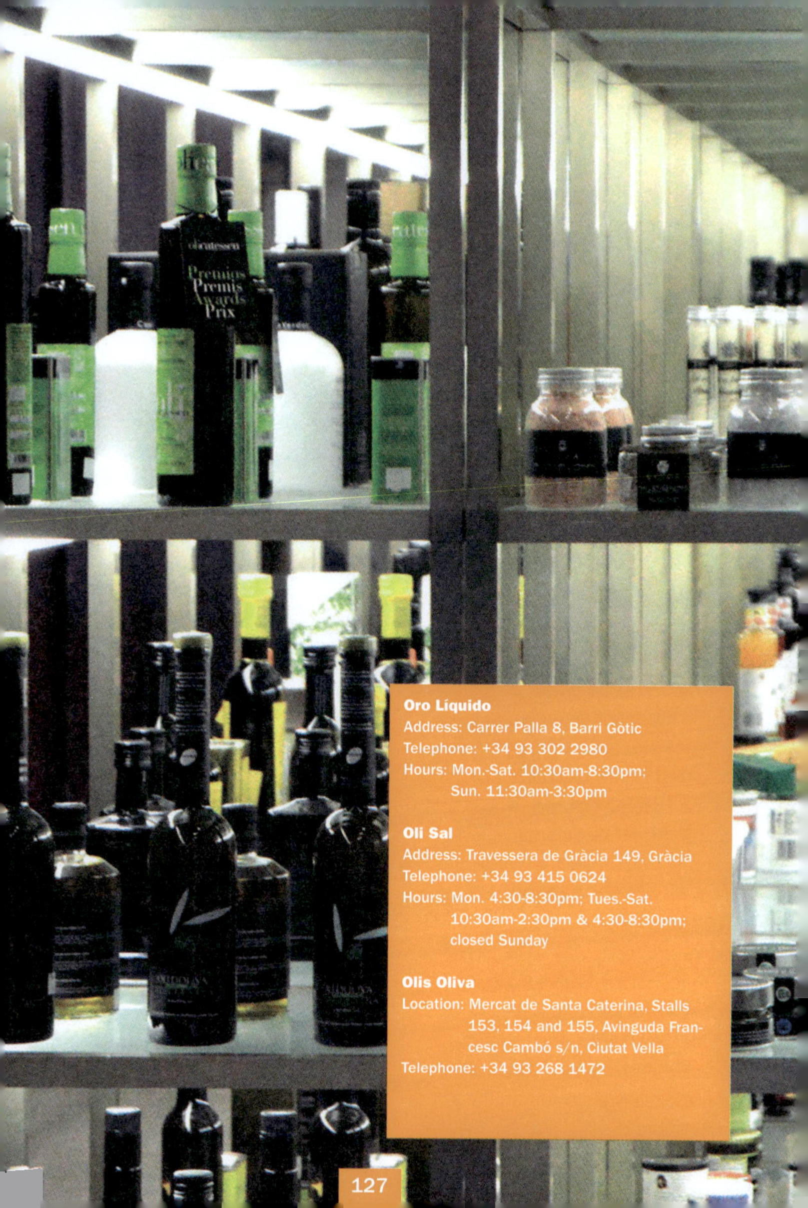

Oro Líquido
Address: Carrer Palla 8, Barri Gòtic
Telephone: +34 93 302 2980
Hours: Mon.-Sat. 10:30am-8:30pm; Sun. 11:30am-3:30pm

Oli Sal
Address: Travessera de Gràcia 149, Gràcia
Telephone: +34 93 415 0624
Hours: Mon. 4:30-8:30pm; Tues.-Sat. 10:30am-2:30pm & 4:30-8:30pm; closed Sunday

Olis Oliva
Location: Mercat de Santa Caterina, Stalls 153, 154 and 155, Avinguda Francesc Cambó s/n, Ciutat Vella
Telephone: +34 93 268 1472

PINTXOS

Basque Bites

Oriol's face lights up whenever a customer selects his favorite pintxo from one of the 49 different trays, beautifully displayed at **Euskal Etxea**, the bar where he works and the first bar in Barcelona to serve traditional Basque pintxos. One wonders how a small slice of bread topped with a chickpea fritter, *jamón serrano* and romesco sauce spiked with a toothpick can make someone so happy. We try one and we immediately see why.

A pintxo (literally "spike") is an individual bite-sized snack consisting of a combination of ingredients, placed on a small slice of bread, neatly pinned together with a toothpick or skewer. In the Basque Country, where pintxos originate, these diminutive snacks are the perfect excuse for socializing with friends while sipping a beer *zurito* (small glass), *txacolí* (local white wine) or cider.

Pintxos took Barcelona by storm a few years ago and Calle Blai in the Poble Sec district soon became a mecca for these tasty bites; these days virtually every bar on the street now offers pintxos. **Koska Taverna** was one of the first pintxo bars to open in the area. "I would come here as a customer to get my daily fix of Gilda," says Koska's manager, Nio, while pouring cider in the traditional northern Spanish way (his right arm stretched and pouring from as high as possible). "Eventually the owners asked me to come and work for them!" The Gilda pintxo is comprised of an anchovy, a spicy *guindilla* pepper and a pitted olive, all secured by the customary skewer; this is probably the most classic pintxo of all time. Nio's current addiction, however, is the delicious *tortilla de txaca*, which consists of layers of potato omelet and crab salad. This cozy little bar also offers less conventional, more inventive pintxos using top-quality artisanal ingredients, such as Gorgonzola cheese with cardamom-pear compote.

Blai Tonight is just a stone's throw from Koska but serves up a very different take on pintxos; they specialize in what Spaniards call *pintxos de batalla* ("battle pintxos"): 40 different basic bites made with just a few ingredients. While not the most sophisticated in

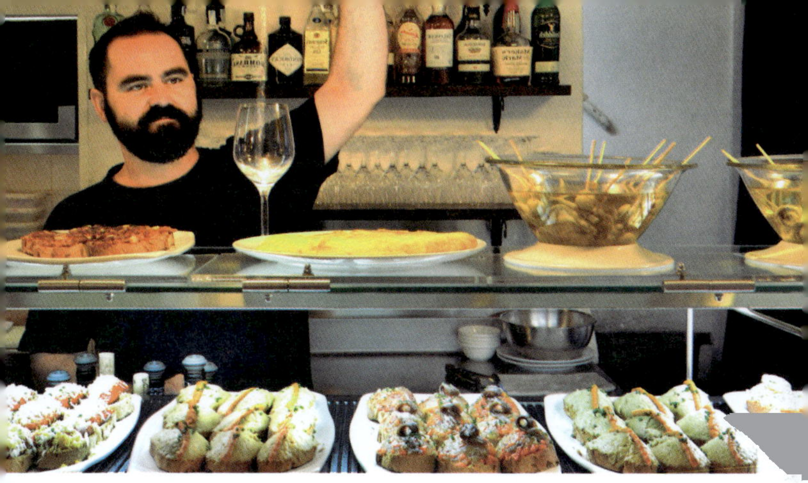

town, they certainly hit the spot. The mini-burger and the croquette are particular favorites with the hungry young crowds of locals, students and backpackers this noisy bar attracts.

Businesspeople with empty stomachs and more discerning palates usually head to the stylish **Els Pinxus Barra de Tapes,** in the business district of Diagonal. Toni, owner and chef, wanted to put a Catalan twist on the traditional Basque pintxos and created a range of 25 extremely elaborate masterpieces, such as his superb *tartar de fuet* (dry-cured pork sausage tartare) and his mouthwatering white sausage with sautéed mushrooms, caramelized onion and aioli mousse. Toni's mother, who helps behind the bar, told us how he served 600 servings of the tartar de fuet one year at Barcelona Fashion Week. "They vanished within minutes! Even the most calorie-obsessed models fell for them."

Euskal Etxea
Address: Placeta de Montcada 1, La Ribera
Telephone: +34 93 310 2185
Hours: 10am-12:30am

Koska Taverna
Address: Carrer de Blai 8, Sants-Montjuïc
Telephone: +34 93 127 0313
Hours: Tues. 6pm-midnight; Wed.-Sat. noon-midnight; Sun. noon-4pm

Blai Tonight
Address: Carrer de Blai 23, Sants-Montjuïc
Telephone: +34 64 873 3200
Hours: 6pm-1am

Els Pinxus Barra de Tapes
Address: Carrer de Marià Cubí 81, Sant Gervasi
Telephone: +34 60 907 1043
Hours: Mon.-Thurs. 12am-11:30pm; Fri.-Sat. 12am-midnight

SALUT!

Barcelona's Top Vermouth Spots

Why are you seeing colorful, 1960s-era carbonated water siphons everywhere in Barcelona? Because they're the symbol of our beloved *vermut* ritual – a fresh drink accompanied by tapas composed usually of preserved food, cold cuts, cured or marinated fish or seafood – that has long served as a way to bring people together before meals.

The partners behind the Morro Fi project, with its four bars, have put out their own line of vermuts (red, red reserve and white), made in a fresh style, with real love for the original ritual. Their original venue, **Morro Fi,** has a younger namesake inside La Illa Diagonal shopping mall. We also recommend the other two in Gràcia/Sant Gervasi: **Mitja Vida** offers a bit more elbow room, and **Dalt de Tot** has a few tables on the street and a little kitchen that turns out more elaborate dishes, such as eggs, *butifarres,* omelets, croquettes and more.

More than a simple bar, **Casa Mariol** is a winery from Terra Alta that produces several kinds of wine and vermouth with accessible prices, available by the bottle or in bulk. The Carrer Roselló shop near the Sagrada Familia also offers bar service with tables. Here you can have a glass of vermut made from *macabeu* grapes and 150 different herbs in the company of a very good selection of cured and preserved foods – from cockles and stuffed olives to ham and cheese.

The lovely restored bodega **Lo Pinyol** (see p. 54) connects vermut, wine and tapas with art and culture. Paintings, illustrations and other works adorn the interior, and one corner has been given over to book swapping. There's an excellent selection of wine, cava and vermut by the bottle or in bulk from barrels. Owner Pau Raga hails from Valencia, and the influence of that city can be seen in some of Lo Pinyol's tapas – like the *esgarraet*, for example, a cod salad very similar to Catalan *esqueixada*. We love to sit at the marble tables of the bar to enjoy a drink and a nibble.

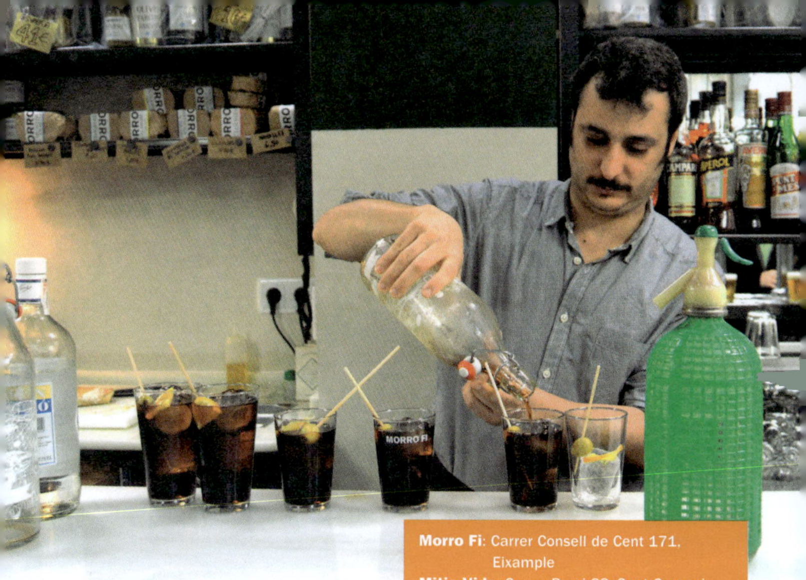

The original 1950s décor of **Bodega Quimet** (see p. 58) is a large part of why this place feels so charmingly old-fashioned and welcoming. Quimet makes the classic combination for vermut, mixing cured anchovies, tuna, cockles or razor clams with the typical dressing of olive oil, vinegar and paprika. We also love the more elaborate tapas here, including baby fava beans with poached eggs and ham and scrambled eggs with chorizo. Besides vermut, there's also a wide selection of great wines and craft beers.

Morro Fi: Carrer Consell de Cent 171, Eixample
Mitja Vida: Carrer Brusi 39, Sant Gervasi
Dalt de Tot: Carrer Saragossa 66, Gràcia
Hours: Mon.-Thurs. 6-11pm; Fri. & Sat. 12-4pm & 6-11pm; Sun. & holidays 12-4pm

Casa Mariol
Address: Carrer Rosselló 442, Eixample
Telephone: +34 93 436 7628
Hours: Mon.-Fri. 9am-10pm; Sat. & Sun. 10am-3pm

Lo Pinyol
Address: Carrer del Torrent de l'Olla 7, Gràcia
Telephone: +34 93 217 6690
Hours: Tues.-Sat. noon-4pm & 7pm-mid night; Sun. noon-4pm; closed Monday

Bodega Quimet
Address: Carrer de Vic 23, Gràcia
Telephone: +34 93 218 4189
Hours: Mon.-Wed. 10am-11:30pm; Thurs.-Sat. 10am-12:30am

THE GREAT OUTDOORS

Top Terraces for Eating and Drinking

The favorite outdoor pastime of most Barcelonans is eating and drinking on a terrace. From the simplest bars to the most sophisticated, multi-starred *alta cocina* restaurants, something like half of our fair city's eateries have space where diners can enjoy their meals *a la fresca* (and smoke a cigarette, too). Many of the best-known terraces sit on the rooftops of hotels, providing lovely tables and astonishing views that extend to the limits of the Mediterranean and menus that fill the pages of the latest Michelin guide.

But to get a real taste of a neighborhood, with some excellent food to boot, we prefer Barcelona's more humble culinary gems, where you can kick back under the sun, the clouds or the city lights at night.

In the appropriately named Plaza del Mar, located between the beach and the port, **Kaiku** ("bowl" in Basque) offers a wonderful seafood menu with imaginative touches. On the restaurant's terrace, the tables and chairs sit among gently swaying palms with a clear view of the sea on the horizon. The menu varies according to the season and what's available at the market. Most of the fish and seafood come directly from Barceloneta's *lonja,* the wholesale fish market in the port area just in front, and are identified on the menu with the date of the catch and the name of the boat that caught it. Much of the produce, such as the squash blossoms, comes from the restaurant's own garden.

Specialties include the smoked rice, a permanent fixture on the menu that's chock-full of ingredients like octopus and green asparagus (the smokiness comes from a brief pass through embers), fish and meat carpaccios, battered and fried anemone, grilled cockles and scallops, and local red prawns. Reservations are a must. Take your sunglasses by day and a cardigan by night.

In Barcelona's historic center, the grand boulevard Rambla del Raval runs through the neighborhood of the same name. This old "Chinese

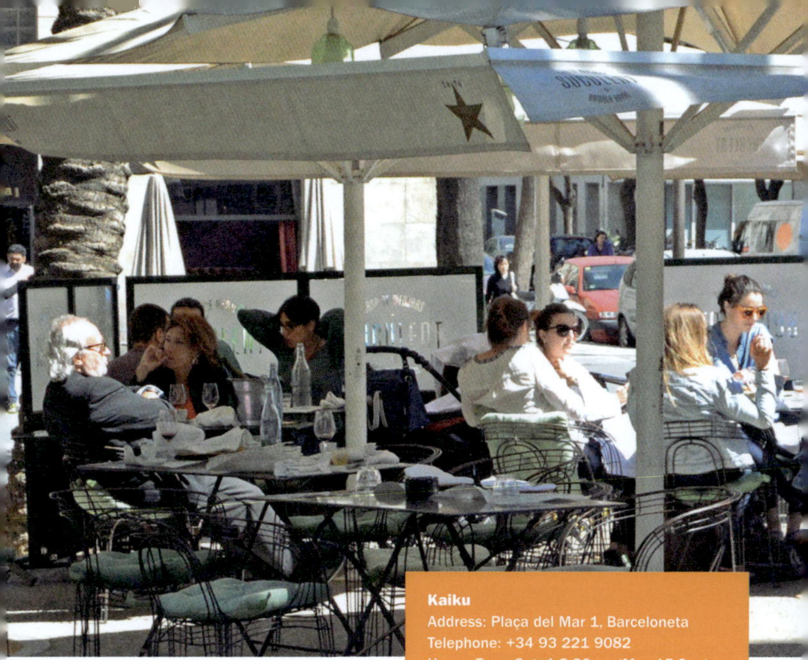

Kaiku
Address: Plaça del Mar 1, Barceloneta
Telephone: +34 93 221 9082
Hours: Tues.-Sat. 1-3:30pm (May 15-Sept. 15 also 7:30-10:30pm); Sun. 1-3:30pm

Suculent
Address: Rambla del Raval 45, Raval
Telephone: + 34 93 443 6579
Hours: 12:30pm-12:30am

quarter" of watering holes and cabarets is nowadays densely populated by Pakistani and Filipino immigrants. And it's in El Raval that **Suculent** serves an amazing kind of cuisine that fuses old and new, reinventing traditional recipes with high-level technical wizardry by renowned chef Toni Romero.

The small venue was a restaurant *de barrio* in its former life, and its lovely terrace abuts the boulevard, which is filled with palms and the sparkling life of families, locals and, on weekends, the market. The menu lists appealing small plates to share – or not – including cod "snout" with snails, *capipota* (head and leg of pork), El Prat artichokes with *cecina* (smoked veal) and truffle mayonnaise, and oxtail with chocolate and baby carrots. This is definitely the place to observe the local *vermut* ritual.

THE RED & THE WHITE

A Guide to Catalan Wines

Catalonia has the greatest number of protected wine appellations, called *denominaciones de origen* (D.O.), in Spain. Of the 11 D.O.s, the four most significant, in terms of quantity, are Penedès, Costers del Segre, Priorat and Montsant. Although Catalonia is renowned for its cavas (p. 114) and white wines, some of Spain's best reds are made here as well. All Catalan D.O.s produce good reds, but the most compelling and critically acclaimed wines come from Priorat, which is further distinguished by a Qualifed D.O., or D.O.Q., and its younger brother, Montsant.

Encircled by the Serra de Montsant mountains, Priorat has a sunny Mediterranean climate, with hot, dry summers and steep hillsides covered in poor volcanic soil composed mostly of slate. Stands of centuries-old vines yield a small quantity of excellent wine with a great deal of power and concentration. Some locals believe that the Romans constructed the oldest stone terraces on the craggy hillsides 2,000 years ago. But the old vines and terraces are just a part of the greater viticulture in the region that flourished until the 19th century, when phylloxera, an aphid that destroyed much of Europe's wine production, and political crisis interrupted production.

In the 1980s, a group of passionate winemakers led by René Barbier and Álvaro Palacios began the difficult task of cultivating the old grenache and carignan vines, as well as introducing such international varieties as cabernet sauvignon and syrah. These producers became known for making intense, structured, big-bodied wines that are also remarkably fresh, elegant and somehow both jammy and mineral in flavor. Two of the best-known wineries of the region are Clos Erasmus and Palacios's L'Ermita.

The wines of Montsant come from vineyards adjacent to Priorat, and while the grape varieties and terroir are similar, Montsant is known more for its new vines, new concepts, younger winemakers and high quality

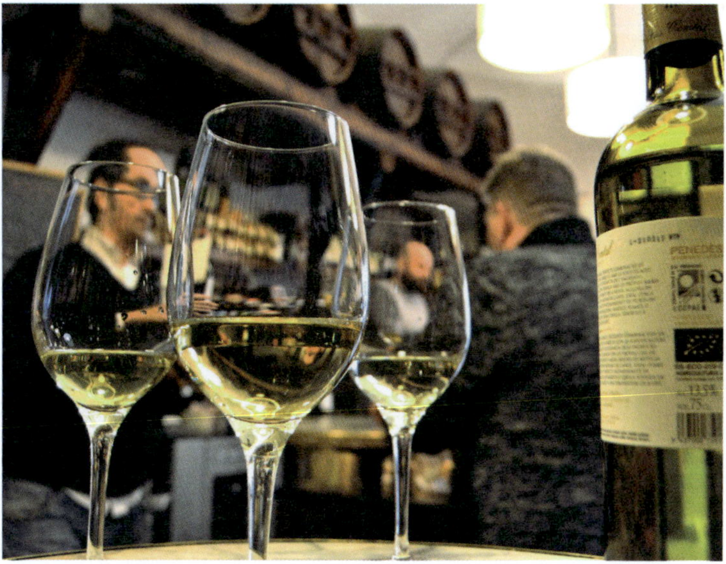

at lower prices. Montsant wines, with their more integrated tannins, are largely less structured and more rounded and delicate than Priorats.

When we think of white wine in Catalonia, we think of its seemingly endless possibilities. Production of whites here has a 2,000 year-old history. The wide-ranging diversity in the climate and calcareous soils, from the mountains to the sea, and the combination of old grape varieties and newly introduced "foreigners" with traditional and experimental methods of production make for innumerable styles and no taboos.

The traditional Catalan grape varieties used to make white wine are mainly macabeo, xarel-lo, parellada and garnatxa blanca, but this area has the largest number of white grapes included in all of Spain's D.O.s. Where other Spanish D.O.s usually are defined by one or a few varieties, in the Catalunya D.O. there are more than 16 – 35 counting the reds. In fact, this umbrella appellation, which covers wines that do not fall under the 10 subregions (Montsant, Penedès, etc.), was created to allow the use of all the grapes of the other Catalan designations in the entire area.

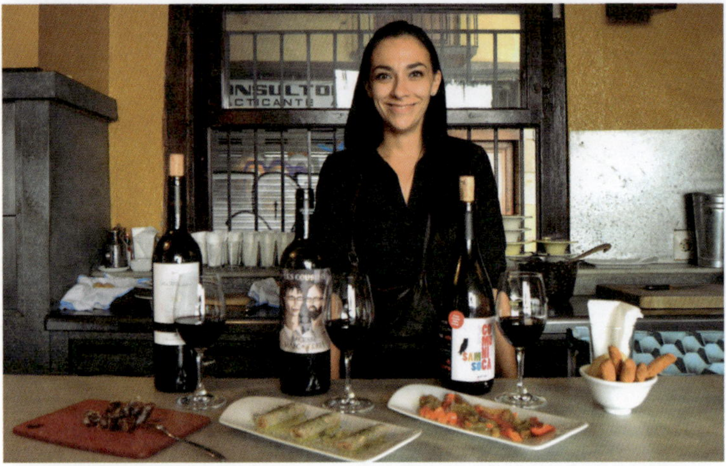

Penedès is the largest area in Catalonia specializing in white wine, in no small part because of all the juice from there that's destined for cava. Although producers can vinify all the varieties included in the D.O., including such international varieties as chardonnay, sauvignon blanc and riesling, the main varieties grown and used are still the traditional macabeo, parellada and xarel-lo. Xarel-lo in particular is winning more and more fans as a varietal wine. This extraordinarily delicate grape possesses aromas with tropical notes and has just a touch of minerality in the glass.

In contrast, the Terra Alta D.O. specializes in garnatxa blanca, a Catalan variety that makes a full-bodied, structured wine, perfect for combining with strong-flavored, oily fish, white meat and even powerful sauces. Terra Alta also produces blends of garnatxa blanca with a small percentage of other Catalan varieties, such as macabeo or vinyater.

For a taste of the full range of Catalan wine, we recommend the shops listed to the right, all of which have friendly staff who are happy to help you navigate the D.O.s and D.O.Q.s. **La Vinya del Senyor** is a proper wine bar, **Bodega Bonavista** has a few tables to taste wine, cheese and charcuterie and **La Vinacoteca** offers free wine tastings on weekday evenings and Saturday mornings.

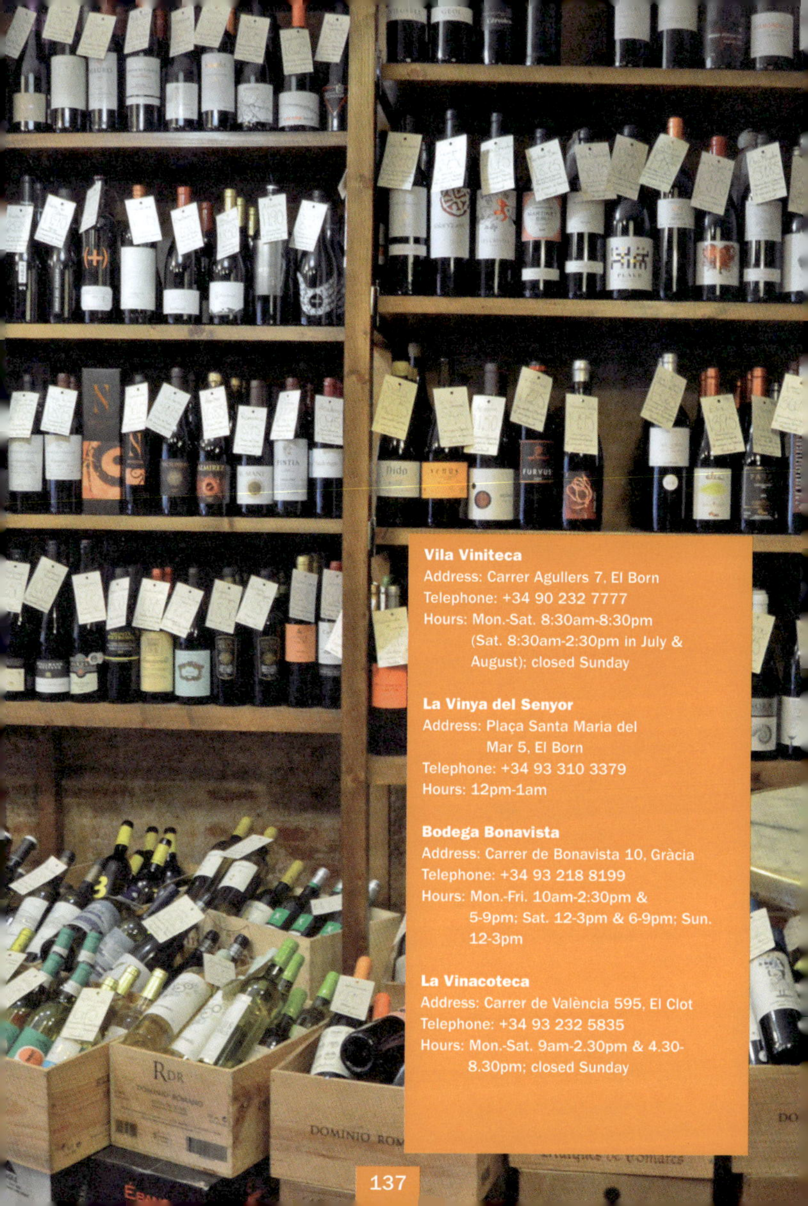

Vila Viniteca
Address: Carrer Agullers 7, El Born
Telephone: +34 90 232 7777
Hours: Mon.-Sat. 8:30am-8:30pm (Sat. 8:30am-2:30pm in July & August); closed Sunday

La Vinya del Senyor
Address: Plaça Santa Maria del Mar 5, El Born
Telephone: +34 93 310 3379
Hours: 12pm-1am

Bodega Bonavista
Address: Carrer de Bonavista 10, Gràcia
Telephone: +34 93 218 8199
Hours: Mon.-Fri. 10am-2:30pm & 5-9pm; Sat. 12-3pm & 6-9pm; Sun. 12-3pm

La Vinacoteca
Address: Carrer de València 595, El Clot
Telephone: +34 93 232 5835
Hours: Mon.-Sat. 9am-2.30pm & 4.30-8.30pm; closed Sunday

TORTILLA DE PATATAS

The Hometown Favorite

It's the *tortilla española*, also known as *tortilla de patatas* (*truita de patata* in Catalan), and not paella, that really holds the place of honor in the hearts and stomachs of Spaniards. Often translated on menus as "potato omelet," this hearty round cake of potatoes, eggs, olive oil and salt has nothing to do with the traditional French omelet, nor does it have anything in common with a Mexican tortilla. At its most basic, the Spanish tortilla is made by frying up a thick mass of sliced potatoes and eggs in olive oil and then slicing it into savory wedges.

The tortilla is also incredibly versatile and can incorporate a dizzying array of supplementary ingredients, including (but certainly not limited to) spinach, garlic, leeks, parsley, asparagus and onions. It can be eaten for breakfast, lunch, dinner or a snack, and not only will you see it in every tapas bar you pass, but it also makes appearances on school lunch menus (at least once per week), at birthday parties and at picnics. You will even see this already carb-heavy dish stuffed between two slices of bread and served as a sandwich! In short, it is the ultimate go-to comfort food and the dish that Spaniards throughout the country most associate with home.

What makes a good tortilla? The answer depends on personal taste, and everyone will tell you something slightly different. There are debates on everything from whether or not a tortilla should include onions, to how the potatoes should be sliced (in thin rounds or in chunky squares), to just how runny the eggs in the middle should be, with some liking their tortilla *un poco crudita* (a little undercooked) on the inside and others preferring a more well-done version.

This classic Spanish dish is available virtually everywhere that serves food in Barcelona, and it is rare that you will come across one that falls flat. But there are exceptional versions to be found. **Taktika Berri**, a

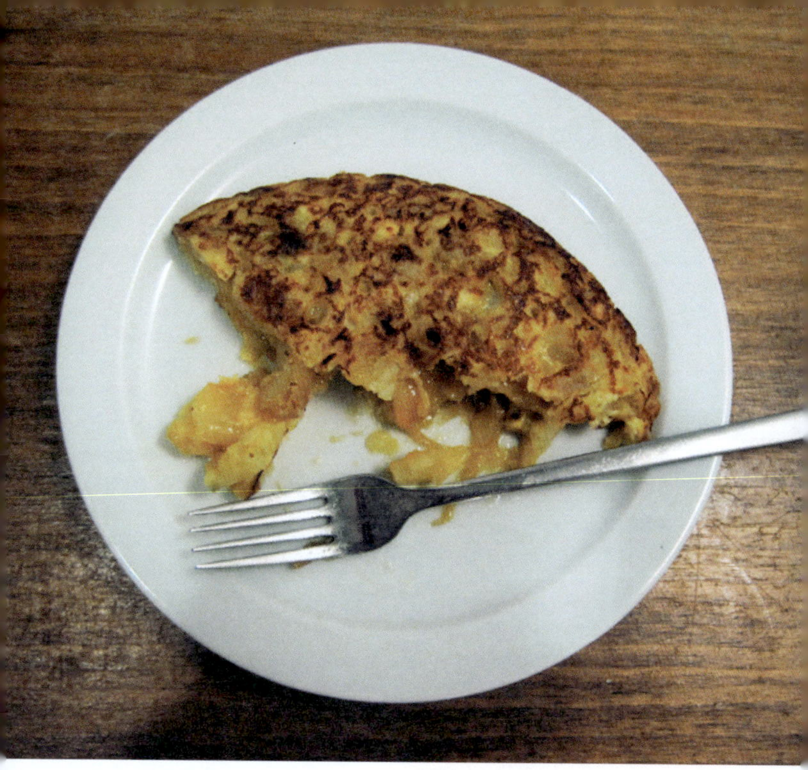

family-run Basque bar and restaurant in the Eixample, makes an especially good *tortilla de bacalao*. **Flash Flash**, the city's most famous *tortillería*, serves an astounding 70 varieties of tortilla, including ingredients such as *morcilla* (blood sausage), artichokes, black truffles and potato chips. (If in doubt, order the Catalan classic *tortilla de samfaina*, with a filling similar to ratatouille).

Taktika Berri
Address: Carrer de València 169, Eixample
Telephone: +34 93 453 4759
Hours: 1-4pm & 8:30-11pm; closed Sat. night & Sunday

Flash Flash
Address: Carrer de la Granada del Penedès 25, Eixample
Telephone: +34 93 237 0990
Hours: 10am-1:30am

TURRÓN

Have Yourself a Chewy Little Christmas

Typically eaten at Christmastime in Spain, *turrón*, a type of nougat, originated centuries ago. Traditionally produced in the region of Alicante, turrón comes in several varieties. Turrón de Alicante, or "hard turrón," is made with whole almonds set in a honey-egg white mixture so brittle that it's often broken with a kitchen mallet. The village of Jijona is famous as the main producer of turrón; in the old days, in the months leading up to Christmas, the inhabitants of Jijona would traverse the country, selling turrones from their horse carts. In the 19th century, Jijona artisans developed a delicate "soft turrón." This turrón de Jijona (or Xixona in Catalan and Valencian) is made with toasted, ground almonds combined with honey and egg white, the oil from the almonds lending a moist, chewy texture completely different from that of hard turrón.

At Christmastime, it is not uncommon to see lines of people at the city's most popular *maestros turroneros*, waiting to buy the hard Alicante variety, the soft Jijona kind, turrón *de yema tostada*, Catalonia's most typical nougat, made with egg yolk and a caramelized crust, contemporary adaptations made with chocolate truffle and many other types.

Since 1775, the Vicens family has produced *torró* (as the sweet is known in Catalan) in Agramunt, a village in the heart of Catalonia. This torró d'Agramunt has Protected Designation of Origin status. Vicens's nougat, which is similar to hard turrón, comes as a round disc made with toasted hazelnuts, sugar, egg whites and honey and sandwiched between thin wafers. **Torrons Vicens** has a number of shops in Barcelona.

On Carrer Cucurulla, in the entrances of **Casa Colomina** and **Planelles Donat**, two families have been selling turrón since the 19th century. Planelles Donat in particular makes some of the best nougat in town. Its soft turrón is

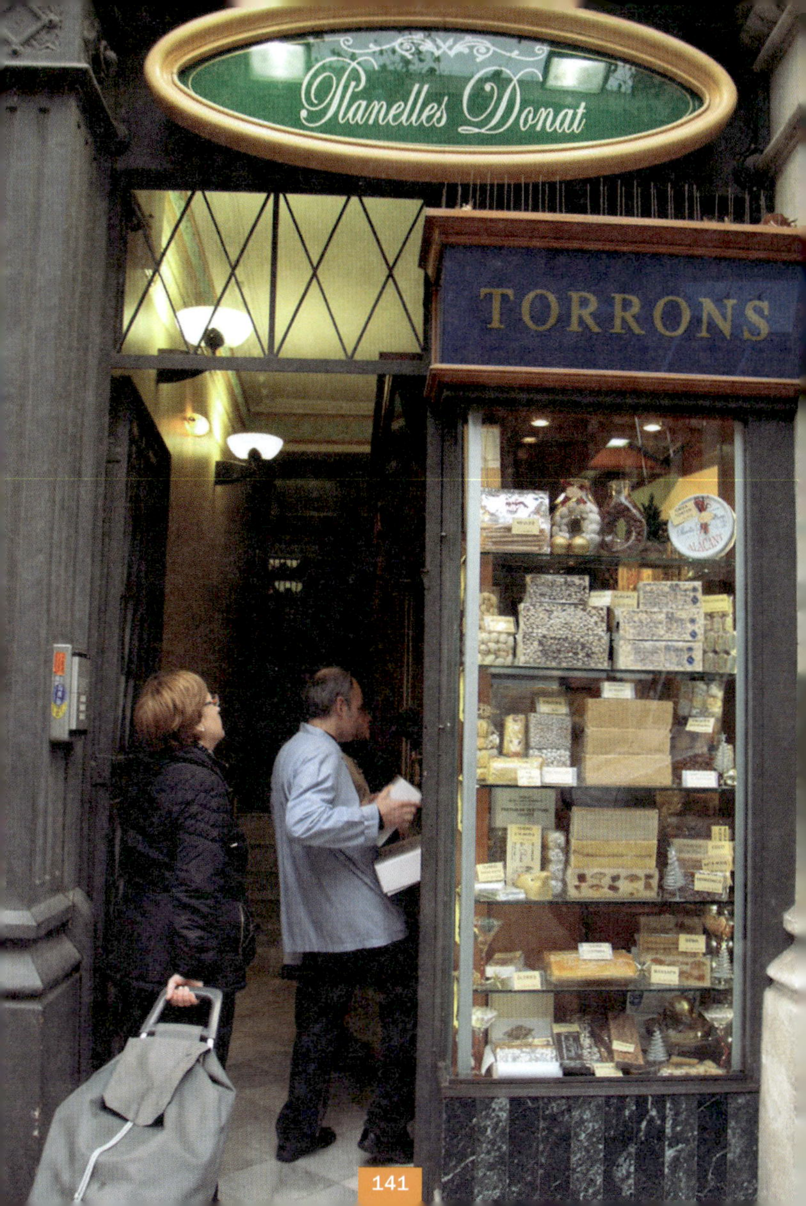
Planelles Donat
TORRONS

chewy and buttery, has the right balance of sweetness and melts in the mouth. It's also known for its marzipan-like turrón de yema tostada.

La Campana, a lovely little patisserie founded in 1850 by Francisco Mira Miralles, a native of Jijona, uses top-quality raw materials to make turrón with concentrated flavors and textures, whether from the extra-crunchy caramelized sugar in the egg yolk nougat or the exceptionally smooth almond paste in the soft variety.

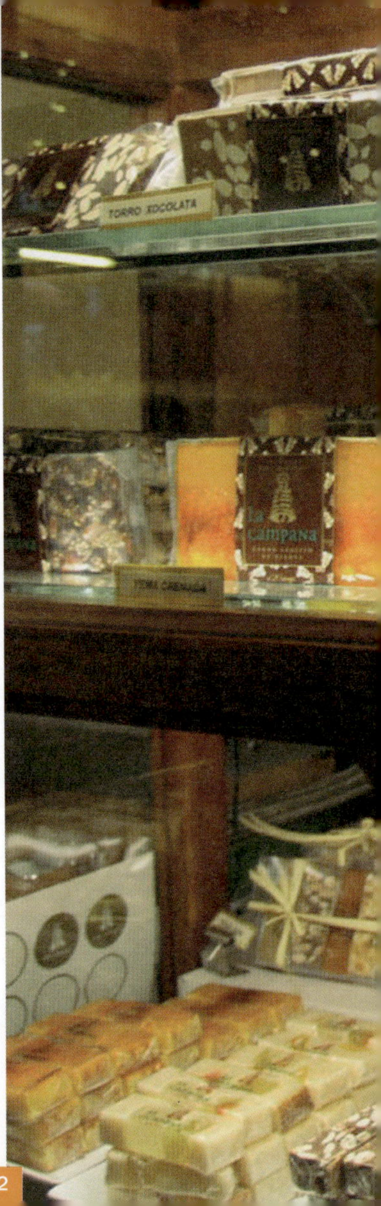

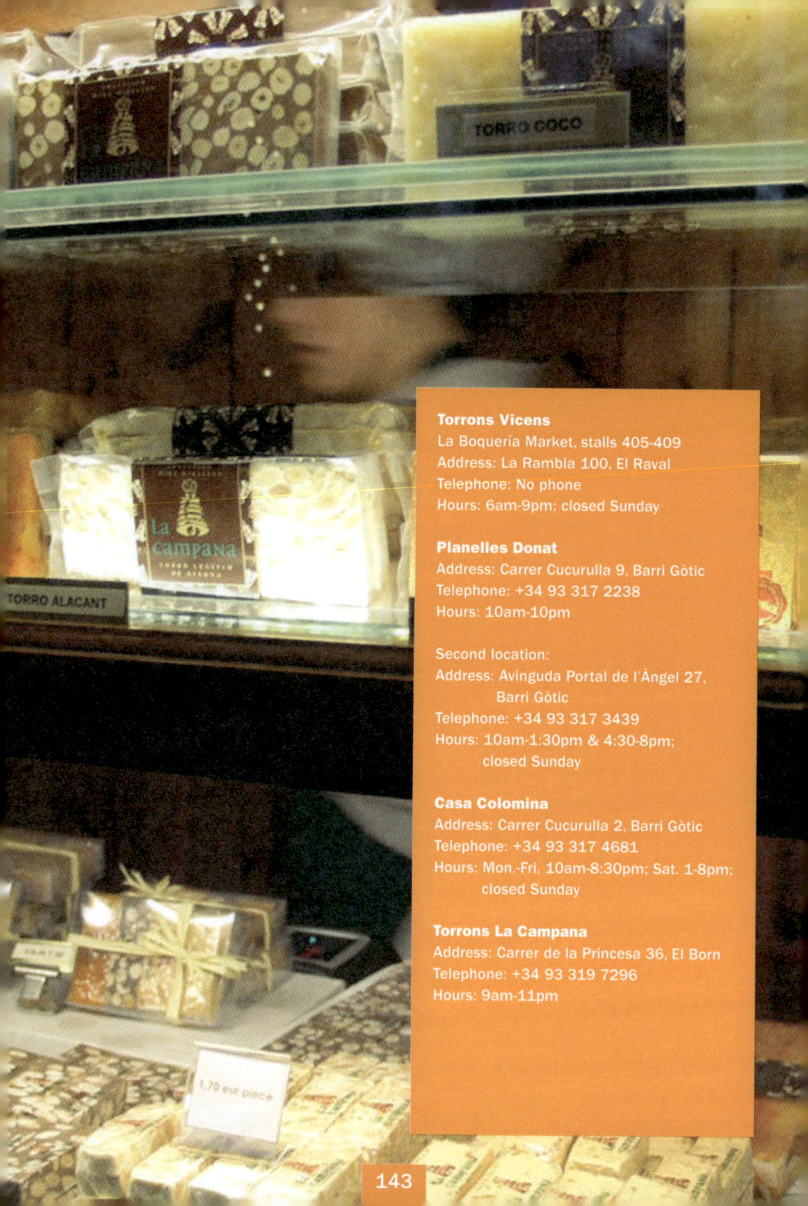

Torrons Vicens
La Boquería Market, stalls 405-409
Address: La Rambla 100, El Raval
Telephone: No phone
Hours: 6am-9pm; closed Sunday

Planelles Donat
Address: Carrer Cucurulla 9, Barri Gòtic
Telephone: +34 93 317 2238
Hours: 10am-10pm

Second location:
Address: Avinguda Portal de l'Àngel 27, Barri Gòtic
Telephone: +34 93 317 3439
Hours: 10am-1:30pm & 4:30-8pm; closed Sunday

Casa Colomina
Address: Carrer Cucurulla 2, Barri Gòtic
Telephone: +34 93 317 4681
Hours: Mon.-Fri. 10am-8:30pm; Sat. 1-8pm; closed Sunday

Torrons La Campana
Address: Carrer de la Princesa 36, El Born
Telephone: +34 93 319 7296
Hours: 9am-11pm

XURRERIAS

Where Every Day is Fryday

Churros, the long, skinny, crenellated, sweet fried crullers made from just flour, water and salt, have been enjoyed for centuries in Spain, with hot chocolate and without. However, in Barcelona, *xurros*, as they are called in Catalan, are becoming an endangered species. In recent years, more than half of the *xurreries* in the city have disappeared. The best way to save this endangered species is to eat it, so here are our five favorites, all worth seeking out.

Churrería Manuel San Román opened back in 1968 and still makes crunchy, non-greasy, loop-shaped xurros with perfect consistency and at top speed, ensuring that you always get the freshest batch. Owner Manuel San Román, whose grandmother was a *xurrera*, has been making xurros for 55 years, his son Luis for 30. Both belong to the trade union Gremi Artesà de Xurrers de Catalonia. San Román makes his dough out of hard wheat flour, altering it as needed to account for the ambient temperature and humidity, and keeps a close eye on the temperature of the oil (a combination of peanut, sunflower and olive oils that has a high smoke point). San Román is widely acknowledged to be one of the city's masters of this craft.

Comaxurros is a recently minted (2013) xurreria, the brainchild of Marc Muñoz and Lluis Estrada Canal (of the family with the famed patisserie, just next door). The xurros here are thin, light, imaginatively and expertly made. They make versions topped with fruit and cream and all kinds of chocolate, as well as innovations like the "Xurritos Bravos," which substitutes xurros for the spuds in *patatas bravas* in a bravura mashup. Everything here is fried in pure virgin olive. Muñoz and Canal are also members of the trade union.

The perfect spot for a coffee break, **Churrería Laietana**, which opened in 1975, makes wonderful thin, light xurros and *porras*, which are similar but bigger, made with

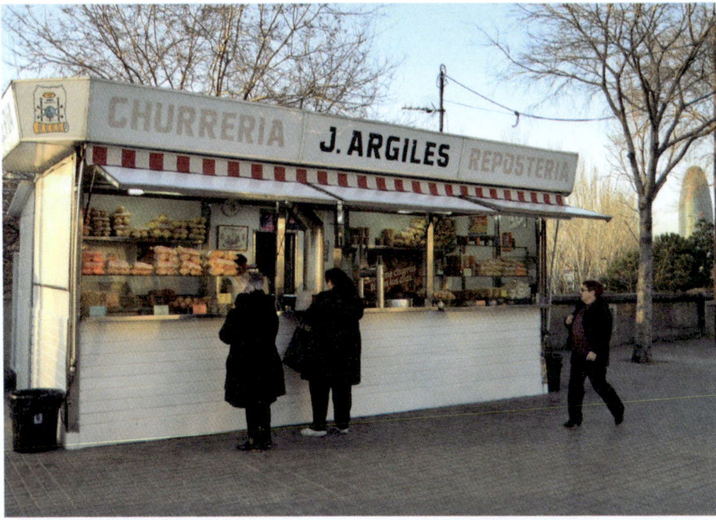
CHURRERIA
J. ARGILES
REPOSTERIA

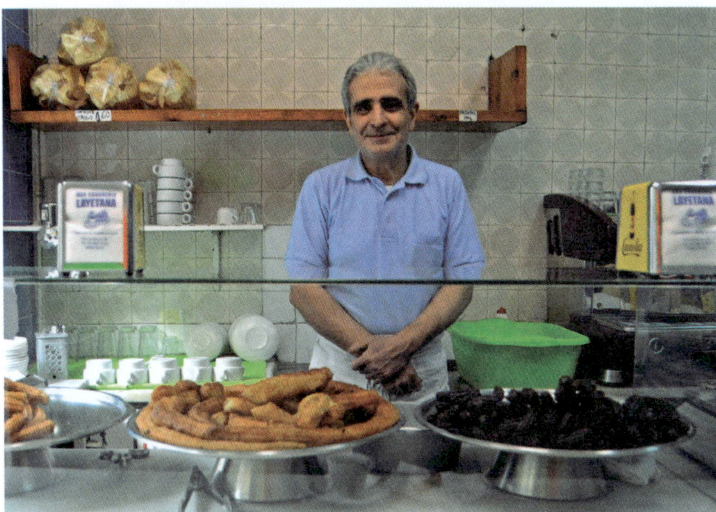
LAYETANA
LAYETANA

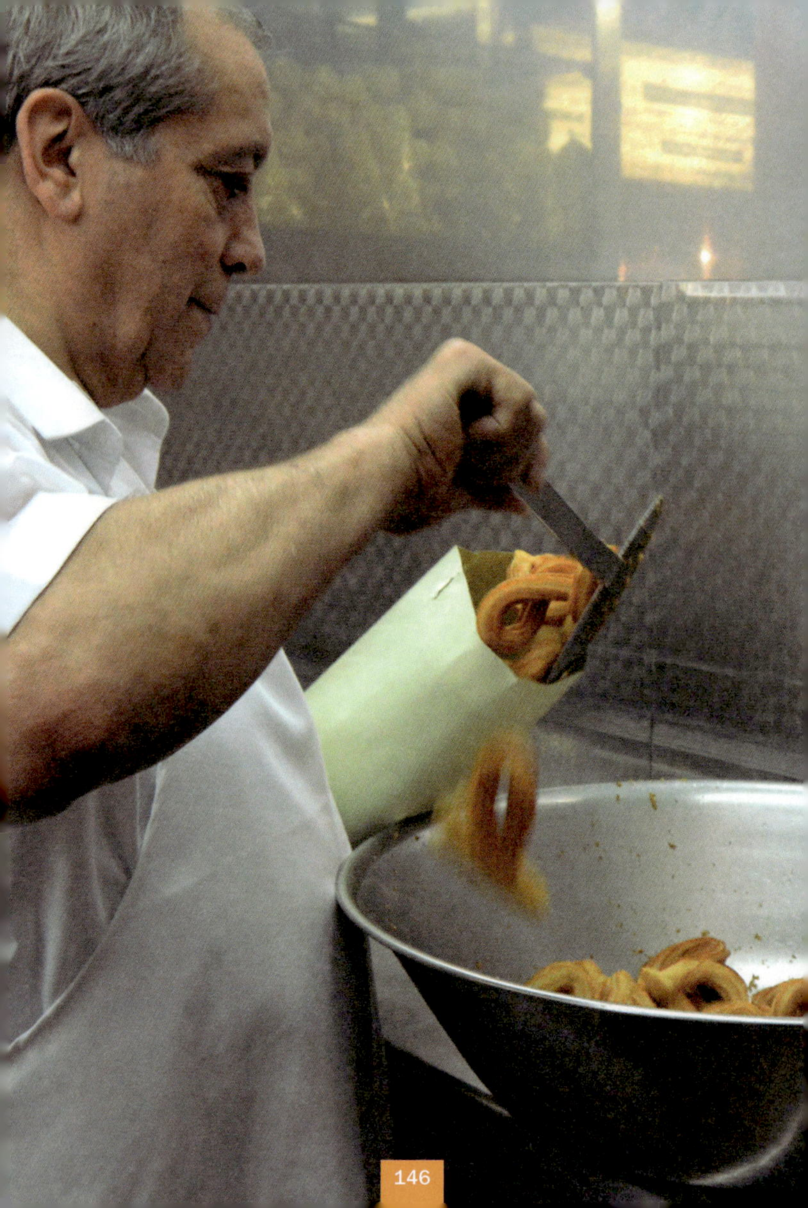

yeast and more commonly found in Madrid. José Ruz Martínez, a cheerful man with 43 years of xurrero experience, grew up in his father's xurreria. His cozy, bare-bones shop is frequented mostly by locals and area office workers, who come for good coffee or hot chocolate with xurros and porras for breakfast or on their breaks.

Churrería J. Argiles is a street xurro icon. The stall's long, thin fried batons can come with sugar, extra salt or in any number of other delicious variations. José Argiles, who founded the operation in 1958, is the president of the trade union. His stand is now lovingly managed by Montse Roche, while Argiles runs a small factory that makes fried items such as potato chips and supplies the original stand as well as other shops throughout Catalonia. At the stand, Roche makes fresh xurros and great *xuxos*, soft crullers filled with a decadent cream and topped with sugar, and also serves hot chocolate and cold beverages.

The xurros at **Xurreria El Trebol** are extra long, thick and very crunchy, a bit on the toastier, well-done side. Cecilia Martínez and her husband, Juan Bacells, started making xurros in the 1940s, and around 1950 they opened this shop in front of the original one, which is long gone. El Trebol was the first xurreria in Barcelona to branch out to other fried items, such as cod fritters and *cañas* with Argentinian *dulce de leche*. Martínez's son, Ramón Bacells, runs the business with her grandson Alex, who is likely the one you'll find behind the counter. They also have good hot chocolate and sell cold drinks.

Churreria Manuel San Roman
Address: Carrer de Banys Nous 8, Barrio Gótico
Telephone: +34 93 318 7691
Hours: Mon.-Sat. 9am-8:30pm

Comaxurros
Address: Carrer Muntaner 562, Sant Gervasi
Telephone: +34 93 417 9405
Hours: Tues.-Fri. 9am-1:30pm & 4-8:30pm; Sat. & Sun. 8am-1pm & 5:30-8pm; closed Monday

Churreria Laietana
Address: Via Laietana 46, El Born
Telephone: +34 93 268 1263
Hours: Mon.-Sat. 7am-1:30pm & 4:30-8:30pm; Sun. 7am-1:30pm

Churreria J. Argiles
Address: Carrer Marina, at the corner of Carrer Meridiana, El Fort Pienc/Parc Llacuna Poblenou
Telephone: +34 93 232 4307
Hours: Mon.-Thurs. 8am-9pm; Friday 8am to Sunday 9pm, round the clock

Xurreria El Trebol
Address: Carrer de Còrsega 341, Gràcia
Telephone: +34 93 217 9594
Hours: Mon.-Thurs. 9am-9pm; Friday 9am to Sunday 9pm, round the clock

THE OLD CITY

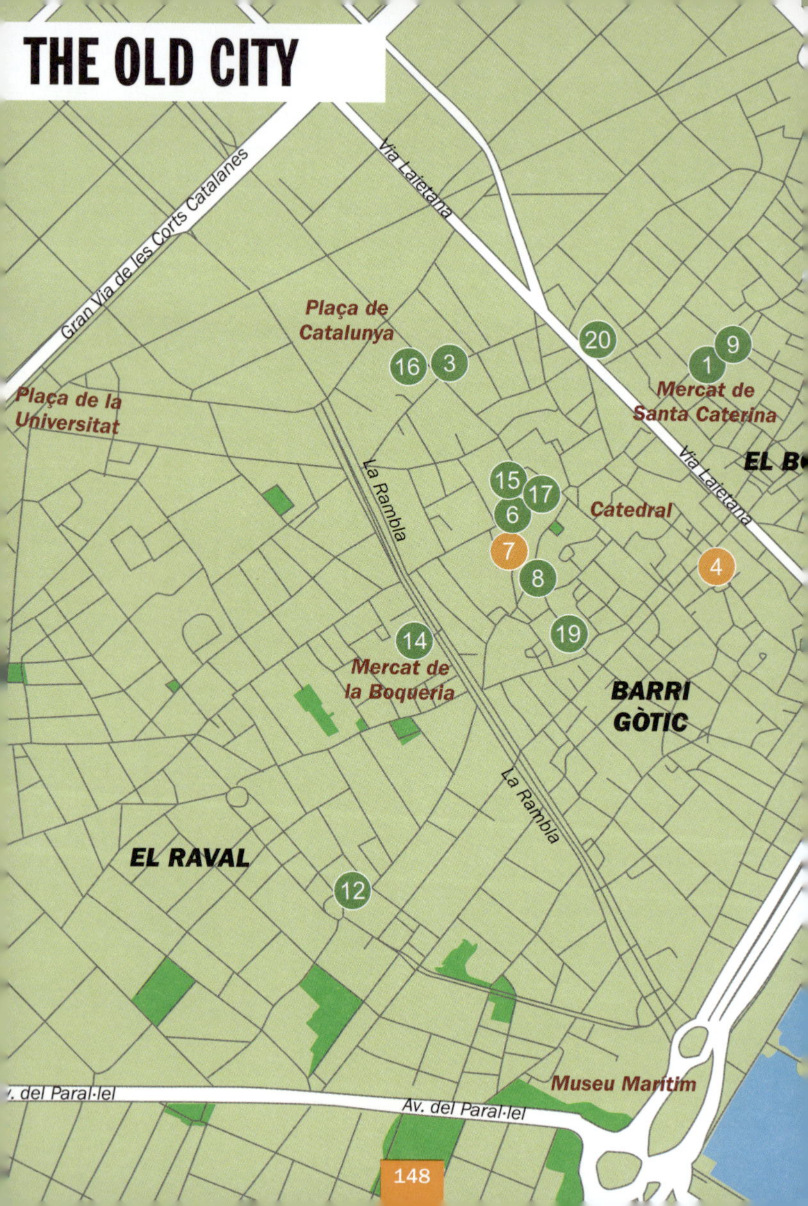

Gran Via de les Corts Catalanes
Via Laietana
Plaça de Catalunya
16
3
20
1
9
Mercat de Santa Caterina
Plaça de la Universitat
La Rambla
15
17
6
7
8
Catedral
4
EL B
14
Mercat de la Boqueria
19
BARRI GÒTIC
EL RAVAL
12
Museu Marítim
Av. del Paral·lel

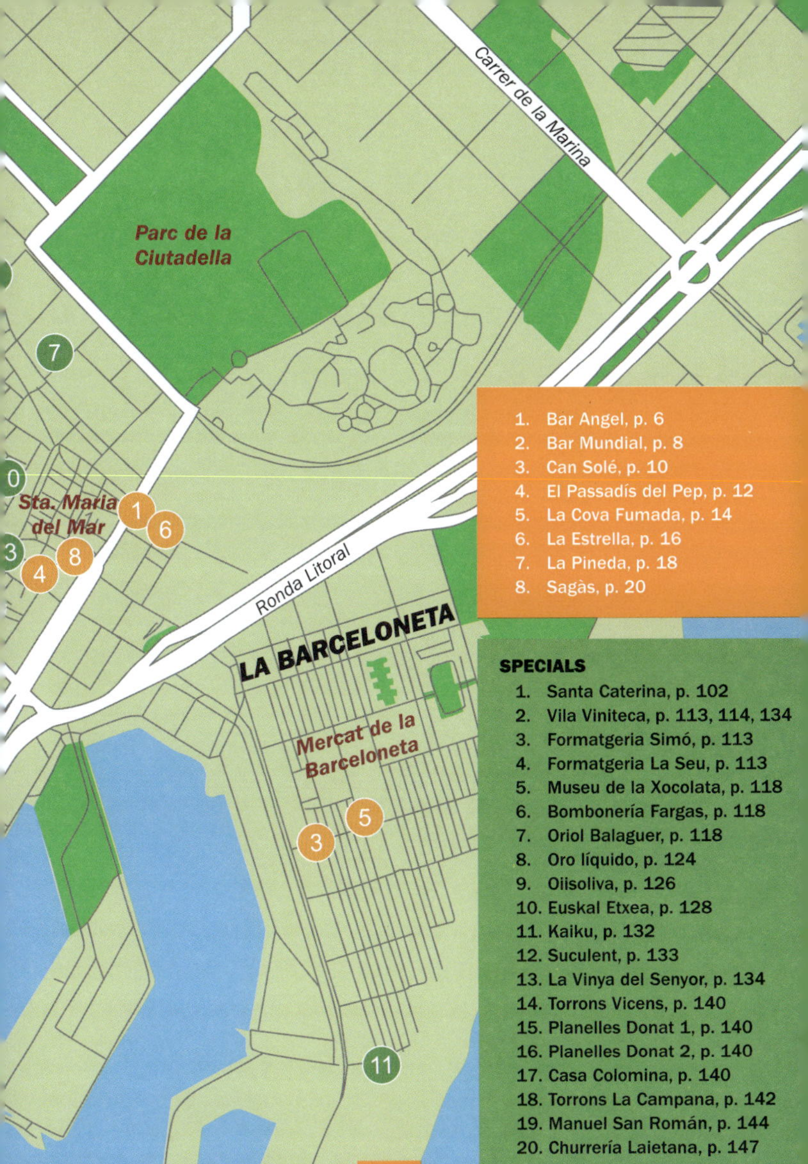
Carrer de la Marina
Parc de la Ciutadella
Sta. Maria del Mar
Ronda Litoral
LA BARCELONETA
Mercat de la Barceloneta
1. Bar Angel, p. 6
2. Bar Mundial, p. 8
3. Can Solé, p. 10
4. El Passadís del Pep, p. 12
5. La Cova Fumada, p. 14
6. La Estrella, p. 16
7. La Pineda, p. 18
8. Sagàs, p. 20
SPECIALS
1. Santa Caterina, p. 102
2. Vila Viniteca, p. 113, 114, 134
3. Formatgeria Simó, p. 113
4. Formatgeria La Seu, p. 113
5. Museu de la Xocolata, p. 118
6. Bombonería Fargas, p. 118
7. Oriol Balaguer, p. 118
8. Oro líquido, p. 124
9. Oiisoliva, p. 126
10. Euskal Etxea, p. 128
11. Kaiku, p. 132
12. Suculent, p. 133
13. La Vinya del Senyor, p. 134
14. Torrons Vicens, p. 140
15. Planelles Donat 1, p. 140
16. Planelles Donat 2, p. 140
17. Casa Colomina, p. 140
18. Torrons La Campana, p. 142
19. Manuel San Román, p. 144
20. Churrería Laietana, p. 147

THE EIXAMPLE DISTRICT

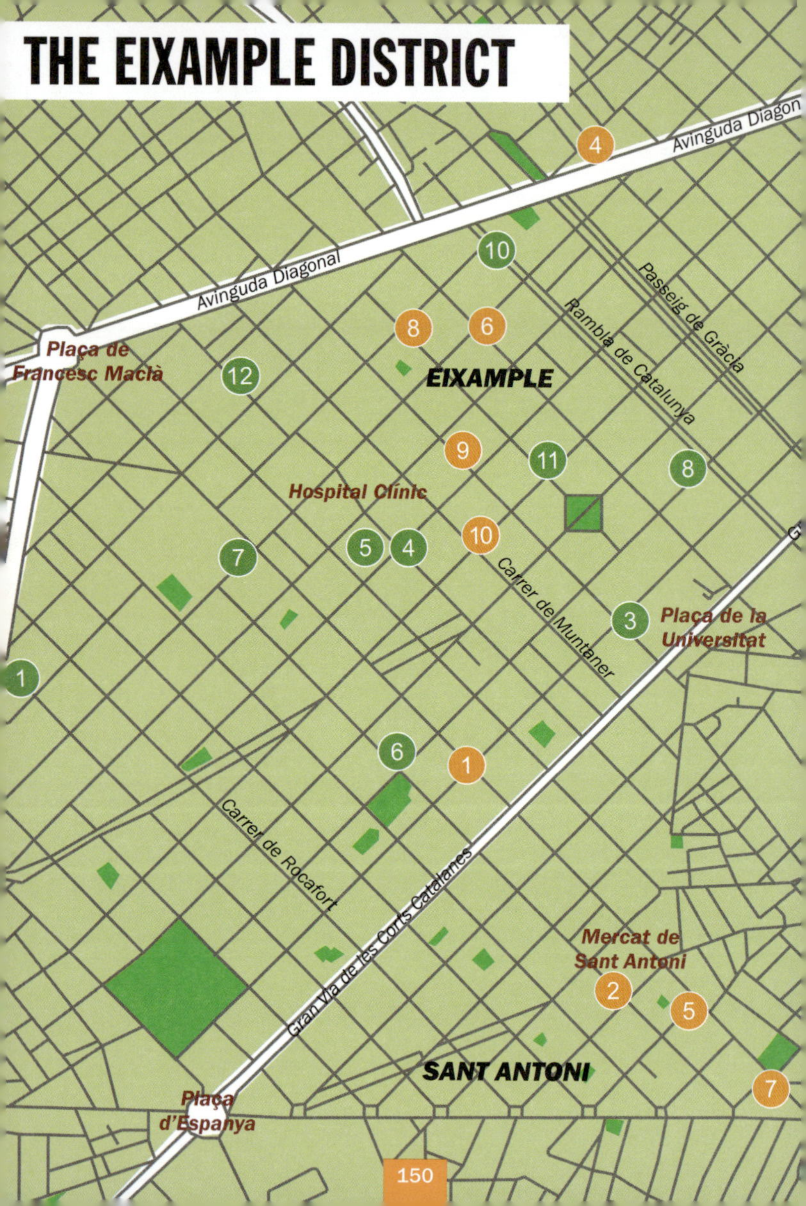

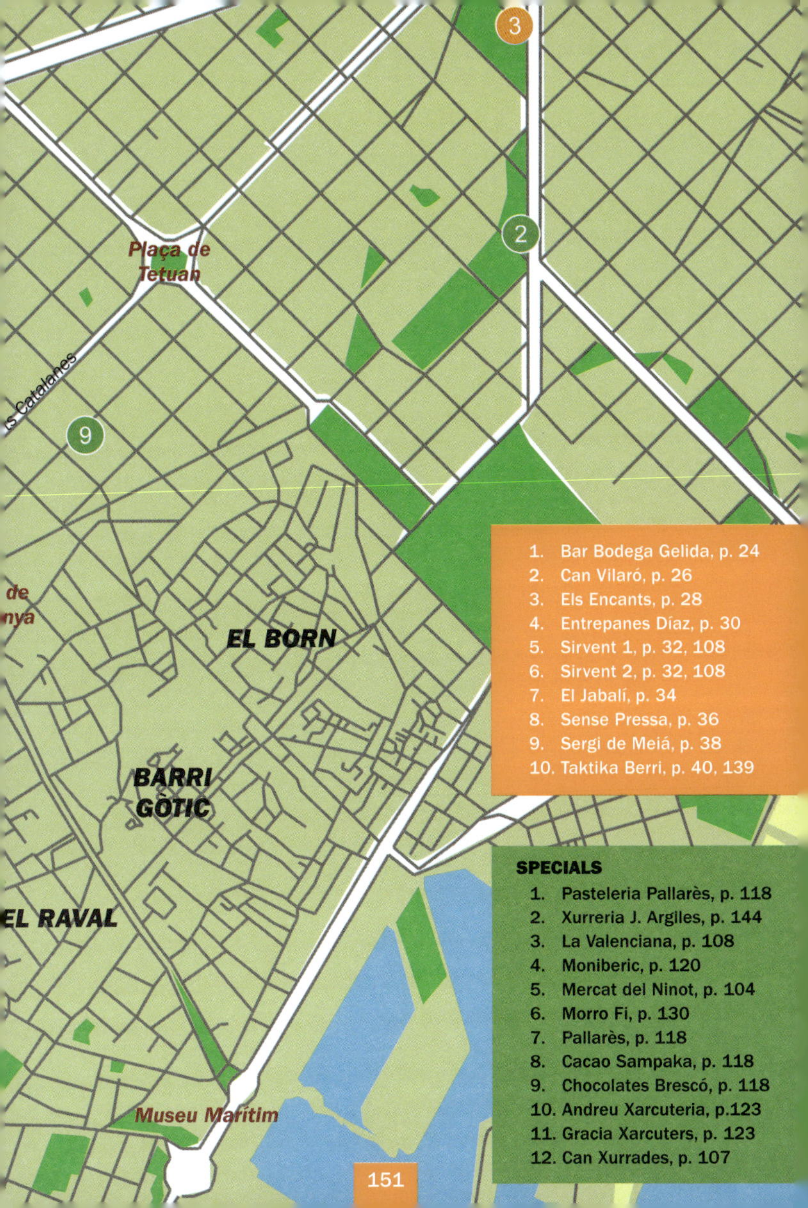
3
2
Plaça de Tetuan
ts Catalanes
9
de
nya
EL BORN
BARRI GÒTIC
EL RAVAL
Museu Marítim
1. Bar Bodega Gelida, p. 24
2. Can Vilaró, p. 26
3. Els Encants, p. 28
4. Entrepanes Díaz, p. 30
5. Sirvent 1, p. 32, 108
6. Sirvent 2, p. 32, 108
7. El Jabalí, p. 34
8. Sense Pressa, p. 36
9. Sergi de Meiá, p. 38
10. Taktika Berri, p. 40, 139
SPECIALS
1. Pasteleria Pallarès, p. 118
2. Xurreria J. Argiles, p. 144
3. La Valenciana, p. 108
4. Moniberic, p. 120
5. Mercat del Ninot, p. 104
6. Morro Fi, p. 130
7. Pallarès, p. 118
8. Cacao Sampaka, p. 118
9. Chocolates Brescó, p. 118
10. Andreu Xarcuteria, p.123
11. Gracia Xarcuters, p. 123
12. Can Xurrades, p. 107

UPPER BARCELONA

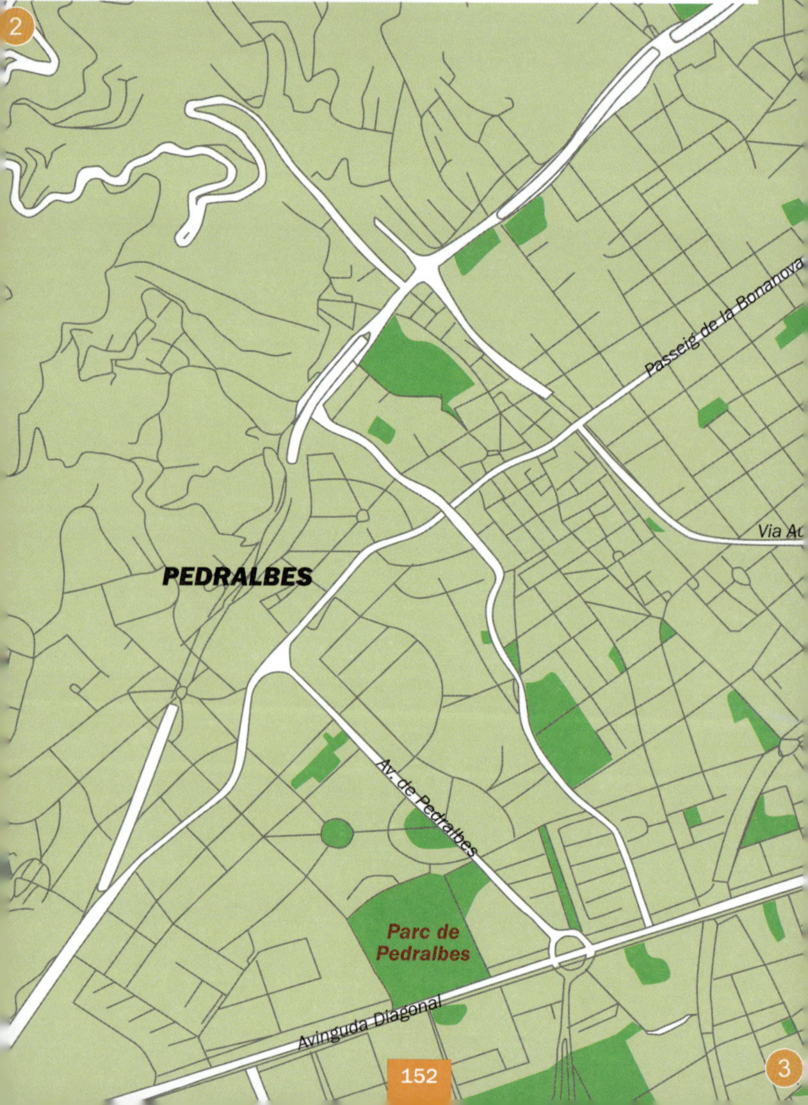

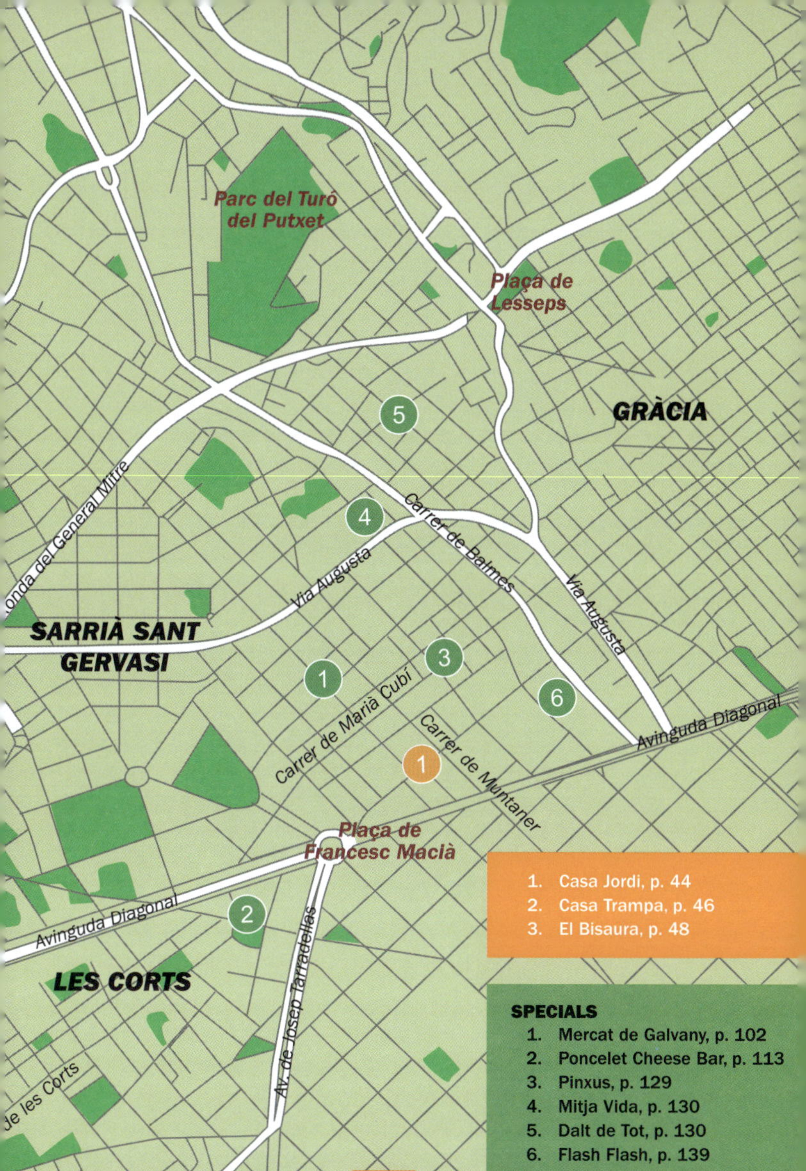
Parc del Turó del Putxet
Plaça de Lesseps
GRÀCIA
Ronda del General Mitre
Via Augusta
Carrer de Balmes
Via Augusta
SARRIÀ SANT GERVASI
Carrer de Marià Cubí
Carrer de Muntaner
Avinguda Diagonal
Plaça de Francesc Macià
Avinguda Diagonal
Av. de Josep Tarradellas
LES CORTS
de les Corts
1. Casa Jordi, p. 44
2. Casa Trampa, p. 46
3. El Bisaura, p. 48
SPECIALS
1. Mercat de Galvany, p. 102
2. Poncelet Cheese Bar, p. 113
3. Pinxus, p. 129
4. Mitja Vida, p. 130
5. Dalt de Tot, p. 130
6. Flash Flash, p. 139

THE GRÀCIA DISTRICT

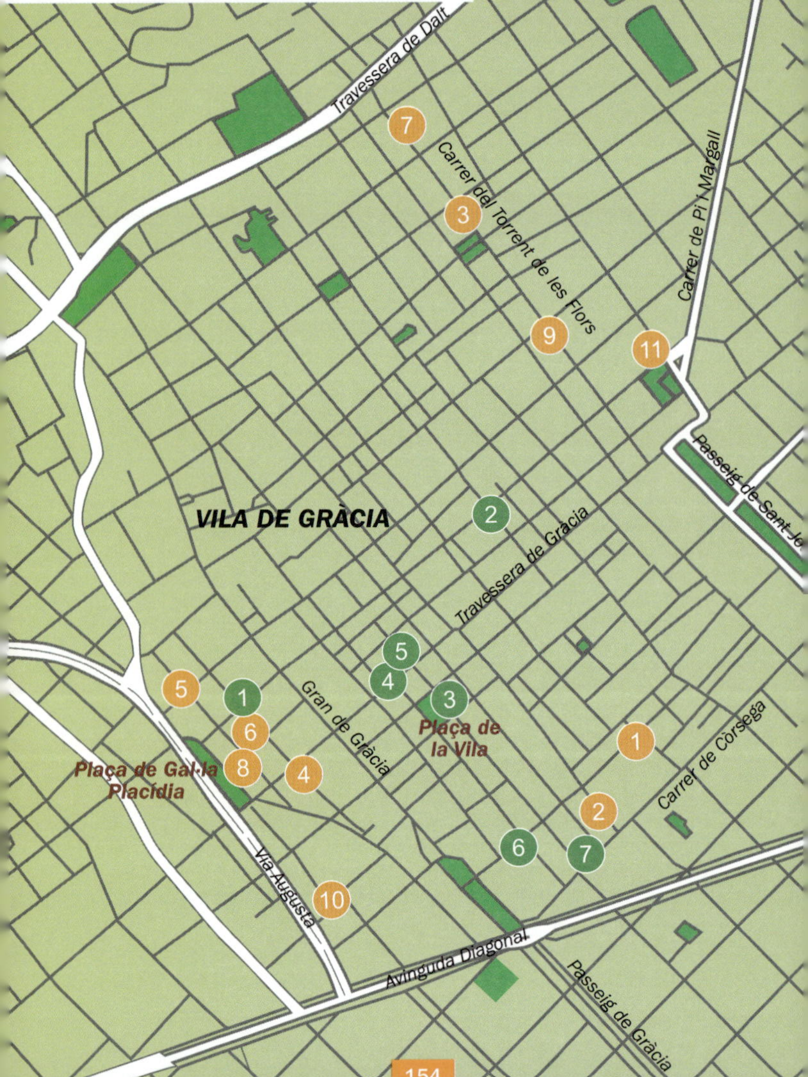

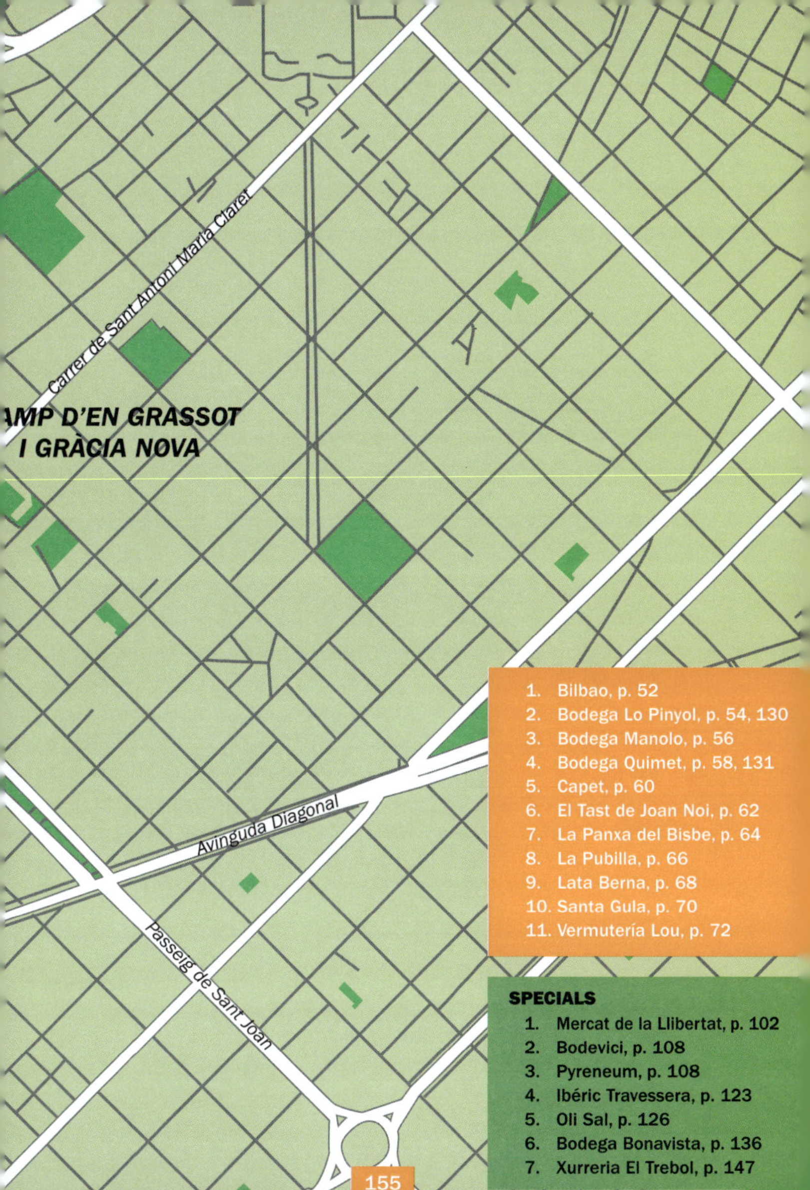
Carrer de Sant Antoni Maria Claret
AMP D'EN GRASSOT
I GRÀCIA NOVA
Avinguda Diagonal
Passeig de Sant Joan
1. Bilbao, p. 52
2. Bodega Lo Pinyol, p. 54, 130
3. Bodega Manolo, p. 56
4. Bodega Quimet, p. 58, 131
5. Capet, p. 60
6. El Tast de Joan Noi, p. 62
7. La Panxa del Bisbe, p. 64
8. La Pubilla, p. 66
9. Lata Berna, p. 68
10. Santa Gula, p. 70
11. Vermutería Lou, p. 72
SPECIALS
1. Mercat de la Llibertat, p. 102
2. Bodevici, p. 108
3. Pyreneum, p. 108
4. Ibéric Travessera, p. 123
5. Oli Sal, p. 126
6. Bodega Bonavista, p. 136
7. Xurreria El Trebol, p. 147

BEYOND THE CENTER (SOUTH)

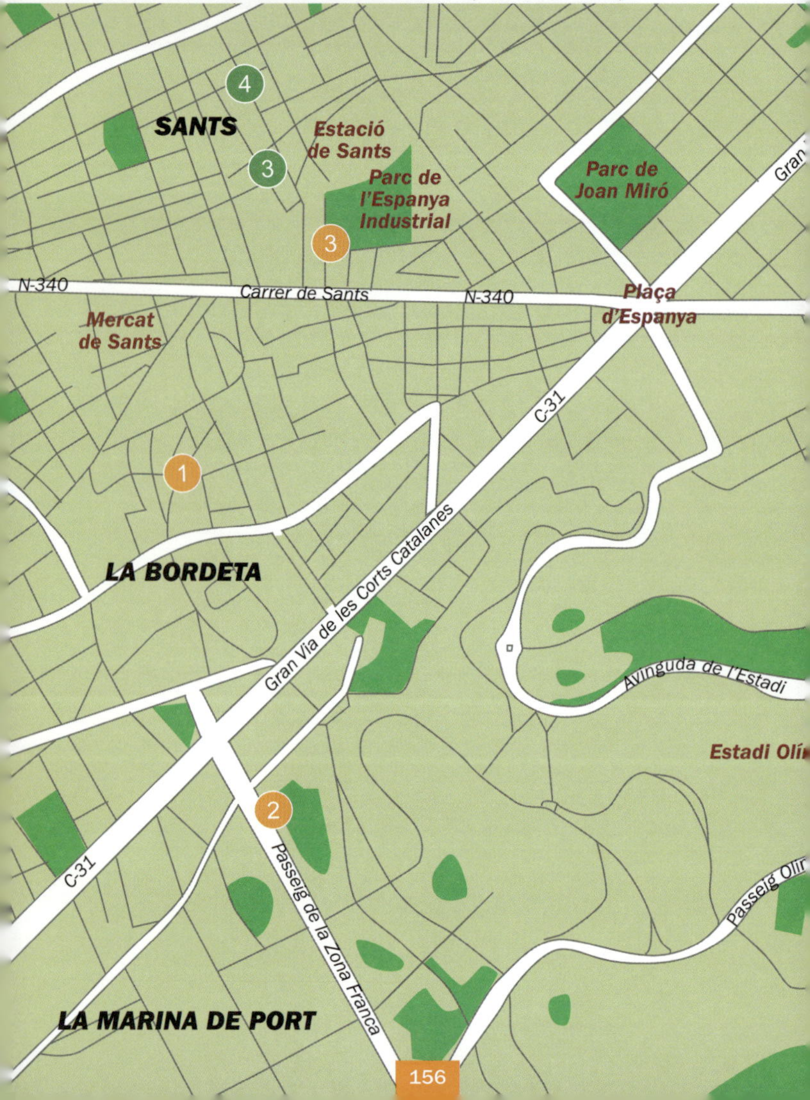

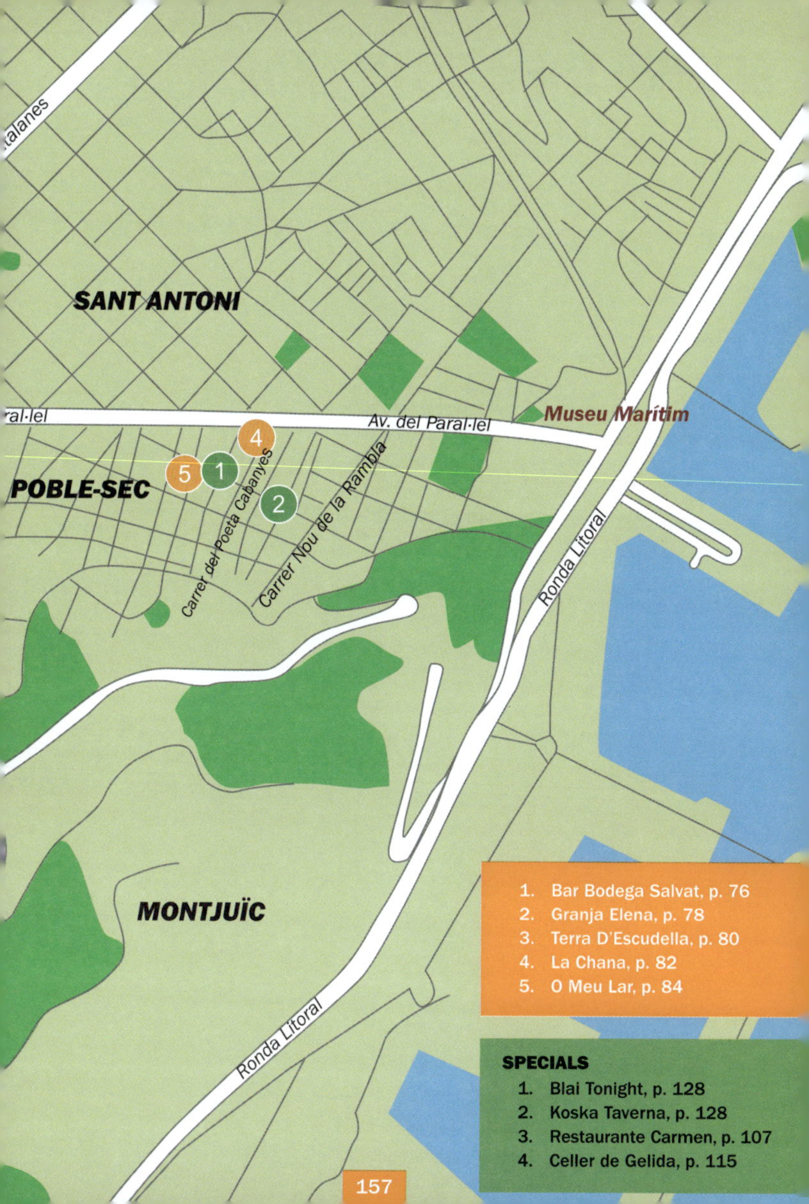

1. Bar Bodega Salvat, p. 76
2. Granja Elena, p. 78
3. Terra D'Escudella, p. 80
4. La Chana, p. 82
5. O Meu Lar, p. 84

SPECIALS

1. Blai Tonight, p. 128
2. Koska Taverna, p. 128
3. Restaurante Carmen, p. 107
4. Celler de Gelida, p. 115

BEYOND THE CENTER (NORTH)

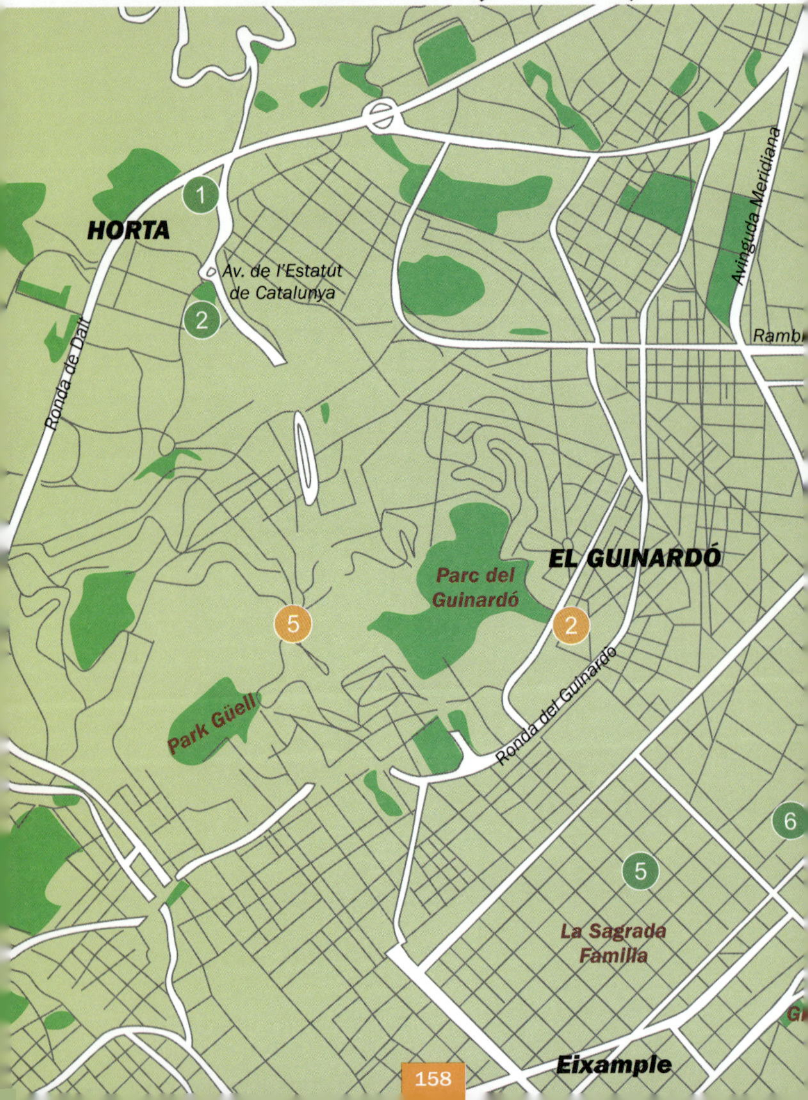

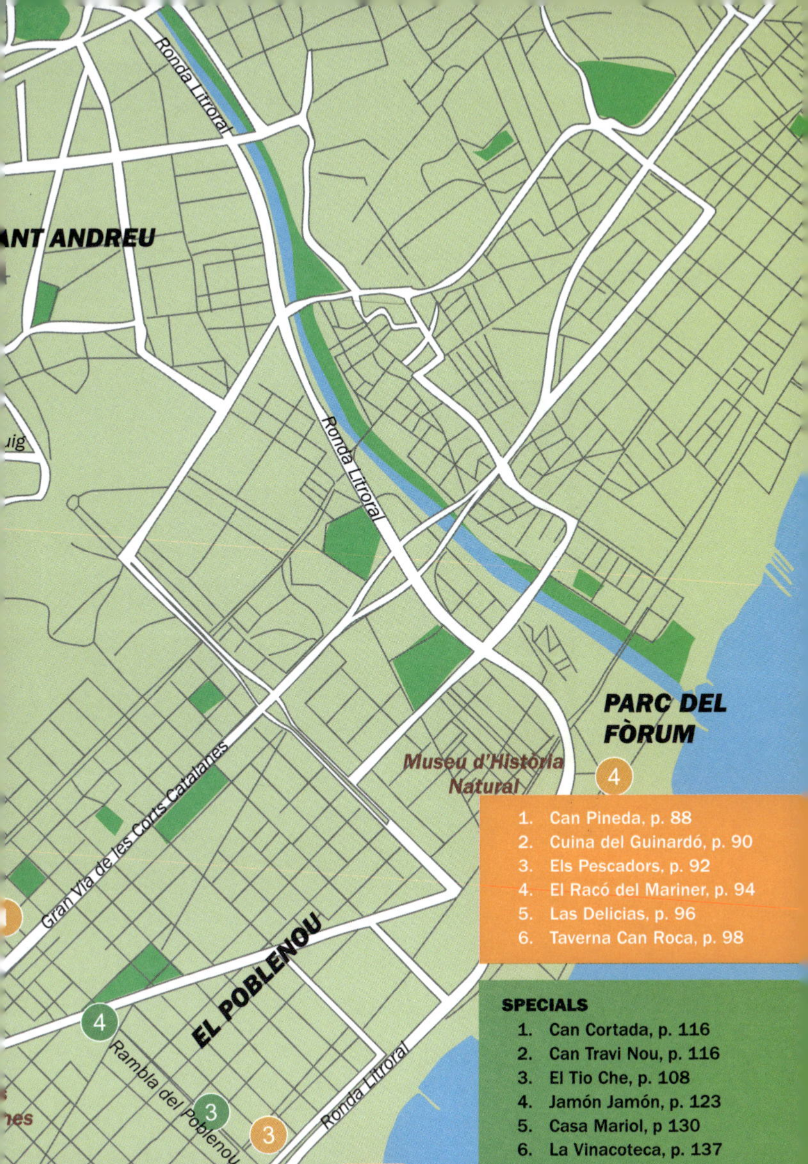
Ronda Litoral
ANT ANDREU
Ronda Litoral
PARC DEL FÒRUM
Museu d'Història Natural
4
Gran Via de les Corts Catalanes
EL POBLENOU
4
Rambla del Poblenou
3
3
Ronda Litoral
1. Can Pineda, p. 88
2. Cuina del Guinardó, p. 90
3. Els Pescadors, p. 92
4. El Racó del Mariner, p. 94
5. Las Delicias, p. 96
6. Taverna Can Roca, p. 98
SPECIALS
1. Can Cortada, p. 116
2. Can Travi Nou, p. 116
3. El Tio Che, p. 108
4. Jamón Jamón, p. 123
5. Casa Mariol, p 130
6. La Vinacoteca, p. 137

TRIANGLE ▼ BOOKS
www.triangle.cat

Carrer Pere Tudurí, 8
07710 Sant Lluís, Menorca

Printed in Barcelona
CeGe
Ciutat d'Asunció, 42
08030, Barcelona

ISBN 978-84-8478-803-4
D.L. Me 491-2018